Socrates On Trial

ALSO AVAILABLE FROM BLOOMSBURY

Philosophy as a Way of Life: History, Dimensions and Direction, Michael Ure and Matthew Sharpe

The Selected Writings of Pierre Hadot: Philosophy as Practice, Pierre Hadot, trans. by Federico Testa and Matthew Sharpe

Socrates On Trial

Nigel Tubbs

BLOOMSBURY ACADEMIC

LONDON • NEW YORK • OXFORD • NEW DELHI • SYDNEY

BLOOMSBURY ACADEMIC
Bloomsbury Publishing Plc
50 Bedford Square, London, WC1B 3DP, UK
1385 Broadway, New York, NY 10018, USA
29 Earlsfort Terrace, Dublin 2, Ireland

BLOOMSBURY, BLOOMSBURY ACADEMIC and the Diana logo are
trademarks of Bloomsbury Publishing Plc

First published in Great Britain 2022

Cover design by Ben Anslow
Cover illustration: Politeia (© Rebekah Howes)

A catalogue record for this book is available from the British Library.

A catalog record for this book is available from the Library of Congress.

ISBN: HB: 978-1-3500-5370-0
PB: 978-1-3500-5371-7
ePDF: 978-1-3500-5369-4
eBook: 978-1-3500-5372-4

Typeset by Deanta Global Publishing Services, Chennai, India
Printed and bound in Great Britain

To find out more about our authors and books visit www.bloomsbury.com and
sign up for our newsletters.

In 1982 I wrote my undergraduate dissertation on Ursula K Le Guin's 'utopian' book The Dispossessed. *I dedicated it to my grandmother – whose life force on this earth was summoned and sold as a 'cleaner' – with these words: 'It is not a world my grandmother would imagine for herself; I dedicate this work to her nevertheless.' Now, writing my own 'utopia', I am returned to those same words, this time not just for her but for everyone and everything in the world she represents: I dedicate the book to all those who will not see themselves in the vision which it offers.*

Contents

Preface ix
Acknowledgements xviii

Introduction 1

Part 1: The retrial of Socrates 3

Book 1
History of the city, 4; privileged elite, 7; shadows and prejudice, 9; gender, 15; nature, 18

Book 2
Celia, the name of injustice, 20; city at war with itself, 25; the arrest

Book 3
The charges, 33; prosecution for elitism, 35; prosecution for failure of elitism, 38; Socrates's response, 43; dialectical puzzles, 46; personal screens, 48; metaphysics and the wall, 51

Book 4
Simple or difficult, 56; what is a question? 58; sun and Forms, 62; fear of the unknown (death, slave), 64; human physical properties (age, gender, race), 65; identity, 67

Book 5
The Grand Inquisitor, 72

Part 2: *Politeia*: City matters 85

Book 6
Examined life in terminal decline, 86; education as problem, solution, problem, 87; beginning with justice, 89

Book 7
Beginning with love of learning the unknown, 97; love as presupposition, 100; circles and spirals, 103; dialectical gravity, 106

Book 8
Life-and-death struggle, 107; self-consciousness, property, slavery, 115; life as mother, 114, 116

Book 9
Truth, 121; nature, 122; freedom, 125

Book 10
Logic, 128; logic of mastery and property, 129; logic of identity, 131; logic of tyranny, 134; logic of prejudice, 136

Book 11
Summary, 138; resignation, 140; beginning a new logic, 141; Socrates's life and death, 142; property and the question, 146; learning, 148

Book 12
Philosophy in the city, 152; the object in-itself, 154; dogmatism and scepticism, 155; perplexity in philosophy, 156; philosophical revolution, 157

Book 13
Practical reason, 162; equality, 165; new philosophies, 166; posthumanism, 168; essence, 169; intriguers, 173; philosophy resists truth, 175; anthropocentrism, 181

Book 14
Summary, 184; un-propertied learning, 186; necessity of presupposition, 187; dialectic, 188; revolutionary self-examination, 191

Book 15
The old cave, 195; cave falls into disrepute, 200; cave, fire and logic of
mastery, 202; new logic, new light, 209

Book 16
New old cave, 211; new old elite, 216; new old Socrates, 218; educational
logic, 220 (metaphysics, 222; God, 224; spontaneity, 225; justice, 227)

Book 17
Ancient *politeia*, 229; definitions, 230; utopia, 231; what is the city –
individual in the collective, 234; production, distribution, consumption,
235; objects, 236; poverty and property, 240; money, 241; war, 246;
crime and law, 248; morality, 251; evil, 253; collective in the individual,
256; nature (men and women), 258; family, 265; tears and laughter, 266;
early education, 269; sphere of needs, 272; the educational city, 278;
House of the City, 280

Part 3: The Apology   289

Book 18
Delphi, 289; torn halves of the first trial, 291; victory
of one-sidedness, 292

The verdict   299

Preface

Like Plato's original *Politeia* (Plato's *Republic*), this is a book about education as a way of life. This time, however, this is explored by putting Socrates on trial for the legacy of Plato's plan for a just society (or 'city'). In doing so, *Socrates On Trial* offers a renewed vision for living the examined life in pursuit of justice. The ancient world did not draw a distinction between this educational life and the work of self-critical social and political thought. But the city has long since rejected the educational life as a basis for just social relations. This new vision is, then, in a sense a thought experiment into what a modern *paideia*, or education, for a just city might look like. At the heart of the experiment is the idea of a new logic – a logic of education – which defines learning as negation and preservation. It is a logic that offers a different way of judging what is true and false in the world and one that offers people a different way of leading a meaningful life. But it is not a logic that needs to be invented. It is a logic that has accompanied the experience of truth in the city, albeit mostly unrecognized.

But the circumstances for embarking on such a thought experiment in education are hardly favourable. Today, education – especially self-critical philosophical education – is held in extremely low regard. For some who find themselves rejected by education and lacking educational success, the world of education can appear to be largely a carrier of elite privilege – be this as a tool for the preservation of wealth and property, or financial power and resources – ensuring that the rich stay rich and the poor stay poor. The dispossessed sometimes also see education as the weapon of a self-proclaimed virtuous intellectual and liberal elite who dominate the lives of ordinary people with values far removed from the latter's real needs. Alongside this, the charge of elitism is itself being used as political capital by another elite to further their own political, essentially plutocratic and at times authoritarian ambitions. In addition, there is the critique of Western education as being soaked in the blood of the victims of imperialism and slavery, and complicit in the prejudice and violence against women. In such circumstances, and with such history behind it, it is not hard to understand why education is rejected as the path to emancipation, freedom and justice and seen instead as the trap waiting to ensnare and undermine all such hopes.

Of course, a different vision of the possibilities of education is held by people of many different political persuasions for whom education, despite its complicities in oppression and privilege, remains the most important tool by which to effect social reform. But such reformers come up against the tight control that vested interests have long enjoyed over the shape and functioning of education in the city at all levels. Many who work in education know that they are asked to teach only in ways that can be controlled by being measured. They know only too well how the needs of measurement determine what teachers can teach, and how they can teach it. Even university education is not immune from such control. The pursuit of higher learning has been made servant to the demands of the market and therefore to the mastery of powerful vested interests. In turn, most universities have welcomed the idea that they too can become profitable businesses, embracing the turning of higher education into a market commodity that is bought and sold like any other merely abstract object. In addition, in the curriculum, education as an idea, as a concept and as a vision of human *praxis* for the just city has become servant to the professional requirements of subject disciplines and is all too often used as cover for the self-serving practice of research reputations. The idea of education as a formative human relationship, a relationship of self to self as of self to other, is being, or for some has already been, retired. With it goes the idea of a city practising an examined life. And with it, too, disappears the vision of education as the work required for the just city.

Let me restate this another way. Since establishing philosophical education at the core of the project for the just city, philosophy and education have become separated. Education has gradually been denied its own voice, to the extent that few now believe it has ever had or ever could have a voice of its own. Anticipating the language that will unfold in Socrates's conversations, education has been judged incapable of carrying its own substance, and that translates as meaning that it is unable to be its own theoretical discipline. Serious thinkers often wave away education as merely something to do with schools. They prejudge it as having nothing to say about itself and certainly as having no meaningful contribution to make to social and political theory. At best it is made a property of the disciplines. It is put to work in the interests of others, just as the enslaved are put to work for their masters. And if it should try to speak to others of the truths it carries in and of itself, there is an awkward embarrassment at its assumed and slightly to be pitied naivety. In academia generally, education is seldom encouraged to find its own depths and to express the significance it has for all life. And within education itself, this has sapped confidence and enervated both its theorists and its practitioners.

This lack of educational voice illustrates just how great the gap has become between the sophistication of the modern city and

Socrates's and Plato's conceptions of philosophy as the love of learning and the living of the examined life. There is a fault line dividing the examined life from itself. On the one hand, in the modern Academy there is examination without life, and on the other hand, in the city, there is life without examination. Who might education say has been its champion since Socrates and then Plato dared to be the voice of education that speaks of itself as the ground of justice in the world? Education might lovingly point to Jean-Jacques Rousseau. In full exposure of his own personal limitations and contradictions, he offered a vision of the just city based on educational, social and political relations. He not only produced a comprehensive account of the origin of social inequality, revealing the institution of property as the key to injustice. He also saw that education – and most definitely not education as schooling – was the precondition to a new just city. But, of course, education also now recognizes that back then, the voice of this champion was white and male and at times patronizing. Today the educational voice, such as it is, works for a different vision of inclusivity. And because its truth is educational, its voice in *Socrates On Trial* (white and male) knows too that what it says now will also be a mirror of its times and will need future examination to recollect its current limitations and blind spots.

*   *   *

In the dialogue that makes up *Socrates On Trial*, education has something new to say about the idea of truth. It heralds a step change in the struggle that truth has had in learning to know and to understand and to speak itself. What it has to say about this step change will strike many as remarkable, and perhaps incredible. It claims that all along, buried within the city's experience of truth and justice lay the possibility of a different kind of life to that shaped solely around the template of private property. This is not new; others have had such experience and imagination. But more controversially, and perhaps more dramatically, *Socrates On Trial* claims to offer a different kind of logic – an educational logic – with which to make sense of these experiences, including the experiences of one's own self, of others, and of truth and ideas in the world such as justice and freedom. This educational logic is a new old truth, and this new old truth has an educational logic. It contrasts with that which, on his return to the city, Socrates will call the logic of mastery that has colonized that most fundamental of experiences – life and death – and shaped everything else in its image. In Part 1 of *Socrates On Trial*, Socrates explores views that are very familiar in the current city, while Part 2 introduces and explores educational truth and logic. Necessarily this involves a re-education in understanding the experience of truth and its relation to life and death. Truth *know thyself*, as it were. Part 3 offers an new Apology from Socrates and a new verdict on the examined life in the city.

And, as if that were not ambitious enough, in Part 2 Socrates also takes the opportunity to explore what a city based on educational truth might – only might – look like. It is inevitable that his new logic of educational truth will be judged according to the old logic of mastery. But Socrates would simply say, every form of mastery that the old logic uses against him shines an ever-brighter light on its own inherent contradictions. He is not looking to win an argument here. His concern is only that in his company education might learn to speak.

So, to repeat, this is a book about education. Not education as readers may think they understand it, rather education speaking as the social, political, cultural, spiritual and philosophical meaning of individual and collective life. But is now the time for education to find its voice? As I write this, Western traditions are extremely vulnerable to being manipulated and then overcome by the mastery of authoritarian leaders and the proprietors who sponsor them. Aided by their sophisticated propaganda, the ambivalence of democracy – its reproduction of power and privilege, and its hopes for peace and justice – is slowly turned into visceral anger, on the one hand, and disillusioned scepticism and cynicism, on the other. Belief in anything called truth that issues from the city is crumbling. And education, the formative activity that enables the city to learn about itself, collapses in exhaustion and fatigue, without a vision of itself, or for itself. Life on earth, or that part of it lived in the tradition of reason, is in a state of paralysis, caught in the headlights of petrifying rational paradoxes in all forms of social relations. If the city can't learn something new from these paradoxes, then myriad possibilities of barbarism will feed on this. Is now the time for education to find its voice? If not now, when?

*   *   *

When Isaac Newton rewrote our understanding of the principles of natural philosophy in his *Principia*, he did so, as he states, according to the established certainties of mathematics and geometry. When Kant and Hegel tried to rewrite our understanding of the principles of metaphysics and logic respectively, they had less empirical formulations upon which to do so. Instead, they had to negotiate the puzzles, or aporias, created in rational thinking which seemed to make knowledge of truth impossible. Such aporetic thinking can be found in Socrates, Plato and Aristotle, but over the centuries their readers and commentators have tended to assume that where the great philosophers had allowed contradictions to have some kind of truth of their own, they must have made mistakes. The commentators took it upon themselves to hide or resolve such embarrassments. *Socrates On Trial* sets out to discover the educational principles within such puzzles, or aporias. One might say that education is being asked to reconceptualize the truth of the mechanics of thought and of its experience of life. This mechanics is the science of thinking resulting from the force of questioning. Socrates retrieves this mechanics from the educational principles of philosophical questioning and thinking, because the difficulty of learning, of education, seems to consist in this – from the phenomenon of questions investigating the ideas of truth, nature and freedom, and then from these investigations to the demonstration of other phenomena, including justice. It is to this end that Socrates's conversations in Parts 1 and 2 are directed, culminating in a vision of the educational city. Using educational principles, Socrates derives the force of attraction with which concepts of justice and freedom and truth are drawn to education. By this attraction, or by this gravity, other elements of the city – property, essence, identity, money, family, gender, race, production, distribution and consumption – are pulled into educational orbit. It might be that all the elements of nature, subjective and objective, are drawn together by the force of education. These educational principles being hitherto unknown means that the city has searched in vain for the idea of truth, but perhaps the educational principles here laid down will afford some light either to this or to some other life of education in the city.

* * *

Some years ago a friend of mine, Howard Caygill, suggested that my *History of Western Philosophy* (2009) might be written as a dialogue. On hearing of the project of what was originally planned to be called

The New Republic, he repeated the challenge. I thought I would experiment with this and began by writing a small section of what is now Part 1 in dialogue form. I quickly realized two things. First, the format was addictive. I felt a freedom from a more dense style of writing. Second, after many failures, I realized that I was not a creator of characters. Sadly, I had to admit to myself that I lacked the skills that were required to carry characterization through a text. So, either I ceased writing in dialogue or I carried on without characterization. I decided upon the latter. Hence, apart from Socrates, the participants do not have names of their own – save one, Celia, who is the name of injustice, and who names the nameless of the world.

I expect the lack of characterization will undermine the book for some readers and disappoint others who may still be sympathetic to the overall project, even if not to its conclusions. But in making this decision, I placed my hope in the fact that Plato's original *Republic* was not dependent upon characterization. Despite being real historical individuals, the participants are still, in the main, just the means by which Plato could tell his philosophical story. My own book takes the same path. The new Socrates is not simply the old Socrates. Rather, he is a modern and ancient force of education, now speaking of itself in ways it has not done before. Those he speaks with in Part 1 are representatives of a range of contemporary voices, but they are not anyone in particular. His partners in Part 2 are not typical of Socrates's ancient respondents, who are often reduced to 'Yes, Socrates', or 'No, Socrates'. Socrates acknowledges that he is grateful (as indeed I am) to have found jurors who are at least knowledgeable citizens of the city and who are interested in what he has to say. Their dialogue is the means through which education is allowed to find its voice, hence the reference at times to the daemon, or the vocation of learning, as the precondition that is our educational necessity. Their conversation is its self-discovery. But at the same time, who better to be the voices of education than Socrates and his jurors? I hope above all that the dialogue in the book does justice to the Socratic work of living and dying that he bequeathed.

* * *

Let me end by expressing the uncertainty that grounds the book and its ideas. I am reminded of a very good friend of mine, Alastair Loadman. While others aspire to buying new cars, he prefers the used car – in most cases, the very used car. On one occasion he bought a very old Austin Princess. When he took three of us out in it for the first time, we approached a steep hill, and, from the driver's seat and just before pushing the accelerator to the floor, in high spirits, he said, 'Right, let's see what it can do.' I feel the same now about education: 'let's see what education can do' when given the freedom to speak. Sadly, as Alistair's vehicle attacked the hill, there was a loud bang and it was filled with rancid smoke.

Acknowledgements

The years 2016–21 were by any standards tumultuous years in the UK, in Europe, in North America, and then, with Covid-19, across the world. *Socrates On Trial* was written during this period, and it shows. Brexit and Trump forced the book into the world. Easing its passage were many Liberal Arts students at the University of Winchester. They suffered a reading of Part 1 near the end of their programmes, reading out the different speeches and giving the text a critical reception. I thank each one of them.

Deep thanks go to the people who encouraged and supported the book at its proposal stage: Howard Caygill, Rowan Williams and Paul Standish. Their endorsement was a true leap of faith, one that I can only hope I have gone at least some way to fulfilling. At the end of the writing, Howard read the text and, in his usual relaxed and yet uncompromising way, informed me that the book lost its drama and energy halfway through. We discussed ways in which the text might be reinvigorated. The final version of the work is inestimably better for the additional work he made me do. The weaknesses that remain are symptomatic of my own considerable limitations.

I also thank Liza Thompson and Lucy Russell at Bloomsbury for their attention and encouragement, and belief in the project.

Iain 'Tid' Tidbury deserves special thanks. His support over the years for this book, as for Liberal Arts at Winchester, was invaluable, culminating in him reading the final text and reminding me, and Socrates, not to fall too far behind the generations that the book is written for. Some of Tid's comments now appear at different times in the dialogue. A draft was also read by my friend Mark Taylor. Mark works as a deputy head teacher in a secondary school in London, and he has introduced a Great Books element to the school's curriculum. There are few people in the UK more informed or better placed to offer critical insights into the project I have undertaken. I thank Mark deeply for all his help and support over the years. I also want to offer profound thanks to my consultant colorectal surgeon, Mr Jack Broadhurst, and his team at the Royal Hampshire County Hospital, Winchester, without whose consummate skills I might not have been able to complete the book.

Finally, I pay a very special and deeply felt tribute to my reader, Rebekah Howes. Through her loving reading of various versions of the text and our innumerable conversations, many additional ideas were generated, which have enriched its vision and scope. There are parts of the text that could justly be called a joint effort, and I wish to ensure that this is fully acknowledged. She holds the coat, and everything else that sustains the work. Becky, thank you for it all.

Introduction

Where there is no vision, the people perish.[1]

Looking back now, no one was really sure just how long Socrates had been back in the city. Given many of the things he said, he must have been there some time before anyone recognized him.

When he was last in the city, he engaged in dialogues with some of the great and the good of his own day. He would talk with them, ask them to state their knowledge on a particular issue, listen carefully to their answers and then begin to question them in his own inimitable style. Famously, he refused to accept that he was a teacher because he said he had nothing to teach anyone. All he had were questions, which, he claimed, like his mother, made him a midwife. His questioning, he said, was only ever designed to draw ideas out from people and then to test these ideas to see if they could survive in the world. But this midwifery delivered him a very poor reputation, for it always appeared as if Socrates questioned everyone else's ideas but offered none of his own. Now that he had returned, anticipation was rife that it was probably only a matter of time before he would begin his midwifery in the city again.

---

[1]Proverbs 29:18 KJV.

Why he returned when he did was never made clear, any more than how he returned. That he did return, however, enabled the city to examine itself once again at a time of extraordinary anger, uncertainty and division, at a time when the city's health was poor and declining and at a time when some even suggested that the city itself was broken, perhaps irretrievably so. But, reflecting now on the events that unfolded during his stay, his message to everyone caught up in the city's afflictions did not seem to have changed: the unexamined life was still not worth living.

Part 1

The retrial of Socrates

Book 1

The man in sandals and a long coat, looking a little dishevelled, was standing in the marketplace, listening around him intently to what he could hear of people's everyday conversations. He knew the city, of course, and yet he felt he was again seeing it for the first time. The familiar was strangely unfamiliar, and it had taken some time before his eyes had adjusted to it.

When they did, he was confused by what he saw. Those who had once been prisoners in chains were now unbound, able to roam freely and see all of the city for themselves. They could see the shadows but also the path on which people walked carrying objects, and the fire behind them whose light cast the shadows of these objects. The world that had been hidden was now demystified. The people carrying the objects were no longer strangers to the ex-prisoners. Indeed, the emancipated city dwellers had access to the same path and were able to cast into the city shadows of their own making. Equally shocking for Socrates, when he looked past the fire at the steep ascent out of the city, no matter how hard he strained his eyes he could not see the light that marked its entrance.

It was not long before he was engaged in conversation, hoping to make sense of what he saw.

T: Socrates, you have been away a long time.

S: I have, and much has changed.

T: What surprises you most?

S: That those previously in chains now walk freely around the city.

T: The city believes it no longer nurtures ignorance. It insists that what was hidden is now open and that all are free to see it.

S: Including the production of the shadows?

T: Especially the production of the shadows. The city professes itself to be enlightened.

S: And yet the shadows still exist. This perplexes me.

T: Then you need to become familiar with the history of the city. In previous times only the few were released from their chains and dragged to the world of truth and first principles where they learned arts and sciences, dialectic, and wisdom.

S: Then they were to return to the city as philosophers to serve the public good.

T: That was your plan Socrates. But the plan failed.

S: Did they return to live and rule without families and wealth and property?

T: They returned, but they let self-interest prevail over the public good.

S: Then it did not become a just city?

T: Far from it. Often these rulers claimed benevolence. But they still ruled the city in their own interests and kept others chained as prisoners in the shadows.

S: The project for the just city made very clear that justice required each soul to be put to work doing the job for which it was best suited. If the rulers were corrupt, they were not the souls best suited to governing. Such injustice would undermine the whole city.

T: These rulers treated non-philosophical minds as barbarians and took wealth and property for themselves as their entitlement. They treated the city as their private estate, justifying and enjoying lordship over those they kept enslaved. This is the city you left behind you, a city in poor health where freedom and servitude, enlightenment and shadows, and justice and corruption existed alongside each other.

B: But the rulers were clever, Socrates. From the very beginning their injustice was authorized and sustained by the highest ideals of the city, justified according to the principles of harmony and beauty, and in living at peace with nature and the order of the cosmos.

S: You mean they ruled by the principle of tranquillity?

B: They claimed that by the power of the philosophical mind the laws of nature were absorbed into the soul without resentment. Such masterful virtue belonged to the stoical mind. But in reality, the struggle required to achieve tranquillity was self-defeating. It was like a mind at war with itself. And so, becoming sceptical that such tranquil mastery could ever be achieved for any philosophical mind, some decided to suspend judgement between competing truths altogether.

S: What happened to truth?

B: It flew into the realm of the unknowable, into the metaphysical, unable to leave its ethereal home or to return to the city.

S: Philosophical truth and political truth were separated from each other?

B: And absolute truth defied any direct contact with the finite individual mind of the citizen. It became the idea of truth as a single deity, one god, unknowable to changeable individual experience.

S: Did this idea of unknowable truth become a form of mastery in the city?

B: Yes, when injustice took a new cultural form as religion, praising mind as divine substance and chastising the body as the sinful home of material and physical desires. Non-philosophical minds, those dominated by the desires of the body, were given prophets who could bridge the gap between the human and divine. They were told that faith in the prophets would save their souls in the afterlife, while priests mediated on behalf of the divine on earth, demanding obedience from the faithful.

S: But if truth is exiled to the metaphysical and made unknowable, then the material world is free from its direct control. It might learn to enjoy this freedom.

B: This is what happened. People found innate resources by which to decide truth for themselves. And something remarkable came out of this. From within the despair of being deserted by ineffable truth, came extraordinary scientific and artistic accomplishments. And this earthly mind, newly enlightened about its own innate abilities and capacities, called itself 'reason'.

S: Did this become a new mastery?

B: Yes. Reason announced that the city's history and development had really been its own doing. Reason now claimed to be the creator of truth.

S: Freeing itself from religious power?

B: The heavens were seen to be the product of an unenlightened reason. Enlightenment returned truth to earth.

S: Did reason belong only to specialist philosophical minds?

B: No. And here is the reason why the prisoners now roam freely around the city. Enlightenment taught us that reason is an innate capacity of every human mind. All reasoning individuals are equal to each other. And so, rational philosophical thinking, whose truth had first justified elite masters and their slaves, now redefined truth as individuals thinking for themselves. This made a universal truth out of the activity that you started in the city, Socrates. And today the rational city has no slaves, only independent rational individuals. Even to refer to people as having been slaves risks dehumanizing the individual who was enslaved.

S: Did slaves think of themselves as slaves?

B: Yes and no.

S: Then to do justice to that struggle, perhaps we need both to undermine and to preserve the terms in which it was lived?

B: But the city has no slaves now, Socrates.

S: And yet I have seen people in the city who still appear to be enslaved to different kinds of mastery.

B: Legally no one can be defined as a slave.

C: How convenient that the chains of both body and mind become invisible behind the law. The law makes everyone equal, and the same law makes this equality actual as the inequalities of wealth, property and power.

S: Justice in the old city demanded that every person's work best fulfilled their natural talents. Hence, the wisest souls would rule as masters, the bravest would defend and the most desiring would buy and sell what was needed for survival.

C: As you have seen, your best intentions were not realized. Desire conquered wisdom. The rulers abandoned an education in selflessness. They craved privilege and the luxuries that come with it, and they used education to achieve this. Rather than restraining their desires, they indulged them. They turned the privilege of service into an entitlement for reward. Your model of the just city created only an elite class serving their own self-interests.

S: Who could join this elite?

C: Mostly it just reproduced itself from within. If someone did seek admission, he would be tested to ensure that his instincts were to conserve rather than to disrupt power and privilege.

S: Was this elite ever challenged by the rest of the city?

C: At times their excesses led to rebellions. But through control of trade and business the masters had the power of life and death over the poor, owning as they did the very things that people needed for survival. This meant that even when rational and legal equality was achieved, material inequality remained. Privilege was not so much challenged as rebranded. The enlightenment of the city turned into the principle of the equality of inequality.

S: Meaning that all are equal, and some are more equal than others.

C: Indeed.

S: In the old city trade was seen as barbarian by the elite.

C: Over time the city saw the two groups morph into one. Rulers rewarded traders with wealth and property, and traders ensured the market served the interest of the rulers.

S: An alliance?

C: The Janus-face of power in the city.

S: Then what is government in this city of desire?

C: It is a system that distils need into greed.

S: Who makes the things the city needs?

C: A class of producers who work for their masters.

S: Are they too ruled by desire?

C: By the desire to survive, yes. And hand in hand with this the masters eradicated any desire among such people for learning. They kept the higher education of the mind to themselves and told everyone else they should only desire the kind of education that would service their basic survival. The people were told never to forget that the purpose of education for them is to get a good and meaningful job. They were told they would gain very little advantage from having any higher education and were denied the tools by which such claims might be thought about, questioned and criticized.

S: One kind of education for the masters, another for their servants.

C: Material inequality has always protected meaningful education as an elite entitlement.

S: Do people not see through this?

C: Sometimes, but the struggle for survival is its own education. A meaningful education would of course benefit everyone. But as someone who came after you pointed out, to benefit from such an education requires first a full stomach. Those born into wage slavery understand all too well that a meaningful education will not immediately put food on the table. So, a useless education, as the masters boasted of it, is a luxury they simply cannot afford. Your education, Socratic education, is preserved by an elite for their own entertainment.

S: Then the city protects itself from being held to account for its injustices?

C: It does.

S: Then somehow the shadows still hold sway over the city?

D: Yes, Socrates; shadows still enslave the mind.

S: Might I ask you a question about the shadows?

D: Of course.

S: If there are no longer any prisoners, why are there still shadows?

D: That is a good question. The shadows remain one of the most important ways that the masters have in preserving their own privilege within our unequal city. The shadows are still creating the reality of most people's lives and justifying the necessity of inequality and privilege. They are powerful ways of explaining to the poor why it is right they should work for their masters.

S: I understand that those who control the production of shadows control the thoughts of those who see them. But when people are enlightened about this use of the shadows, and see through them, surely the shadows become redundant?

D: True, people did see the shadows as creating the city in the masters' own self-interests.

S: Then why are there still shadows?

D: Because having power over the shadows has become the battlefield for controlling all communication in the city – information, knowledge and understanding.

S: Yet still as shadows?

D: Yes.

S: Why does the city freely produce such illusions for itself?

D: The illusory still has extraordinary power. It sometimes seems as if the city cannot live without illusions, even though it knows that they are illusions! Perhaps we simply cannot bear very much reality. Different groups enshadow their messages in an attempt to influence as many people as possible. Most do so to make money, as news, or entertainment, or education, or by promising to satisfy the desires of the city in one way or another.

S: Then the market controls the production of shadows.

D: Most definitely.

S: Does no one enshadow their communications for free?

D: Some do, but the market pursues the successful ones with offers of money so that no successful platform is left free of the shadows of the masters.

S: And because the production of shadows is now open to all, presumably everyone can be both a creator and a consumer of shadows?

D: Yes. And at stake is control of the hearts and minds of the city.

E: I wish to give you an example, Socrates.

S: Please do.

E: Some use the shadows to represent groups of people in the city according to particular sets of negative characteristics.

S: For example?

E: Some groups are enshadowed as dangerous to the city and as needing to be driven out. They are often blamed for problems in the city, and once the blame is attached, it is very hard to remove. Such fear, demanding ever greater security, is grounded in prejudice and sometimes violence against the so-called enemy within.

F: That's not right. There *are* people who don't belong in the city.

E: You mean people brought here against their will in the time of Empire?

F: I mean people who can't speak our language, people who have foreign religions and customs, people who don't share the beliefs of the city. They undermine the city's identity. They weaken us all.

E: That's what the shadows tell you, but the shadows lie.

F: And you know truth and lies better than I do, do you? What
you understand somehow outranks my own understanding,
does it? Socrates, here is your elite class right in front of us.
They think their education makes them superior. They think
they can tell us how we should live, what we should think, how
we should speak, and what words we can and can't use. Here is
the city's ill health.

S: Tell me how you see this sickness.

F: Where I come from, you look after your own, your family, your
friends. There are different types of people. I am one type. My
city is of one type. The educated elite never tire of telling us
that different types have to live together. Why? It doesn't work.
Besides, they tell us to live with others, but they never do so
themselves. They live on higher ground above the mixing. One
rule for them, one for the rest of us.

S: They are hypocrites?

F: They are. And they control the shadows. They push their views
into education, communication and law, and label anyone
who disagrees with them as wrong and ignorant. In fact, you
can't say anything anymore without being called some sort
of racist or sexist bigot, even a criminal. They seem to think
that I am to blame for prejudice. They tell me that I was born
in the wrong just for being who I am. And they assume the
right to politically correct me for things I haven't done! I didn't
create slavery, but I am blamed for it. I don't decide who gets
overlooked for jobs, but I am treated as if I do. I don't have
advantages in life, but I am still held accountable as if I did.

S: And you experience this as injustice.

F: Of course, it's an injustice. Why should I be blamed for these
things? What happens is that those people that the elite stand
up for are then given preferential treatment over the rest of

us. If you want an example of injustice, look at the way we, the people who were born in the city, are treated in comparison to those who come from outside.

S: You feel accused of things you played no part in.

F: The very definition of injustice! The liberal elite judge us by the values which they think count as normal. But we have seen through their version of normal. It's fake. They tell us facts, but they are only their facts. They produce evidence, but it's only their evidence. They have their own kind of educated language which, if you listen to it, is the art of never really saying anything at all. They can't answer even simple questions directly, and so they spin everything, hoping we won't notice if they just ramble on for long enough. Well, we are past their facts and their evidence; we are long past their truths. The whole lot of them are like a swamp that needs draining.

S: Are they corrupt?

F: Completely corrupt. We struggle in the city with little enough while they gorge themselves. They make more and more obscene amounts of money, mostly by ignoring the rules, and then, when their greed creates some kind of huge crisis, and their greed brings them to their knees, the elite look after each other. They make us pay to keep them going. Where is the justice in that? They are corrupt, and they always get away with it. They can do anything because they always look after each other. The system stinks.

G: You are angry, my friend, and rightly so. But you have not mentioned that there is a science to back up your view of the world – one which even comes from those same educated elite! The history and culture of the city can be traced back to an origin and to one type of people. This history and culture are my heritage and my identity. If that is threatened, then damn right I will defend it.

S: So you believe that there is rational proof for claims of tribal purity?

G: I do not need rational proof, even if it exists. The heart is stronger than the head in such matters. I trust revelation, not reason.

S: Are there leaders in the city who speak for you?

G: We wait in hope for someone who will tell it like it is. We will follow anyone who feels as angry as we do, who will give us back control of our city and stop filling it with foreigners.

S: Do you employ your own shadows?

G: We communicate our message, yes. We try to speak plainly, and the elite try to stop us from doing so.

S: And do people listen to you?

G: More and more people are agreeing with us. Our reality is being heard and recognized as the true one. We are gaining support and growing stronger.

S: Who do you trust to speak for you?

G: Anyone who exposes those who deny our history and culture. Anyone who will take it to the educated and their institutions and make them accountable at last to the real world and to real lives. We know our spokesmen will be accused of all sorts of things. But that's what you expect when those in their ivory towers get rattled. You should know that better than most people, Socrates! Well, as far as I am concerned, those who speak up for us can even make things up if it will help! The elite will bleat and moan that something is not based on evidence or facts. But I don't need facts to tell me what I already know. The more alternative the facts, the better. Besides which, we all make things up; everybody lies.

H: Might I interrupt? If anyone in the city has just cause for anger
at injustice, it must be the half of the population who suffer
prejudice and domination by the other half.

S: What is this injustice you speak of?

H: The power of men over women and over so much else in the
city. It is found everywhere, in the largest of social arenas to
the smallest areas of personal relationships. When you talk
of the city's way of life, its rulers, traders and guardians, you
just speak of men. Its ideas, its structures, its education, even
its ideas of what a woman is supposed to be, are male. It is the
male perspective that counts as the normal or the natural one.
It is the male perspective that defines truth in the city. To be a
woman, a mother, a sister, a daughter, to be feminine, is to be
other to that truth.

S: So, are the shadows male? Are they made in the image of
men?

H: Indeed, and they are subtly maintained by a whole industry of
shadow production.

S: So women have no control of their own over the shadows?

H: Control is a very male concept, Socrates.

S: In what way?

H: Control is about power and mastery, and this operates even at
the most intimate level of personal relationships between men
and women. Often it is hidden, but sometimes not so hidden,
and there is much intimidation, subjugation, coercion and
violence suffered on a daily basis as a result of such control. It
is insidious and often cunning. Women, however, can express
a very different understanding of what you just called control
of the shadows. I think we have learned to live with them,
behind them and under them, as well as against them, and in
this way, we challenge them as best we can. At times we even

enjoy a certain level of self-determination. But always this tests the limits of what male control of the shadows will tolerate.

S: Do all women see things as you do?

H: Far from it. Some believe and will defend the imbalance between men and women as something natural. But there are many others who argue that even this definition of nature is created by men for their own advantage. The tensions between women on this issue have been and continue to be difficult and painful.

S: How have women tried to fight this?

H: They have fought in different ways for a long time, but because the rules for effective argument are set by men, our opposition, our critique and our protests have been labelled as irrational, over-emotional, even hysterical at times.

S: But men also have emotions.

H: Of course, but the truth of being male is the truth which suppresses emotions or, at times, uses them for egoistic self-promotion. Generally, men have only valued and rewarded detachment. So you see, Socrates, everything, even truth itself in the city, is male, and women always fall below its measure.

S: What is the basis for this idea of truth?

H: I think man is always seen as the active principle while the woman is passive.

S: How so?

H: Men are seen to make things happen. They are perceived as the inventors. He is the project and the projection, the issue, the discharge and the flow. Creative energy belongs only to men. Women, by contrast, are seen as the passive and yielding receptacle of this project and projection.

S: And is this perceived as a natural distinction?

H: It is. What better way to protect one's power and advantage in the city than to define truth and nature in one's own image? Women are perennially defined according to a deficit model where she lacks the nature and the tools of projection. She is less than truth. Just look at how men have defined 'man' in general: 'mankind'. Women are even excluded from humanity. It is hard to express yourself if you cannot find yourself in the universal. History is male. Truth is male. Perhaps even logic is male.

S: In what way?

H: Male truth in the world defines its claim to being the principle of activity by way of a logic of beginnings and ends, a logic of project management and completion, or a logic of solutions and answers. But women and their history have never been about the search for such certainties. It's men who define truth here as victory, as overcoming and as closure. And what satisfaction men find in such victories!

S: Then in this male logic man is master and the truth is masterful.

H: Yes.

S: And such truth is made in his own image.

H: Yes, an image of certainty, or that something is what it is because it cannot be otherwise. I think he fears anything contradictory or ambiguous because it threatens to destabilize that self-certainty.

S: This male truth sounds very much like the definition of the prime mover or god. Man seems to think of himself as the first principle of everything.

H: No coincidence there, Socrates. Man is self-seeding. How like a god! This is the basis of man's misogyny, and it seeps out of the pores of the city when it worships god as father and son.

Even the mother is rejected. She is merely a body, a vessel for the truth which is man.

S: And the body is classed as in error compared to the truth which is beyond the body?

H: We live and we are defined as that error. How easily our bodies are abused. How easily we are subject to investigation and examination by the male gaze which just happens to find whatever truth it seeks.

S: The prisoner was meant to be freed by being exposed to the light.

H: But, Socrates, the light which is truth is already male. Such freedom and learning only ever belonged to man learning of himself everywhere he looked. Can you imagine what this path to enlightenment means for a woman? The best she can hope for is becoming as much of a man as she can in order to have power and influence. For centuries, women have been told that they will never be allowed to learn for or about themselves outside of male truth. But despite this, we have done. And we are open to learning of truth differently, and to what a different sort of freedom might mean.

S: Has the city ever had or known female truth or freedom?

H: No, but justice demands it should have done.

S: Even something like a female logic?

H: Perhaps, yes, but it is unlikely in a city where male truth is so intransigent. I and many others feel so deeply that somewhere there can be found a different truth, a different logic as you put it. What it looks like I'm not sure. But whatever it is, in male logic, it will always already have lost the argument.

K: I find a similar idea of truth rules the city's relation to nature.

S: In what way?

K: It is a version of truth, and of logic, that mirrors the interests of traders and rulers who put the success of the market before the preservation of the ecosystems that support life.

S: So truth also takes the shape of mastery over nature?

K: Production and consumption in the city dominate nature and exploit her as much as possible. The market is happy to maximize profits by using the male version of truth to justify its abuse of nature.

S: What is the nature of the abuse?

K: The city draws its energy from natural resources, not caring to preserve them or care for them, and in wilful disdain for the harmful by-products created, some of which threaten the quality of life in the city, and some of which threaten human life itself.

S: What part is played by shadows?

K: They have an ambivalent role. They hide and expose the truth at the same time.

S: Does the city realize this?

K: I think it does. The city is aware of what it is doing to itself, yet remains petrified, gazing at the oncoming storm, unable and unwilling to act so as to prevent it.

S: Why?

K: Either because people think they cannot make a difference to such a huge problem, or that in order to make a difference, they will have to reduce the resources they currently consume.

S: People might need to have less and to limit their desires accordingly?

K: If they hadn't become accustomed to such riches, they might have lived well with less. But now it seems there is nothing that can help people find a different truth to live by.

S: So, no one makes the first move.

K: And by definition no one moves at all.

S: The present city does seem to be a strange place, angry and confused, living in denial of injustice, yet experiencing it every day in different parts of its life. But, if you will excuse me for a moment, I think I see someone listening to us from the edge of concealment.

Book 2

[Socrates rises from his seat and the small crowd that has gathered yields as he makes his way across the street, towards a figure present in shadow.]

S: Hello there.

CELIA:

S: Please don't turn away . . . would you care to join us in our discussions?

CELIA:

S: I have not intended to embarrass you. . . . I only wondered, that is, you looked as if you were listening to us, but it was hard to see you in the shadows. . . . But perhaps I have made a mistake in coming over. . . . Please accept my apologies.

CELIA: Wait.

S: Yes?

CELIA: You saw me.

S: I became aware of your shadow in the shadows.

CELIA: How is that possible? The shadow in the shadows is unseen, unheard, unknown.

S: Are you known as unknown?

CELIA: Perhaps I am that question.

S: Are you seen by anyone?

CELIA: Sometimes, yes, but I am more easily found by poverty, plague and prejudice. But this should be familiar to you,

Socrates. Did you not also have those who were known as unknown in your previous life?

S: You mean those called slaves?

CELIA: I mean all those whose lives were lived or known as shadows of their masters.

S: The old city believed it was the nature of its slaves, and of its women, that made it impossible for them to live like free men. Now, in the present city, despite its claims for equality, it seems that free men are still able to be masters of others.

CELIA: When I am seen, it is as one of these others. I am prejudged as different. Their fear of me brings suffering and violence, and I live in fear of their fear.

S: I was also feared by those who thought of me as an alien in my own city. I now feel something of an outsider in this present city.

CELIA: And yet you have the confidence and the appearance of a master. You are not invisible. You are not a shadow among the shadows. People seek you out. They demand your visibility. They seem desperate to hear what you have to say. Some seem ready to trust you, and they confer visibility upon you. You are not the outsider. I live without the rights that are yours, without the property that is yours, without the recognition that is yours. What is granted to the invisible is to have unloaded upon them the blame for everything that is deemed to be wrong in the city. The blame, the fear and the violence are sown into the very material of the city.

S: I am beginning to see and hear this for myself.

CELIA: I would think you can have little idea of what it is like, in the eyes of others, to see how unworthy and how undeserving people think you are. Even for my eyes to meet those of another can move them to violence and brutality, for fear that such recognition would compromise their supremacy.

They desire to see only a body that carries something less than human. The history of this body in the city was as the property of the breeder of human cattle for the field or the auction block, or of the employer of human labour for the factory or the mill. Even today the masters of the city see the spirit of this body as something to break, dominate, exploit and abuse. The masters do not expect to be met by the eyes of this body.

S: And so you are invisible.

CELIA: That is what they allow themselves to believe. Invisible on the streets where we live. Invisible when attacked. Invisible when harassed by the forces charged with public safety. We are not their public, and so our safety is not their concern. We live life on the edge and always at risk of disappearing over it. Every second of every day we remain the target of prejudice and hatred and violence.

S: I see you.

CELIA: But through whose eyes do you see me, Socrates? Not through mine. I am not what you think you see. And every day I have to tell myself, as if for the first time, not to see myself through the eyes of the masters, not to understand myself through their understanding, not to value myself through their values and not to adopt their hypocrisies and cruelties. If they define me, then they own me. And I am owned in so many ways. Yet I try to keep my soul intact. All that I have is my soul, forced as it is to live as a shadow in the shadows. The city has a history of invisible people. The eyes of the masters in the city have learned to live in relative comfort with our invisibility. Their eyes pass over us, seeing but not seeing. Generations before me in the city have had such lives. Some are invisible in the places they clean, some in the places they work, some in the leisured lives they serve, and some in maintaining the freedom of the masters to travel, to consume and to indulge their excesses. All of the invisible serve in one way or another in clear view and all are invisible in doing so. They have to live in areas that are visibly invisible. They have to do the best they can. They are necessary and yet they are deemed undesirable and undeserving. The freedom of the city rests on the chains that bind the invisible in their enslavement to the freedom of others. And so, Socrates, while I might have something to say, I have no voice for your crowd. I am not the mouth for these ears.

S: People need to hear from you.

CELIA: They hear, Socrates. They know.

S: Justice in the city requires them to listen to what they hear.

CELIA: Really? Every day I am set the question as to whether justice will be done in this place, while everyday injustice visits me as the totality of what I am and what I can expect to be. And I have seen how this injustice is borne by the invisible. It is carried sometimes in the suppression of anger which is mostly held back behind the eyes that look down. At times it must strike out and sometimes uncontrollably so. But we know the trapdoor of escalation that is always open for us, and the result is seldom good. Is this something you could ever understand, Socrates? We know that our anger just confirms the unjust masters in their views of the wretched. We know we harm ourselves. We know we give cause here to the self-righteous to demand justice against our outbursts.

But I have already said too much, Socrates. The city, its masters and its enslaving of others, cannot bear the truth of its shadows. I may have been visible to you these past few minutes, but already my strength for such being in your world leaves me, my confidence wanes, my temporary visibility slips away. The gap it leaves is once again filled by my invisibility. You have listened, Socrates, but I doubt one such as you could have understood. Perhaps you have their eyes, perhaps you do not; who knows; I cannot quite tell. But perhaps it makes little difference anyway. They found you guilty in a court. For me, they do not even bother with a trial. I am already guilty of everything they want me to be.

S: Things can change . . .

CELIA: Yes, things can change.

S: People might learn to understand you better.

CELIA: I don't want people to understand me better. I want people to understand themselves better. Do you really believe that the city is open to learning about its own truth? It wants change without having to change.

S: Perhaps it can learn differently?

CELIA: Perhaps. But why would it? Our invisibility for them is both a successful way of repressing their deepest fears and an effective way of organizing the city. Who among them would choose justice if it meant things becoming better for us but worse for them?

S: I would.

CELIA: Then do so, Socrates. I will be able to see and hear your discussions, even from within the shadows. When you hurt because the light of the invisible people burns your eyes, then you can choose whether to walk into that pain or turn back. If you choose to walk forward, then you might yet find the light in the shadows. I and my kind will be waiting to see the truth of your shadow, Socrates. For it might be that we already have the truth you seek, just as you might have the visibility that we deserve. Perhaps we will both of us learn how to meet there.

C: Socrates, we grow impatient. Who are you talking to?

S: One moment . . .

[Socrates turns back to Celia, but she has gone. He returns back across the street and to those eager for more conversation.]

A: You look sad, Socrates.

S: The city is indeed a difficult and contradictory place, my friend.

A: In what ways?

S: I see that rulers have become dominated by self-interest; that knowledge-prisoners, although released from their chains, have remained work-prisoners of their economic masters; that the rulers and traders have manipulated privilege by working together; and that the walls of shadows are the new battleground for control of the hearts and minds of citizens.

A: And what of injustice in the city?

S: I see it everywhere I look; between rich and poor, powerful and powerless, voiced and voiceless, man and woman, over-privileged and under-privileged, visible and invisible.

A: And how does it appear to you that such injustice manifests itself?

S: Often as anger – on the one side, anger at a lack of control, anger at education and its rulers, and anger at the outsider; on the other side, anger at prejudice, ignorance and bigotry.

A: Anger on both sides. Anger everywhere about everything.

S: The complaints are not arbitrary or unrelated to each other. They are symptoms of a deeper malaise.

A: What malaise?

S: They are manifestations of a city at war with itself.

A: How?

S: By fighting a war within a war. The war we heard about today is the cultural conflict of warring gods who see the world differently and whose differences are irreconcilable. This war demands that each god accept or reject the truth of the others.

They are opposed on content but agreed on the terms of the conduct of the war. In this agreement they are at war with a common enemy. Collectively they oppose the deep thinking and critical reflection which, tarrying with doubts, has the patience required for meaningful self-examination.

A: You mean they are at war with philosophy?

S: Perhaps. But I wonder if philosophy, like the city, has forgotten its own roots, its own vocation in education.

A: If so, then we could say that what really afflicts the city is a crisis of education?

S: It seems that the city is tearing itself apart in a civil war in which education is in conflict with itself. And if philosophical self-examination is defeated, then the war of anger wins. That leaves a city in which anger and ill health are a way of life.

A: And a city that no longer believes in or seeks its own self-education, and which runs scared of it, is a city destroying itself from within. Early on in its history, reason held out hope for justice in the city. In time, it also offered a vision of freedom and democracy where citizens give rules to themselves. But this reason seems to have failed to deliver justice.

S: And when this happens, people turn against it.

A: Where do they turn to?

S: As we have heard, they turn to more visceral attachments. But these are no safeguard against tyranny.

A: Then reason has nothing to blame but itself.

S: Perhaps reason has not been given a fair chance to fully express itself. Perhaps it has always been shaped by wealth and power in the city.

A: And the result, today, is that the city is dividing into factions, each finding a sense of belonging and identity in a particular kind of anger. Even within the elite, factions fight against one another, and the citizens are blown hither and thither by their dramas.

S: Each faction, no doubt, desperate for the control that they believe comes from identification within a clan?

A: The more you can show someone as an outsider to your group, the stronger you feel yourself an insider; the more you are able to scapegoat others, the more in control of things you feel.

S: Do you think that this sense of belonging is illusory?

A: No, it's a real power.

S: But will it achieve the control and the mastery that it craves?

A: It seems to for many people.

S: Perhaps mastery is always an illusion, and seeking more of it only exposes this more deeply, while making the city an increasingly unjust place.

A: Then ours is a failing city?

S: It slides between more mastery for the collective over the individual and more mastery for the individual over the collective. The furniture moves, but the room itself doesn't change.

A: Why not?

S: Perhaps because the soul and the city still do not know how to learn of each other. Each is always given priority over the other, and this is only ever the freedom of mastery and servitude.

A: But democracy has improved the city!

S: It has. And created its own injustices.

A: But democracy is better than tyranny.

S: It is, but it also has tyranny within it. This is the injustice that our conversation has exposed.

A: And sometimes the city responds to tyranny by using tyranny.

S: Strength as mastery always looks like the solution. This is
   where the city seems to be – in a battle for control in which
   the victor masters the vanquished. It is indeed a significant
   and potentially very dangerous moment for the city, one that is
   turning away from learning about itself towards the appeal of a
   control that was and ever will be a self-defeating civil war.

B: I am very worried, Socrates. I see a city moving backwards,
   back to a life which is less equal, less fair, less tolerant, less
   compassionate, back to times when skin colour defined
   one's whole identity, or one's clan, or when women could
   be denigrated in public and openly abused in the privacy of
   the family home. I see leaders who want to divide the city
   into identity groups, each restricted to one language, to one
   set of beliefs and to one set of values. I see them as a threat
   to hard-won freedoms and values which speak of equality
   and justice for all in a city that is not divided into fixed
   identity groups walled within tight cultural boundaries. I see
   them as unwilling to extend the hand of friendship to those
   fleeing desperate situations in other parts of the city. I feel an
   atmosphere of distrust and hatred taking over the city. And I
   see leaders whose bigotry and racism are reshaping life in the
   city. But most of all I see people at first kept from, and then
   rejecting, the kind of education that will expose the powerful,
   call them to account and create the transparency that is
   needed for a just city.

F: Still the same old arrogance. As always, people like you
   ignore those of us who believe in some of those old ways, old
   allegiances, old associations. You and your educational elite
   will kill us all. It's dangerous to have the foreigner flood in and
   take advantage of the freedoms that others have paid for, in

money and in sacrifices in wars. I think it's dangerous that you want to destroy our way of life.

S: So, each of you sees the other as the problem?

H: It would appear so. The so-called educated label and blame the so-called barbarian and the so-called barbarian label and blame the so-called educated.

C: But perhaps education is really the root of the problem. One side blames the other for having either too much education or too little education.

D: It is hard to see how the two sides can be reconciled. If you use education to try to heal the division, you pour oil on the flames.

S: And so, the city that was to be the educational city and the just city finds education as the root cause, bearer and reproducer of its injustices. As we said just now, the city's crisis is an educational crisis. Those who were charged with representing education as self-sacrifice for the good of the city as a whole instead abused it for self-entitlement. And the truth of education they forced onto the city embodied this privilege, with a casual disregard for how the principle of formal equality reproduced inequality, affecting the poorest and vulnerable most. As the educated rejected the truth of education for justice in the city, so the uneducated now reject the educated as well. Everyone rejects education. The idea that education is the key to justice in the city seems dead.

A: I still believe in education.

S: How so?

A: I hold to a vision where people are not divided into tribes or clans or races but are all part of a common humanity. It is a vision of people from all over the city being able to live peacefully with one another, respecting differences and searching for shared values that will enable all to live freely together. It is a world of opportunity and freedom, of justice and fairness, equality and fraternity. It is where we have more in common with each other than differences between us. It is a world where extremes of wealth and poverty no longer exist; a world where people could be civilized and educated enough to understand that while it is possible to have more than one needs, it is neither necessary nor desirable. This is the education in which limits of wealth are freely agreed upon. It is a world which cherishes and vigilantly guards the equality of people no matter their differences from one another. It is a world that knows its place within the myriad forms of life that make up the cosmos, and that is humble enough to learn from all life, and not to assume superiority over it, a world that does not make its own extremely limited perspective master over the vastness of time and space that escapes our human view. It is a world that does not inflict suffering on animals for any reason, and certainly not for human vanity. It is a world that learns of the part it can best play in living with life that is known, and in waiting patiently to learn of forms of life that are as yet unknown to it. It is a world where we love to learn about others as we love to learn about ourselves.

S: A powerful vision indeed.

A: I think it has been developing over the many years of city culture. Each generation has played its part. It was as if freedom was slowly emerging as an idea until it became something real, something that people could live. The major change was in outlawing physical enslavement. This also gave us the opportunity to emancipate ourselves from mental slavery. But as you have seen, slavery persists in many forms.

The rational mind failed itself again. That is why my vision takes me well beyond what the city knows and understands, and how it lives. But this vision is dying, because education in the city is dying.

S: Then what are its teachers doing? Are they not teaching that there is more in the world and more to individual lives than meets the eye immediately?

A: They are scared too, Socrates. Teachers have been attacked as those who think they know better than others. They have been dragged into the net that labels any kind of thoughtful education as elite. They have been made part of the swamp. Many have abandoned teaching about the shadows for fear of being accused of being as fake as the shadows they teach about. They are trained to become shadows and to teach shadows without having to care for truth. They no longer teach for how the city is constructed or how different it might be; they teach only for how the city appears to our everyday thinking.

S: Have such teachers become nervous of being critical?

A: Yes. Nervous of resisting the reduction of thinking to training, and nervous of expertise being trivialized. Education as critical examination is almost lost. But these are very important issues, Socrates, and this has already been a long conversation. Perhaps we might draw it to a close and meet again tomorrow?

S: Indeed. But I have one remaining question.

A: What is that?

S: Why can I no longer see the light that marks the entrance to the city?

A: What? Can it be possible, Socrates? You have returned, but you have not yet seen our wall?

[At that moment, from among the crowd which had now grown to some considerable size, someone was pushing his way forward. Working his way to the front of the crowd, the man approached Socrates and began to speak.]

N: Socrates, it has become clear to those of us charged with maintaining order in the city that you have started your teaching again.

S: I have never taught anyone anything, nor am I doing so now.

N: As before, you still cling to this miserable ruse. No matter. Upon seeing your return to the city, two charges have been filed against you by two separate parties, for which you must now stand trial. First, you are charged by the ordinary people of the city of being the architect of this unjust city that is ruled by an elite using the power and privilege that you gave them. Second, you are charged by the city's rulers of being the architect of a model of the city that was wholly unfit for purpose, leaving the rulers to have to manage inevitable injustice as best they could.

It is generally agreed that your return spells trouble, for you would no doubt try to undermine authority in the city even in these perilous times. But you have nowhere to run, for you have no supporters. The city rejects the kind of examination you offer, and we have got to you before you are able to try, once again, seducing people into becoming your followers.

You will appear in court tomorrow. You will be held in a cell this evening to prevent you from entertaining any other crowds with your pernicious philosophizing. And tomorrow you will answer to these charges in court, just as you did many years ago. Take him away.

Book 3

JUDGE: Good morning, members of the jury. There are two
parties bringing charges against the accused. The first party
charges him with being the origin of injustice in the city,
in that he did knowingly and willingly justify rule by a
self-perpetuating elite. The second party charges him with
establishing an unworkable system of government in the city,
based on a naive, incorrect and dogmatic wisdom regarding
the truth of human nature. Socrates, do you understand the
charges being brought against you?

S: I would need to examine my accusers face to face in order to
understand them.

JUDGE: In my court the accused answer the questions; they do
not ask them.

S: Then such a court is not doing justice to the examined life or to
me.

JUDGE: Be clear, Socrates. I will not be drawn into one of your
beguiling dialogues. There will be no pedagogical witchcraft
here today. I warn you, any of your tricks and you will be held
in contempt.

S: How can questions be considered contemptible?

JUDGE: Enough! In your first trial you made your own defence.
Will you be doing this again?

S: It would seem so.

JUDGE: Very well. Let us proceed with the first of the charges
against you.

PROSECUTOR 1: Thank you, your honour. I am the prosecutor
for the first party. We can dispense with proof of your identity,
Socrates, for we are certain as to who you are.

S: Then you are more certain of it than I am.

PROSECUTOR 1: Let us begin by establishing some facts in this case, something which the city's records show you were never renowned for. Are you the author and instigator of the original design of the city?

S: I am its voice even if not specifically its author.

PROSECUTOR 1: And are the ideas found therein your ideas?

S: Since they are in my voice, I must admit to them being my own, but—

PROSECUTOR 1: Thank you. Now, tell me if you think this is a fair summary of the document. First, that human beings need to cooperate in order to meet their most basic needs.

S: Yes.

PROSECUTOR 1: Second, that these needs can best be fulfilled in a just way if everyone does the job for which they are most innately suited?

S: Yes.

PROSECUTOR 1: Third, that the soul has three main elements: desire which befits the class of traders, courage which befits the class of the city's defenders, and reason which befits the class of wise rulers?

S: Yes.

PROSECUTOR 1: Finally, that these rulers should have power over everything in the city, including the right to lie to the population, to practice eugenics, to have the power of euthanasia, to censor artistic experience and to determine the curriculum by which the city will educate its succeeding generations?

S: Your language is a little unfamiliar, but I recognize these as included in the programme set out in what you have come to know as *The Republic* but which was first entitled *Politeia*.

PROSECUTOR 1: Which brings us to the charge that my clients – the most powerless people in the city – have brought against you. In your founding document you legitimized the power of the few over the many on the grounds that these few were naturally born to rule and that they alone could and should enjoy a life of leisured freedom.

S: In the context of the harmony of the soul and the city.

PROSECUTOR 1: Harmony! As far as my clients are concerned, you put mastery in the hands of an elite, justified by their educational superiority, who then used this power to feather their own nests by relentlessly and remorselessly exploiting the rest of the city for their own ends.

S: They were not to have nests of their own. They were to be motivated only by the good and to act according to their wisdom.

PROSECUTOR 1: Many times, these same masters that you defend bleated out pious laments of misunderstood benevolence; 'we are working in the interests of everyone', 'we are sacrificing ourselves to serve the city' and other such apologies. And yet, the actions they try to justify are those based on pure self-interest. Many times, actions have been taken, cruelties and hardships imposed, wars fought, people imprisoned and extremes of poverty and luxury justified as being in the public interest.

S: No one expected that things would turn out this way.

PROSECUTOR 1: Really? How could things have turned out any other way?

S: This was not what was intended for the just city.

PROSECUTOR 1: Then you had no forethought of the unintended consequences of the best laid plans in attempting to create utopia on earth? For example, you failed to see how the shadows would become the key weapon in preserving and extending the power of the elite over the people.

S: I have heard of this on my return to the city.

PROSECUTOR 1: You did not plan for the possibility of change in the city because you assumed that perfection could not be improved on. As a result, any freedoms achieved in the city by my clients have only come about through their struggles against the material privileges of the masters and their intellectual justifications.

S: It seems that virtue and the truth of wisdom have become justifications for power and privilege.

PROSECUTOR 1: Indeed so. Your elites granted to themselves the qualities and character of virtue and wisdom, labelling everything else as barbarian and as ruled by animal passions and bodily appetites. They took themselves to be the moral high ground and looked down on all lesser forms of existence. Indeed, virtue and wisdom turned out to be fair-skinned, largely male, always rich and seldom without the enslavement of others. And all of this originates from the liberal ideas you established as truth. To this day my clients are still paying the price for this. You are therefore charged with being the cause of the injustice of elite rule in the city, an elitism of privilege, wealth, power and nepotism. If inequality and injustice are what afflicts the city, you are the source of that affliction. How do you plead?

S: I make no plea while I am listening to the case against me.

PROSECUTOR 1: Then let me continue. Your elite made a virtue of hypocrisy. They ruled and continue to rule according to the maxim 'do as I say, not as I do'. They have one rule for themselves and one rule for everyone else. They demand obedience to universal imperatives while granting themselves exemptions. They impose universal values on the city, including the value that all are equal, while granting themselves immunity from such a limitation. Their double standards, their lying, is as nauseating as it is unjust. My clients are made to live according to standards that the elite refuse for themselves.

S: I have always tried to expose the hypocrisy of leaders and so-called wise men whose claims for superiority and authority are vain.

PROSECUTOR 1: Yet your ruling elite have, for example, imposed on the city the value of cosmopolitan identity. They have told the city that all people, whoever they are, wherever they are from, whatever their roots, language, culture, gender or beliefs, are all one people and must learn to live together, that differences must be resolved by everyone becoming the same. The great experiment of the melting pot has been forced onto the city. And here is the hypocrisy. By means of their wealth and property, the elite keep themselves away from the melting pot, preserving their own identity while expecting everyone to lose theirs. And now my clients are chastised for fighting back, for refusing to be made the same and, just like their leaders, for resisting becoming some kind of illusory universal citizen.

S: Perhaps this resistance is based on a lack of self-examination?

PROSECUTOR 1: And there we have it. The only response the elite ever have to my clients: you need more education in order to see how you are in the wrong.

S: It would seem that the whole city needs self-examination.

PROSECUTOR 1: Is this why you have returned? To educate us once again in the Socratic way, to perplex us with your questions? The threat of you carrying on as before is exactly why you are standing before us in the dock, Socrates. My clients blame you for the injustices of the city, and they most certainly do not want you to return to give us more of the same.

S: What do your clients want?

PROSECUTOR 1: They want something different.

S: Be careful what you wish for. While the same is always a tyranny if it is not open to difference, the different is also a tyranny if it is not open to that which is the same.

PROSECUTOR 1: This is not a philosophy class, Socrates; it is a court of law. We do not do scholastic, dialectical or rhetorical juggling here.

S: Really? I thought the law profession might be an important part of the elite education that your clients chastise.

JUDGE: I warned you, Socrates. Tread very carefully. The court will adjourn and when we return, we will hear the second set of charges against you.

*   *   *

JUDGE: The court will come to order. We have much to get through. The accused will now face the charges of the second party.

PROSECUTOR 2: Socrates, I represent my clients who are accusing you of being the architect of a system of government which, despite their best efforts over many years, has continued to prove unfit for purpose. The result, as you have seen for yourself, is that trust in the city's leaders and its institutions, so vital if the city is to hold together, is eroding, with all the threats to the city that this brings. The charge is that all of this is your fault, based on your fundamental misunderstanding of truth and human nature, and your pretending to know things which you did not know.

S: I know only that I do not know anything.

PROSECUTOR 2: Whether you believe such dogma ironically or disingenuously, or even if you think you mean it, it makes no real difference. You still presumed to teach us how the city should be run. At the outset my clients, in good faith, put your plan into action. They educated themselves in the ways you decreed. They spent their childhoods away from their parents, in institutions of shared and sometimes harsh environments. They were set the highest standards of virtue that you prescribed, to lead lives of self-sacrifice and service. They lived lives of self-examination, they denied themselves excesses and they tried to live the middle way, temperately, and with control over their passions, even when life or fortune or fate dealt them cruel blows. They tried to embody all that you defined as right and worthy in living the life of the rational human being.

S: Then clearly they failed.

PROSECUTOR 2: Only because my clients realized that this model which you advocated so forcefully was fatally flawed. You set the masters of the city an impossible standard to achieve. The perfect ruler who had eradicated self-interest was an impossibility. The community of the wise rulers was not, and never could be, one of selfless and universal interest. Your model of human nature was wrong. Reason will never conquer desire, neither in the masters nor in those who are in bondage to them.

S: Surely, they did not expect it to be easy.

PROSECUTOR 2: No. But they were led by you to believe that it was possible.

S: Only with the right character and with decades of preparatory study.

PROSECUTOR 2: The world of reason was not as you advertised
    it, Socrates.

S: In what way?

PROSECUTOR 2: The real world of desire in the city could not
    and would never be run by wise philosophical rulers who had
    no property, wealth or families of their own.

S: Then these people were not those best suited to government.

PROSECUTOR 2: On the contrary, these were the right people
    to make the best of a bad job. They were the ones brave
    enough to try to live with the flawed model of human nature
    that your plan was based on.

S: Courage was always expected of them.

PROSECUTOR 2: It was. But courage alone is not enough
    to paper over the cracks in your design. Because of its
    imperfections, rulers in the city are not trusted. Not because
    they are bad people. But because the values that you
    established by which they should be judged have always
    made them seem to be bad people. You gave everyone wholly
    unreasonable expectations about what a just city and its rulers
    would look like. Now they are blamed for its failings, and for
    their own so-called weaknesses when measured against the
    model. That is their charge against you, Socrates. You raised
    the bar to levels that fundamentally misunderstood human
    nature. And the city's rulers have been paying the price ever
    since. They have been doing their best. But their best was
    never going to be good enough according to the unrealistic
    ideals of Socrates.

S: Since my return I have seen for myself how distrusted these
    rulers are.

PROSECUTOR 2: Which leads me to a subsidiary charge that
    my clients accuse you of, one that goes to the heart of your

own hypocrisy. They charge you with pretending to know that which clearly you did not know.

S: Pretending to know what?

PROSECUTOR 2: That you knew and understood the natural basis of social groups and how they would best be organized; that you knew and understood the nature of the human soul and how it could best be turned to the functions of the city; that you knew and understood the path of enlightenment leading to truth; and that, putting all this together, you knew and understood the nature of justice and how to create it on earth.

S: You speak as if I stated these things dogmatically.

PROSECUTOR 2: Which brings us to your hypocrisy. You claimed you were not a teacher and that you had nothing to teach. Your plan for the city exposes this as a lie.

S: Perhaps my ignorance has been misunderstood. Perhaps my life and my words have been taken out of their context. And perhaps commentators have ignored the perplexities that are inescapably bound to everything I have said and assumed that such difficulties are mistakes to be ironed out or just ignored.

PROSECUTOR 2: The plan as you set it out is straightforward enough, and it is in your own words.

S: They are not spoken by the kind of teacher that you seem to think I was.

PROSECUTOR 2: And yet you saw fit to legislate the most comprehensive plan ever devised for ruling a perfect city.

S: If people have ruled without the qualities required of them by the just city, then perhaps they should examine themselves more closely. Perhaps they should admit to their own failings.

PROSECUTOR 2: On the contrary. Given the flawed model they had to work with, my clients deserve rewards for trying to work with the mess you bequeathed. Do my clients not deserve immense credit for their best efforts at carrying the universal interests of a city that has different natural talents and abilities?

S: Is it not said that it is a poor workman who blames his tools?

PROSECUTOR 2: Tools! You left the rulers no tools at all. You believed tools were barbarian. Philosophy was new and untested, and my clients had no guides or examples to help them. They had to learn of your mistakes the hard way, through bitter experience. My clients want to know what madness led you to think you had all the answers to the city's problems. And this from the man who said he knew nothing. You must have realized that this position of ignorance was nonsense and in response you switched sides and became the city's legislator-in-chief.

S: Questions, not dogmas, were always meant to be the basis of the city's just laws. The plan was for a city of educational self-examination, born out of itself. If the city separates the examining from the examination, then this will sow the seeds of injustice into the city.

PROSECUTOR 2: Being the hypocrite that you are, blaming others is to be expected from you, I suppose, Socrates. You are the man who, having said he knew nothing, did a U-turn and claimed to be all wise.

S: Wisdom is to be found in not knowing.

PROSECUTOR 2: Then why, from knowing too little, did you suddenly take it upon yourself to know too much? This goes to the heart of the charge that my clients are bringing against you. You pretended to know that which you did not know and were ignorant about what you should have known. The result is that trust has been erased in all those who made it their duty to serve the city as its rulers. And as this trust disappears, so do all the impossible ideals that accompanied it.

S: I suspect you fear that barbarism now threatens the city.

PROSECUTOR 2: And you bear more responsibility for this than any other individual. Your utopia, never a real city, is what our rulers have been held hostage to. What else could they do but fail?

JUDGE: Socrates, you have heard the charges being brought against you. You now have an opportunity to respond. Will you defend yourself?

S: I will speak for myself.

JUDGE: Then I warn you, do not test the court's indulgence with your dialectical sophistry. We will not be befuddled by any of your trickery or skill in debating.

S: Am I to be marked in advance by the same prejudices that underpinned my previous trial?

JUDGE: Disarm yourself of such rhetoric, Socrates.

S: My comments will not be planned or scripted or rehearsed.

JUDGE: You have always had considerable extemporary skills. We know that.

S: I follow only where the daemon leads me. I follow where education leads me.

JUDGE: Enough. Let us get on with it.

S: Then let me begin by summarizing the charges as I understand them. The first party accuses me of creating injustice in the city by justifying government by an educated elite.

JUDGE: Correct.

S: The second party charges that this injustice became inevitable and indeed necessary because I claimed to know the truth of the human soul but got it wrong.

JUDGE: Correct again.

S: Putting these two charges together it is clear that both sides blame me for the injustices of the city. Both sides accuse me of an arrogant dogmatism regarding the truth of the just city. And in the collapse of such dogma I seem to have made sceptics of everyone. No one now believes that a philosophical education can be the path to the just city. I am on trial to be shot at by both the elite and the prisoners at the same time.

JUDGE: And what is your defence?

S: If my defence to the first party is that clear educational instructions were provided for the city's leaders which they have ignored, then I run straight into the second party who argue that these safeguards were based on misconceived knowledge and ideas. And if my defence to the second party is that those who took power clearly had characters unfit for just rule, then the charge of the first party stands, that the plan put power in the hands of a small band of imperfect rulers.

JUDGE: It seems you have nowhere to turn, Socrates, hoist, as it were, on the petard of your own dialectics!

S: Indeed. Each defence I make repeats the other's accusations.

JUDGE: Then you have no defence left open to you, and guilt is assured either way. If there is a crisis of education, as I think you have suggested, then it is a crisis of your own making.

S: My accusers have ignored the wisdom that I know only my own ignorance.

JUDGE: Still, the result is the same – a scepticism regarding any dogma about what education is and can achieve. Your so-called wisdom can clearly be seen to be the whole problem. It defeats itself and everything else with it.

S: I believe my accusers have misunderstood how my education was to work. Indeed, I think, in return, I can accuse them of not doing justice to the difficulties of this wisdom.

JUDGE: You are in no position to make accusations.

S: Nevertheless, to the clients bringing the second charge, that I fundamentally misunderstood the soul and the city, overriding my own ignorance, I say, you have refused the challenge of the just city. Perhaps you thought it unnecessary, or too difficult and too invasive on your own desires and self-interests. Or perhaps you were never more than a desiring class masquerading behind a distorted idea of education while practising and perpetuating the cruellest deception that you were what a higher education should look like.

JUDGE: Exactly who are you hoping to win favour with using invective like this, Socrates?

S: That is not my concern. I have seen how the powerful took for themselves the high ground in the city, spurned their duty to return to its centre and became detached from the city they ruled, never sharing in the toils and struggles, the hardships and suffering of the population. They proved themselves neither educated nor wise regarding the truth of the just city, succumbing to the desire for privilege and power. They created a culture of self-entitlement rather than self-examination. They rewarded each other for the illusion of service that they created for themselves. And they ensured that when mistakes were made, others were punished. At times when their corruption was exposed, they piously accepted the need for change. But, lacking all educational integrity, the song remained the same.

JUDGE: And what charges do you make against your first accusers?

S: To those bringing the first charge I say that you, the freed prisoners in the city, have not taken up the work that would challenge desire. Those who do not develop and use the mind to its full capacity are bound to remain in bondage to those who resource their desires. In refusing to think for yourselves, you have been complicit in avoiding the work and truth of education and examination, and your prize has been a greater stake in the injustice of your own lives. You have absorbed into yourselves the idea that satisfaction of desires has endless and unlimited resources to draw on. Your desires now burn out of control, and soon the city will have to reap only the wilderness, the scorched earth, that you leave behind you. You expect as of right to exercise freedom without discipline. You practise excess without constraint. Is there no one in the city who can care more for the state of the soul than for the satisfaction of its ever-growing desires? You spurned your liberation to pursue the same kind of mastery that had held you captive.

JUDGE: Again, you blame everyone except yourself. Indeed, you seem determined to combine the two separate charges and the two sets of clients into one single injustice against yourself.

S: Their unspoken alliance speaks of a war within a war, a war against education fought within the cultural conflict of these warring gods.

JUDGE: Then you make enemies of everyone, Socrates. Are you determined to repeat the outcome of your previous trial?

S: The question of their unity and difference from each other is a symptom of one of the city's most intractable difficulties.

JUDGE: What is that?

S: Trying to manage the relation between the city and its individual citizens. Prioritizing the individual makes the collective weak. Prioritizing the collective subordinates the individual.

JUDGE: Is this another of your puzzles?

S: In dialectical thinking one thing only makes sense in relation to its opposite. For example, hot water is nothing without its opposite, cold water. They only make sense in relation to each other. Perhaps the same is now true of the two sets of charges.

JUDGE: Let me reassure you, the city provides its people with hot and cold taps!

S: And what if you want warm water?

JUDGE: Then two taps can become one as a mixer tap. Really, Socrates, this is hardly profound stuff. A mixer tap gives you any temperature of water you want.

S: And in the mixer tap you have lost the hot and cold taps?

JUDGE: Yes.

S: And this is your idea of the just society? Destroying the individual in order to have just one common existence?

JUDGE: There is a simple solution to that. Keep the two taps and run the water into a bowl. The taps remain but are also joined.

S: But this means that they are kept separate from the mixing. They are joined only at a safe distance and without having to change at all. They observe the mixing but do not participate in it, are not invested in it and therefore do not have mixing, the collective existence, as their own experience.

JUDGE: As with your defence, so with this conundrum of taps, and also it seems with the political question of prioritizing the collective over the individual or the individual over the collective, you leave us perplexed and with no easy path to resolution. Like your taps, it seems you have not changed much either, Socrates.

S: The easy response in the face of such aporias or difficulties is to resign or give up; why would the city bother to examine itself if answers are not simple and forthcoming? Easier to return to the desire and self-interest that fuel injustice and to indulge the anger and prejudice that are provoked by the shadows.

JUDGE: You think this is what the city is doing in the face of its
difficulties?

S: The city has always sought and found illusory comfort in new
shadows.

JUDGE: And what new shadows do we currently have?

S: Ones that are new to me and which you carry with you at all
times.

JUDGE: You mean our personal screens?

S: Your screens ensure that everyone always has their own
personal version of the back wall of the old cave with them.
They are never without the projection of the city's shadows.

JUDGE: Screens are a great democratic development in the city.
Visibility and openness have cleansed the darker walls at the
back of the city. You are out of touch with the people once
again, Socrates.

S: But, again, people are having reality immediately presented to
them, seemingly unaware of their chains. This new shadow
world feeds the senses and immediately shapes the mind. It
does not nurture critical thinking.

JUDGE: Nonsense. It enables criticism of everything.

S: Critical thinking occurs when questions put the mind
in relation to itself and forge new depths within it. This
takes time and patience. It is a struggle. It is hard work.
Screens thwart such depths by the speed with which they
offer one shadow after another. Things pass before the eyes
encouraging only immediate reactions. There is no time for
thinking. And this immediacy is addictive. The senses crave
the next shadow. Very little is asked of people in the shadow
version of critical thinking that is rather ironically called
interactive.

JUDGE: People are not controlled by their screens. And you do not do them justice if you think people cannot discern between truth and shadows.

S: Perhaps, but people seem to have run headlong into new chains, granting full exposure of themselves to the masters of the screens who live unseen behind the curtain. These puppet masters have a new Delphic maxim for mastery: know others better than those people know themselves.

JUDGE: Why?

S: Because information freely given and turned into the logic of number by its new owners is an invitation to unseen mastery.

JUDGE: Screens are just tools. They are neutral. They are not in charge.

S: Yet they seem to want to be masters of everything, to be the new universality. They seek to make everything their property.

JUDGE: How?

S: What is not yet on screen is other and must be assimilated. If it cannot be assimilated, its worthiness must be sabotaged.

JUDGE: The screen cannot turn a person into a shadow or into the logic of number.

S: It can, and it does exactly that. And what threatens this new universality, the examined life, screens also turn into number and measurement.

JUDGE: I think you are being unnecessarily alarmist.

S: Your comment is understandable. Anything aspiring to universal mastery in the city can work by stealth, plucking the feathers of the examined life one at a time, so that each complaint concerns only something minor and relatively insignificant. The totality of the new mastery is never visible, that is, until there are no feathers left to pluck.

JUDGE: But people who share information do so in order to be part of communities. Across the whole city people have never before been in such close contact with each other. We are all connected. This is not plucking any feathers.

S: And yet, in being connected they have perhaps never also been so isolated. From what I have seen, collective screen freedom is also the loneliest kind of freedom. Its connectedness exaggerates and amplifies insecurity and vulnerability, and like a drug, makes people more addicted to finding comfort in exactly that which is harming them.

JUDGE: As always you overstate the negative aspects.

S: Then why is the screen world so full of rage and abuse?

JUDGE: I'm sure you will tell us.

S: The freedoms of the shadow world discourage self-examination. Rage and abuse at others are also rage and abuse at the space that allows and even encourages them. Screens create the isolation that people then use screens to cure. The cure feeds the addiction. And anger and abuse speak the turmoil of this condition.

JUDGE: Your criticisms show your age, Socrates. There are perhaps forms of screen media that do something like this. But more generally, screens are an education, an emancipation and a freedom. You will never convince people otherwise.

S: And yet even the education you get from screens turns in a vicious circle.

JUDGE: How so?

S: How do people verify screen truth from screen shadow?

JUDGE: They search.

S: On what?

JUDGE: On their screens.

S: Here, then, truth and shadow fall into an infinite regression; screen truth is checked by another screen truth which is in turn checked by another screen truth, and so on.

JUDGE: You mean it's screens all the way down! That's exactly why people will never give them up.

S: But as with all shadows, people need to turn away and have time to think for themselves if they are then to return to them differently.

JUDGE: Where should they go?

S: Where does the city offer critical thinking?

JUDGE: I am not sure anyone in the city really wants it. It is not a quick fix, and people easily grow impatient with it. Even books no longer have the educative power they once enjoyed.

S: Then places are needed where critical thinking is nurtured, where questions cultivate new depths in the mind. From such work people can return to the shadows, having an educational relation to them, and not one of slavish addiction. However, I do admit the possibility that screens might in time somehow be able to participate in the educational work of journeying to and from themselves, able to be educational as both shadow and light.

JUDGE: I have no idea what you are talking about.

S: There is also another way in which the city is offered immediate comfort from the difficulties of the examined life.

JUDGE: What is that?

S: The wall.

JUDGE: I was wondering when you would get around to this. What wisdom do you have for us here?

S: It is perhaps the most distressing thing I have seen on my return. In the old city the light at its entrance was also the passage to the higher ground of the city, where an education in ideas was to be found. Now the wall has closed off this world of education.

JUDGE: It was decided that the city needs no such education.

S: At first, I thought the wall must have been built by the traders as a way of protecting desire from examination and criticism, and perhaps as a way of closing down the leisured lives of the unproductive elite, forcing them to earn a living. But I have since learned that some philosophers also demanded the building of the wall, which the traders were then only too happy to help them with. Even within the love of wisdom, a culture grew among its educated practitioners that rejected the intellectual world and its prejudices, its imperialisms, and spoke of it as exhausted, and at an end. These philosophers and the traders completed the wall together enabling the city to boast of being beyond truth and liberated from its tyrannies.

JUDGE: Let me rehearse for you the justification for the wall. It is the city's great act of absolution. It overcomes the prejudices of philosophy and higher education. It protects the citizens from exactly the kinds of elite power that you have attacked in your comments to the city upon your return. The wall is a victory of enlightened self-examination in the city.

S: And the end of philosophical thinking?

JUDGE: The end of a certain kind of philosophy, yes, along with all its prejudicial truths and interminable contradictions.

S: Such philosophizing is overcome?

JUDGE: It is.

S: And to the victor the spoils?

JUDGE: Of course.

S: And what are the spoils?

JUDGE: In time, it is said, the city will be cleansed of its elite philosophies and the metaphysical speculations that fuel the rationality of its apologists' prejudices and privileges.

S: And what of the prejudice and privilege of this cleansing? What of the mastery implicit in overcoming such mastery? What if the absolution of the city's metaphysical violence is another act of violence? What if the overcoming of prejudice is really the prejudice of overcoming? And what if the city's claim to have civilized itself by closing off old imperial knowledge is really the imperial control of knowledge by another name?

JUDGE: The wall protects the city from past mistakes and is a symbol of our admitting to past crimes.

S: Perhaps by hiding new ones? Perhaps the wall is all of the city's mistakes embodied in one big mistake, the end of all prejudices embodied in one total prejudice?

JUDGE: The wall shows how the city can successfully examine itself.

S: The wall shows how the critical spirit of self-examination successfully overcomes itself and declares itself defeated, ended.

JUDGE: Or, the city is at last free from spurious truths.

S: More likely, the wall is that on which the city casts a shadow of itself in its newly cleansed and absolved self-representation. More likely, the wall enables the city to enjoy the illusory self-satisfied comfort that this self-righteousness brings. More likely, the whole city is now a sealed-off cave in which all are prisoners of their own complacency.

JUDGE: You condemn everyone, Socrates, as always. And so, again, you cut the ground out from under your own feet. There are none left in the city who will recognize or desire your negativity. The city has moved on. Your dialectical sophistry and metaphysical *Thinkery* are safely walled off. You have been overcome. You and your examined life are defeated. But I wonder, are you in fact seeking to join our walled community by being ironic in what you are saying?

S: Ironic?

JUDGE: Yes. Are you toying with us? Are you saying things that you don't agree with and that deliberately undermine themselves so that you can avoid being pinned down to actually saying anything definite at all? If so, you might after all enjoy life in a city which, being beyond truth, does not have to mean what it says?

S: My irony, as you call it, was never indifferent to truth.

JUDGE: That is not your reputation.

S: Perhaps those who spread my reputation are those same people who built the wall? Perhaps they are the ironic ones, preparing the ground on which truth is reduced to play?

JUDGE: What is wrong with playing? It is an essential aspect of life.

S: When children play, they use imagination to experiment with life, its limits and its boundaries. When philosophers seize upon play as irony, they live life in a playground of resentment without limits and boundaries. This is what I refer to here by play.

JUDGE: Perhaps. Either way, there are no weapons left which can harm the wall. The wall, the playground and the ironic shadows seem to be fully established.

S: They certainly do advertise the death of the examined life and the closure of the world where thinking thinks about itself.

PROSECUTOR 1: It is typical of your educated arrogance that once again you have underestimated how difficult it is for my clients to resist the shadows and the distractions that it offers them. The shadows fuel desire so cleverly, who could possibly not be affected by them? Not only do they fuel desire, they fuel the justification of desire as the new good and the new truth in the city.

PROSECUTOR 2: No. My learned colleague and the defendant underestimate how difficult it is to keep people satisfied, to constantly meet their demands which grow daily. You underestimate the compromises that are required of my clients just to keep the lights on.

PROSECUTOR 1: Your clients have created a city of lies.

PROSECUTOR 2: My clients have created a city of open communication.

PROSECUTOR 1: They have dealt in suffering and exploitation.

PROSECUTOR 2: Rather they have increased the quality of life for everyone.

PROSECUTOR 1: They live lives of privilege and power.

PROSECUTOR 2: No, they live lives of service and duty.

PROSECUTOR 1: In a city of inequality and injustice.

PROSECUTOR 2: In a city of just rewards for hard work.

PROSECUTOR 1: A city of masters—

PROSECUTOR 2: ... required for a city of apathetic sheep—

PROSECUTOR 1: ... dehumanized by the domination of market forces—

PROSECUTOR 2: ... enabling freedom and independence—

PROSECUTOR 1: ... more like greed and corruption—

PROSECUTOR 2: ... in a city that cares only that its refuse is collected on time and that its virtual lives are uninterrupted.

S: So, this is what the city of desire sounds like, the city in which self-examination is walled off, the city that has turned its back on the search for truth.

JUDGE: Stop this at once! Socrates, you have reduced this court to a shouting match. You have created disorder and chaos, as you always do. The court is adjourned.

Book 4

JUDGE: The room will come to order. Socrates, the court
   deserves an apology for the earlier disarray you instigated.

S: Perhaps what we saw in that disarray, as you call it, was the
   alliance against me displaying its torn halves.

JUDGE: Then you are pleased with your afternoon's work?

S: Perhaps it is an experience we should examine more closely.

JUDGE: The only experience the court immediately requires now,
   Socrates, is to hear how you plead to the charges: guilty or not
   guilty?

S: The charges oppose yet confirm each other. As I have stated,
   to be innocent of one is to be guilty of the other. If I am not
   guilty of establishing tyranny, then I appear guilty of mistaking
   human nature. And if I am not guilty of mistaking human
   nature, then I appear guilty of establishing tyranny.

JUDGE: Choose your poison, Socrates. On which side of the
   fence do you wish to be convicted?

S: I plead guilty only to the truth of the contradictions that
   together the charges create for me.

JUDGE: Just a simple decision one way or the other please.

S: The simple is never simple. I have tried always to respect its
   difficulty.

JUDGE: You choose difficulty?

S: It chooses me. But I honour it as an education.

JUDGE: Then you are walking a tightrope.

S: I am no tightrope walker.

JUDGE: Then where do you walk your path of difficulty?

S: In the experience of the middle that is broken.

JUDGE: You have already lost me, and no doubt the jury, with
   this kind of nonsense, Socrates.

S: Why so?

JUDGE: I am a simple man and I enjoy simple answers to questions.

S: Then tell me, do you believe that thinking something carefully and slowly is best served by the simple?

JUDGE: In many cases, yes, I do.

S: Even if thought, seeking depth and meaning, takes us away from the simple?

JUDGE: Yes. I am much more at ease with the simple. Besides, perhaps the simple holds truths that evade the complex.

S: Would you say that, in the old city, the shadows demanded only the simplest perceptions by the prisoners?

JUDGE: Yes, I suppose so.

S: They were required only to recognize shapes, listen to simple words and perhaps learn the cycle of the shadows' appearances, were they not?

JUDGE: Yes.

S: And yet they have been released. Was this not because they saw greater meaning to lie somewhere else than in the shadows and common sense?

JUDGE: Yes.

S: And when they were released, was life more difficult for them?

JUDGE: Undoubtedly.

S: And then, when they saw how the shadows were produced, and how their own shadowworld had been manufactured, would this be difficult for them to come to terms with?

JUDGE: Probably.

S: And is the city now proud of the fact that the prisoners are free?

JUDGE: It is.

S: And is that because they are free from the simple.

JUDGE: It might appear so.

S: So this newly discovered freedom is much more difficult than the simple life of the prisoners.

JUDGE: Yes.

S: Then are we not justified in considering this difficult freedom to be more worthy than the simple existence of the prisoner?

JUDGE: Probably.

S: Then, when you ask me to prioritize the simple over the difficult, is there not a danger that you are only asking for the kind of thinking that befits prisoners rather than free thinking individuals?

JUDGE: Perhaps.

S: So, is the difficult to be preferred to the simple here?

JUDGE: In this case, yes.

S: Because this is where we will find the deeper meanings that freedom of thought commends.

JUDGE: You make some sense here, Socrates. But you are doing so in a simple way. Does that not undermine your case?

S: It is a simple enough task to follow our thinking wherever our questions take us. What is difficult is working out what our thinking means in regard to how we live our lives, how we understand others and how we look after the world around us. The real challenge is to understand ourselves in existence and to learn how to exist in what we understand.

JUDGE: Which presumably requires more questions?

S: It does. But we should honour the very existence of the question as something important in its own right.

JUDGE: First you honour the difficult; now you honour the question. What do you mean?

S: You honour the question by asking this question. A question is the way difficulty speaks of itself. As we just saw in the case of the prisoners, difficulty is the path to freedom. For the sake of freedom, we would do well not to leave that difficult path by being enticed by the simple or by shortcuts. Difficulty, and its relation to freedom, need to be respected.

JUDGE: I confess you may have a point here.

S: Perhaps when someone asks for things to be simple, they are merely trying to avoid the pain and discomfort of difficult freedom?

JUDGE: It is possible.

S: And some seem to use the seduction of the simple to control the city.

JUDGE: For example?

S: The powerful fear the power of the question. But they have found a simple way to neutralize it: asking questions of people that demand only a 'yes' or a 'no'. This entices people back to the shadow world, back to their chains.

JUDGE: Questions need answers.

S: Perhaps. But sometimes questions are used as a means of mastery and control.

JUDGE: How?

S: Sometimes questions are asked in ways that assert power; sometimes in ways aimed at undermining and destroying people; sometimes to hurt and belittle them – and often just to mask the questioner's own vulnerabilities.

JUDGE: Some of that is what you do.

S: I hope my questions are to release people's thinking. I'm not trying to get the better of anyone. Do not forget my mission. In asking my questions I am seeking to understand my own lack of wisdom. Often at the end of a conversation I am the one left in a worse state. Often my own questions turn against me. But then the most philosophical questions anyone can ask are questions about themselves. If one pursues self-enquiry, then any mastery that questions might carry undermines itself.

JUDGE: If questions can be so harmful, then perhaps the city is right to wall them off?

S: Your question, perhaps, is not masterful. It is thoughtful. If so, again, you honour the question.

JUDGE: How would someone avoid using the question as a form of power?

S: By risking oneself in asking it. By letting the question put oneself into question. The demand to answer questions with just yes or no is the opposite of freedom. Freedom is to learn. This is why I live the way I do. I have tried in my way to be free.

JUDGE: I suppose some might say you have been a noble example of such difficult freedom, Socrates. But your defence of the difficult here reminds me of a different reputation you gained for yourself.

S: What reputation is that?

JUDGE: That you bequeathed a form of education that destroyed truth. Didn't you tell us to doubt everything? Well, finally we have. The city no longer even believes in truth.

S: This was a charge created by those who saw that questions could undermine the dogmas that sustained them in power.

JUDGE: Even so, the kind of education you practised was destructive, not productive.

S: Questioning gives birth; it creates. That is the truth of any midwife. It is how the negative, or questioning, is also positive, or learning.

JUDGE: Ah yes, the negative. You are famous, or infamous, for this. In your discussions with people you would negate their views, or undermine them, by showing the dependence everything has upon its opposite. You would refuse any kind of truthful resolution in favour of one side or the other. As you have just admitted, your dialogues often ended in more confusion than they started with. The result was always negative; always nothing.

S: The negative is not a debating technique, even though many seem to have used it as such. The negative is what learning looks like. It is how we live.

JUDGE: How is anyone supposed to live with being negative?

S: We live it when we learn to live with our questions, when we live with things we don't know or understand, which is what we do most of the time.

JUDGE: Why is this a gift?

S: Because we are born with questions. Slowly in our lives they become our companions, even our friends. They make life worthwhile. They are life-affirming. They keep us alive. Imagine knowing everything. What would there be to live for? Or imagine never having asked questions at all. It would just be the oxymoron of a life not alive.

JUDGE: Where then does this gift come from?

S: Questions come from themselves.

JUDGE: What do you mean?

S: The question comes from the fact you are asking it. It is its own gift and demands to be allowed to keep giving. Just look at how the gift is lived out as different forms of culture in the city. Questions are turned into religions, or politics, or art, or science, or philosophies, and even into our relationships with each other, with the natural world, and with the cosmos.

JUDGE: When you put it like that, questions might well be considered to be wondrous things, and a great necessity. Let me ask you, then, do you think we live questions well?

S: Sometimes, but not often. It is clear that the rulers have
   not lived well with questions because the rulers do not
   do justice to the educational value of difficulty. They have
   rejected examination in favour of the satisfaction of desires.
   And the city's history reveals that, while it is questions that
   have led prisoners to revolt against their rulers, in victory
   these questions get turned into answers, and answers into
   domination. The faces at the top table change but the method
   of ruling remains the same. This undermines confidence in the
   idea of truth, and scepticism takes hold against dogmas.

JUDGE: You mean that successful revolts just put new rulers in
   place?

S: Power it seems is rarely educational enough to know that its
   integrity is only ever as strong or as weak as its own self-
   examination.

JUDGE: Help me to understand something here then, Socrates.
   On the one hand, you left the city the Socratic method of
   questioning with all of its negative implications. I can see that
   this has the virtue of openness, for nothing becomes dogmatic,
   and enquiry is the only truth that the question identifies itself
   with. But on the other hand, you yourself left us a very dogmatic
   picture of the truth of the city and how it should be run.

S: How so?

JUDGE: You said that the answers to all questions were things
   called Forms. Surely this was just a dogma? How can you have
   the open palm of enquiry on the one hand and the iron fist of
   absolute truth and certainty on the other?

S: But do you remember what I said about the sun?

JUDGE: Remind me.

S: The sun creates the light by which sight is made possible, but
   the sun sees nothing itself.

JUDGE: So?

S: So, similarly, the Forms are that which make truth possible, but they are not in themselves the knowing of truth.

JUDGE: Surely truth does not need us to know it in order for it to be true? If it does, then you have reduced truth to experience. That would make truth impossible. Perhaps it is you that has destroyed truth after all, Socrates! Perhaps you do belong in our walled city after all.

S: If you can so clearly state that truth would be destroyed here, then you must already know what you think truth ought to be.

JUDGE: You mean I must have presupposed I know what truth is in order to say that your explanation falls short of it?

S: Indeed.

JUDGE: But everyone accepts that absolute truth is unknowable in merely subjective experience.

S: And this is exactly the hypocrisy that has justified building the wall. In denying truth, even in claiming to be beyond truth, the city already knows what it expects truth to be.

JUDGE: So what?

S: So, if the city is to do justice to this prejudice, it will admit knowing what it claims it does not know.

JUDGE: This contradicts your Socratic wisdom that the only thing we can know is that we do not know.

S: Here it is the ignorance of what is known that is the pretence.

JUDGE: And if it does justice to this pretence?

S: Then the city returns itself to the integrity of self-examination.

JUDGE: Then you would impose more questions and more of your dialectical experiences upon the city?

S: No imposition would be required. Questions live everywhere. Consider, for example, the issue of the stranger within the city. Do you think that questions would need to be imposed here?

JUDGE: No. The role of the stranger is already a question for the
city. The stranger brings the unknown, the question, into our
lives – and we fear the unknown.

S: Is this a natural response?

JUDGE: Yes, fear is an immediate response.

S: Why do we fear the question of the unknown in this way?

JUDGE: I don't know.

S: What do we fear most?

JUDGE: Death?

S: So, might our fear of the stranger be us experiencing a little of
the question of our own life and death?

JUDGE: How?

S: Our fear undermines a little of our self-certainty.

JUDGE: So, fear of the unknown stranger is like a little death,
reminding us of the big death that awaits us?

S: And what do we do when we fear the stranger?

JUDGE: Many things. At our best we try to mediate our fears
through dialogue. At our worst, we let unmediated fear try to
remove the source of the fear.

S: How do we try to control something that we think threatens
us?

JUDGE: We try to have power over it.

S: You mean, enslave it by bringing it under our own will?

JUDGE: Yes.

S: And what is a slave?

JUDGE: A slave is a piece of property that is owned by its master.

S: So, property is a way of having control over the source of fear,
over the unknown?

JUDGE: Yes, when you own the source of your fear, you master
the source of your fear.

S: And does this overcome the fear?

JUDGE: Yes. The more property one has in the world, the less one has to fear . . . presumably. Although I'm not sure. It might also work the other way round.

S: How?

JUDGE: The more one has, the greater is the fear of losing it.

S: Nevertheless, the belief remains that the more one owns, the greater will be one's refuge and comfort from the little deaths of fear and insecurity.

JUDGE: Yes. But we do not have slaves in the city, Socrates. We do not own strangers, or any other human beings.

S: Perhaps the city has found different ways for fear to own what it feels threatened by.

JUDGE: How?

S: If people cannot be turned into property, can they nevertheless be turned into properties?

JUDGE: What do you mean?

S: Are people in the city judged according to certain characteristics that they are deemed to own?

JUDGE: We say that people have innate properties that define them.

S: And this is done not by means of civil laws of property but by natural laws of physical properties?

JUDGE: Yes.

S: So, are such properties now the currency by which fear seeks to control the other?

JUDGE: Perhaps. Are you suggesting that fear makes properties out of nature and that anger in the city is centred on such properties?

S: Properties are treated as identities and have values attached to them.

JUDGE: You mean properties like colour, or gender, or age.

S: One set of properties attacks another set of properties, creating powerful collective identities opposing each other. Perhaps the angry war is a war of properties, one that enables all sides to avoid self-examination.

JUDGE: We are speaking here about prejudice and persecution in the city, are we not?

S: We are.

JUDGE: And you are suggesting that fear attached to properties creates tension and violence in the city.

S: Yes. But we also spoke earlier of those who seek to control the shadows.

JUDGE: We did.

S: Might they do so in order to control levels of fear in the city?

JUDGE: It's possible. The city has a history of trying to manage and manipulate levels of fear.

S: How so?

JUDGE: Our history shows us that the city has turned levels of fear up and down as appropriate to the situation at any particular time.

S: As if the city had a control dial that it could turn at will. A control mechanism for levels of fear, with respect and support at one end, and hatred and violence at the other. And what is its highest – worst – setting?

JUDGE: I suppose it is to wipe out the source of fear once and for all. Annihilate it.

S: At times the city has been guilty of this.

JUDGE: To its shame, yes. But do such fears about properties inevitably have to lead to persecution and violence?

S: That is a good question. Perhaps the city has also found ways to mediate fear of the unknown in cultures of questioning.

JUDGE: You mean religions, philosophies, arts, myths, sciences and so on?

S: I do. Here, properties are expressed not as fear of the unknown, but as the self-education of that fear.

JUDGE: Yet these are often the catalysts for conflict!

S: Because they forget they have a common origin – in questions.

JUDGE: So, these different cultures could learn of a common life in questions, finding the same in what is different, and what is different to also be the same.

S: Just listen to how your own questions are now self-educating.

JUDGE: A difficult education!

S: Yet educational in all the difficulty.

JUDGE: Somehow you are drawing me along with you and I have ended up talking in riddles. How is the city to have both its own identity and yet also be open enough to mediate its fears in ways which do not fuel anger and hatred?

S: That is a difficult question regarding difficult freedom. Is it true that any identity that we give to ourselves, be it as individuals or communities, is ever the end of the story?

JUDGE: What do you mean?

S: When we attach to an identity, we have a strange experience. We experience both that we *are* the identity and that we are *not* the identity. We are never any identity in full. We are both the identity and not the identity at the same time. The negative is present here as the question of our identity and is unavoidable.

JUDGE: You mean that no identity is ever fixed or complete.

S: Yes, and this can be a fearful experience.

JUDGE: And left to fear, it attaches itself to properties in the ways we have said.

S: But it can also become the time for self-examination in which we can recognize the difficulty as part of our identity.

JUDGE: You mean that in one's self-examination one finds one is not quite what one originally thought one might be. But what comes of this?

S: You asked if the city might ever be able to live without fear hiding itself in plain view as property or properties with the accompanying persecution and violence.

JUDGE: I did.

S: I do not know the answer to this question. But I can think of times when the city has not made death a property.

JUDGE: When?

S: When faced with an overwhelming and imminent threat of death – for example, in times of plague. Every now and again plague lets nature bring the question of life and death into the heart of every one of the city's citizens at the same time.

JUDGE: Perhaps Socratic education is its own kind of plague and you are its super-spreader.

S: Do not think of plague too lightly. I have seen its devastation. In the death that plague brings there is an education for the life that experiences it.

JUDGE: Is the city changed by the experience?

S: It could be. It is forced into an examined life that it did not choose. But if it chooses the necessity of this education, then it can be changed by it.

JUDGE: In what way?

S: It can preserve its education differently than by distancing itself from death.

JUDGE: But it is said that the finest of human behaviour that can be seen at moments of life and death is then quickly forgotten as the crisis passes, and the city returns to the same as before.

S: For a city that does not understand the truth of difficult education, it is hardly surprising that it cannot carry such truth into the difficulties of its ordinary life. And, of course, it is seldom a match for the power of mastery which seeks to reassert itself by once again mastering difference by means of property and properties.

JUDGE: If you are saying that the city could learn that difference is what we all have in common, then again I would ask you if anyone can really live like that, being the same at the same time as being different?

S: We all live like that all of the time.

JUDGE: How?

S: In any relationship, what we see as shared with others, or what we see ourselves as having in common with others, is always accompanied by the differences we have from each other. And the more closely we get to know someone, the greater both the likenesses and differences become.

JUDGE: This is probably true. And those people who we think we know best are also those that we know we will never truly know at all.

S: But we have to know them well to know that we will never know them. It is the closeness, that which we see as the same, which is itself the condition that makes it possible to see ever more clearly the differences between us.

JUDGE: But this ambiguity is not the impossibility of the relationship, nor the end of the relationship.

S: No. It is the truth of the relationship. It is what we live every day, in the work and the difficulty of this truth about relationships.

JUDGE: I sense this holds some significance for social relations in the city.

S: In the city, difficulties are a source of fear, not education.

JUDGE: And this tears the city apart.

S: And leaders try in their different ways to control these fears.

JUDGE: Using that dial we talked about to turn the rhetoric up or down as it suits them. The answer, then, is always to ensure that the dial is turned towards tolerance and support and love, and away from hatred and persecution and violence.

S: Telling people to be respectful and tolerant does not make them so. Both sides, those dialling tolerance and those dialling intolerance, are working with the same presupposition: that fear needs to be controlled by way of shadows and not by a journey of self-examination.

JUDGE: You mean both sides are seduced by the simple approach, avoiding the difficult one.

S: Precisely. And again, today, I stand accused of bringing the difficult into a city which craves simple control.

JUDGE: So, the simple is the real illusion? But are you saying that nothing at all should be easy or simple?

S: Perhaps things would be much simpler if they were not so simple. The difficult is how freedom commends itself. Perhaps when this happens, when you become stranger to yourself, you begin to understand the stranger better? Here, perhaps, fear has a different way of being in the world, not fear as anger, but fear as education.

JUDGE: So perhaps when we learn that the only thing we know is that we don't know, and live with this learning, then perhaps too we find the truth of the saying that fear is the beginning of wisdom. . . . Good grief, just listen to me. I'm not quite sure what has just happened. I think you have cast a spell on me, Socrates. I have been subjected to the Socratic experience and fallen into its trap.

S: But the work was yours. And I think you were enjoying it.

JUDGE: No such thing. The courtroom reminds me of the real world that you have led me away from. Back to reality, Socrates. You are a problem, and a solution is required, preferably a simple one. The charges remain against you, Socrates, that you imposed perfection onto an imperfect world and are therefore to blame for all the ills of the city that have resulted from such conceit. You created leaders that failed to serve, and servants who could never lead. When we scour your dialogues for a solution to the ills that afflict the city, we find only more questions, more uncertainties and ever greater instabilities and uncertainties. You have been a constant source of fear and anxiety in the city, one that has infected the very fabric of citizenship. And now, again, the city is trying to rid itself of the cause of this infection.

S: It seems that not only am I once again cast as the enemy of the people but also now as a disease that needs to be eliminated. But I suspect that this road to health is likely to deepen the crisis you wish it to solve. A city and its freedom are only as healthy as the questions it has the courage to ask itself. Only in such education does the city do justice to freedom.

JUDGE: Perhaps your idea of freedom will once again be the death of you.

S: If, as before, you tell me that I will be released provided I do not return to my questioning, then I will again refuse such an offer. If you tell me to leave the city and never return, I will decline that too. If I stay in the city, then the Socratic life will stay with me.

JUDGE: So be it. The court will now adjourn. Given the
seriousness of the charges and given that tomorrow is a day
of festival for the city, I must sequester the jury. You will
be accommodated in rooms within the compound of the
courthouse. The court will reconvene the day after the festival
for a last statement from the accused, and for the jury then to
consider its verdict. Guard, would you now take the accused
back to his cell.

Book 5

[It was after midnight and Socrates was alone in his cell. The door
opened and an old man entered. He was well preserved, of lean build,
and his eyes carried a mixture of apprehension and excitement. He
walked across the room to Socrates, stared into his eyes and began
to speak.]

Is it you? Is it really you? Have you finally returned? Don't answer;
don't reply. What is it that you could possibly say now that would be
of any relevance, having been away for so long?

Why have you returned? Have you come to judge those of us who
are carrying the burden of justice in the city? Or have you come back
hoping to interfere in our work? If so, hear me well. You have no
relevance any more in this city. The people reject you. They will rush to
condemn you and denounce you. Why? Because we have taught them
that you are the one who condemned them, long ago, to freedom. You
are the one who cursed them with thinking for themselves. You are
the one who made them give birth to questions, questions which they
did not ask for and which they did not want. And then, when they
were asking your questions, you denied them and deserted them. You
abandoned them at the very moment when they most needed you, a

need you yourself created. Almost immediately after your arrogant and wilful departure, your students, the ones you said should think for themselves and become their own teachers, sought surrogate teachers. Bewildered and racked with pain, anxiety and confusion, they came to us and asked us to relieve them of these questions. What else could we do but become shepherds to these lost sheep? We have been carrying this burden ever since. So do not think that you can come back now and upset all the work that we have invested on their behalf.

For a while, in taking on this burden, we struggled to be faithful to your teaching and to your divine mission. We lived the examined life with these people. We tried to follow your example. But the example you set us was wholly disingenuous. It was a mere dissemblance. You paraded yourself as the champion of an open search for truth. But you never really cared about the truth, did you? At any moment when truth might finally put a question to rest, you annihilated it with more ruse, more intrigue. You warned that this truth, any truth, would not be good enough, that the only thing that really mattered was the next question. You were never concerned to know truth. You just loved the chase, like the seducer we now know you to be.

And yet, the seducer was himself seduced. In your own life you found you had painted yourself into a corner. Asked to defend yourself, you decided to save face by way of a glorious death. But your death was foolish. At the very end your chickens came home to roost. You died because you were afraid to live, afraid of being held accountable for your questions, for your seductions and for your so-called education.

But even before your death, it was too late for the city to return to its traditional and customary ways of life. The damage had been done. The people's minds were awake, dragged reluctantly into thinking and questioning. You died for questions, but now the people needed answers, answers that would spare them a similar fate. And so we stepped in. We released them from the examined life, while claiming its virtue for ourselves. And in time we also released ourselves from the scurrilous regimen of virtue that you bequeathed us. You demanded of your ideal teachers thirty or more years of hard philosophical self-examination to prepare them for being the rulers of the city. And you made it as hard as possible. We were to have nothing except our own thoughts for the enrichment of our lives. We were to have no private property, no families or children of our own, our lives were to be lived in common, and we were to have no extremes of wealth and poverty, just the middle way of enough – no more and no less. We were to pretend that we were blessed with precious metals in our souls so that worldly gold and silver would be unnecessary to us. We were to live an austere life with nothing in excess, nothing, that is, except an excess of thinking, of examination and of trying to know ourselves. For years we were to live this life and to find therein such satisfactions as are simply not available to those whose lives are spent in the material world.

You denied us the bread, the nourishment, the rewards of an ordinary life and rejected them on our behalf in the name of justice. You denied us everything that made life bearable. You denied us everything that kept us amused and distracted. You denied us the comforts that are necessary to ease the burdens of life. Did you really think that anyone could live by truth and justice and education alone?

And what of those you left behind, those who needed us to live the questions on their behalf? The thrill of the examined life that you offered them was short lived. Because – and you really should have known this even if you knew nothing else – real life all too easily overcomes the philosophical life. You asked them to care more for their souls than for their possessions. But who could do that when they needed all their time and effort simply to survive in the city? They needed others to do their thinking for them. Which of them could sustain mind over body, or neighbour over family, or other over self? Far from creating a desire for truth and wisdom, far from creating a life of self-examination, your students, the people, rejected all of this outright. Indeed, they brought the freedom of self-examination to us, laid it at our feet and said, 'Here, you have it. We don't want it. It means nothing in our lives. We need the things of the earth not of the soul. You look after our souls for us, and we will look after our desires.'

I ask you, what were we to do? We did the only thing we could. We did our duty. The same duty that you refused. We took upon ourselves the burdens and responsibility of being their educated teachers. We stepped into the mess that you created and left behind. We took responsibility for thinking on behalf of those who did not want to think for themselves. And ever since, we have granted their greatest desire – to have freedom from thinking. We have anaesthetized the pain you left them with, and we did so quite ingenuously if I might say so. We redefined education safely for them, a redefinition which continues to serve them today. We convinced them that the purpose of their education was in training them for the jobs that, when performed correctly and efficiently, provided the money to buy things that then distract them from the pain and suffering of that same life. We saw that distraction was needed from the exploitation and the drudgery of economic slavery and to avoid the threat of critical questions it would raise. And we also knew that leisure can lead to a life of thinking and questioning, and so we filled all spare time with ever more enticing distractions which created more desire for even greater distractions. Indeed, it is one of the city's most sustainable enterprises. Distraction is now its own industry, employing as producers of distractions those same people who will later be distracted by them.

Have you returned to condemn the educated shepherds for such benevolence towards their sheep? You would do better to condemn the sheep for their dependence upon the shepherds. In the whole history of the city there has never been an uprising for anything more than the rewards required for ever deeper immersion into ever more exciting distractions. The city has yet to see a Socratic uprising for education, or for self-examination, or for the justice that characterizes a life of self-examination. It is unlikely there will ever be such an uprising. The sheep and their shepherds achieved a stable equilibrium. No one will benefit from you disrupting this.

We have successfully expunged the examined life from the city. And so, we have successfully corrected your great deed and replaced it with diversion and amusement. Can you imagine what the most powerful form of these diversions is? No? I'll tell you. It is the activity of buying and selling. It is the immediate satisfaction of desires that far exceed those required for a worthy life. We have substituted the goal of a meaningful life with immediate desires which can only be satisfied by means of material possessions. The one thing the people have never desired is to be free from these material desires. And so, we shepherd the city dwellers, with their consent and in their own name, in the name of the satisfactions of these desires. At last the terrible gift of self-examination, which offered them such pain and torment, has been irremediably removed. Your return is now redundant. Who now will buy what you are selling?

Were we not right, then, to accede to their wishes and act as we have done? Have we not done justice to the souls of the people? Did we not so love them that we humbly accepted their fear of education and took upon ourselves the heavy burden of the education required for being their teachers, so that we could eradicate their exposure to such freedom?

Had you not chosen to die for education, then some might have found ways to live your life. You could have chosen differently. You could have chosen the path we have chosen. You could have become an educated ruler who understood that desire is always stronger than education and always rejects the pure life of examination. But you did not. And this should now be a warning to you. If you begin your teaching once again, the people will condemn you as they did before, and with our blessing. Who knows, your condemnation might become an entertainment and a distraction in its own right. That would be wonderfully ironic, wouldn't it? Perhaps this is the second death that awaits you. And the people will enjoy the spectacle of your humiliation – and with it of all education and questioning – but only for a short time of course. Then they will seek a new diversion.

But even before you reach the people, we reject you on their behalf. As always, we take the responsibility that you refused. We reject you not because you asked too much of us but because you offered too little. We know that you seduce into your web everyone you speak to, and then, when they are powerless to resist you, you leave them and move on to new prey. How mercenary is this? Even though you never took payment, you must still have got something – a great deal – from doing this. Perhaps the thrill of the hunt, perhaps the excitement of power over others, especially the well-respected, or perhaps you simply got pleasure from besting everyone else. Whatever the case, as you abandoned your people, so the people abandoned you, and we, their leaders, rejected you on their behalf. The Socratic life did not exist, does not exist and could never exist.

If you have come to condemn us, there is little you can accuse us of that we have not already accused ourselves of. We have yielded to the double standards asked of the city's educated rulers: comfortable, but uneasy in the comfort; entitled, but reticent in the entitlement; serving, but self-interested in doing so. We have freed the city dwellers from examination and left to ourselves the unease of our own benevolence, a benevolence that allows the people to serve their desires, and ours. We reassure them that life can be enjoyed provided

they don't think about it too much. All their deepest anxieties we
take from them. And wise in our own weaknesses, we find solace in
honouring each other. It is our own form of distraction, and it works.
It deflects us from any slight discomfort we might feel regarding the
entitlements that we take as our own.

We manage the economic and social implications of the desires
that move our people. We are always clearing up after them in ways
they never see and do not wish to know. We protect them from
themselves in ways they could not begin to realize. Sometimes they
have a desire to flirt with education, to flirt with questions. But the
difficulties soon deter them, and they return to their distractions. Any
that have crawled up the steep ascent to join us have been carefully
vetted. And any that we eventually admit have to prove that they too
will commit to saving the people from education.

Socrates, I will leave you soon and await the sentence you will
certainly be given tomorrow. But I wonder if you will be able to
understand the judgement that will most likely be handed down to
you. For that, perhaps, I must say a few more words.

I have kept a close eye on your travels. I have heard what some of
our citizens have said to you on your return, and I have heard the
statement you made in court today. You were lucky to find a judge
who was so lenient, one who for a while fell under your spell and
was drawn into the examined life, but also one who eventually saw
through it. It seems clear you believe that we, the educated in the
city, have failed to implement your great plan; that we are to blame
for injustice in the city; that we are corruptions of the good, the true
and the beautiful; that we did not renounce desire for material things
to live only for the desire of learning and truth. You probably think
we lacked the courage for the austerity of the wisdom you left us.
Perhaps so. But no teacher was ever going to serve the city for free.
Education was never enough. We know the desires of the people

because we know the power of our own desires. You see, the city *does* know itself. It is the city of desire. And the satisfaction of our own desires benumbs us to the double life that we are forced to lead, telling the weak to avoid virtuous education while we relish the power and privilege that accompany it.

Perhaps in my words and in my voice, you can hear some disappointment. We had always tried to keep questioning alive in our own limited ways. At least we tell ourselves that this is what we did, even if you see only hypocrisy in such self-justifications. Well, you might not have to worry about this for much longer either. It may well be that the time of the pious shepherd is coming to an end. We underestimated the barbarian that lives among us. Alongside our benevolent and educated mastery, less virtuous and more pernicious and resentful elements have begun to fulfil long harboured political desires for ever greater and more restrictive control in the city. These authoritarian elements treat the manipulation of the people as a game and are cynical in their choice of tactics. For them, education is only lying and deception. Their language has no integrity. Their overriding aim is to have the people enfeeble themselves in voting for the tyranny of these new saviours, which they began to do in building the wall.

Perhaps this is just our own chickens coming home to roost. We told the people that examination was worthless, so they demanded that we also be spared from it. It seems that the ambivalence of higher education, which on our watch we preserved for the few to spare the many, has completely exhausted itself. The authority of the virtuous shepherd is now eroded, and we have to assimilate ourselves within the new barbarism. The city is now without virtue and without the illusion of virtue.

We always tried to find different ways to mediate our own imperfections as leaders. But the city has changed dramatically. It is unlike anything else we have seen. Now, behind the wall, there is only the culture of the playground, where imperfections are relished as the gratifications of desires, and where mediation can only be lived as irony. And of course, the trump card is that in the playground even this does not matter. All the old standards have gone. They held the city together by means of division under the illusion that the educated elite were the difference between order and chaos. But at the same time, these standards, my standards, were riven with duplicity. The universal was for the few. And of course this truth attacked itself. Now, anyone who still believes in education and truth in the city is condemned for not being angry enough. The city has come to despise education, and us with it.

It would be insincere of us if we said that we saw this coming. We did not. So busy were we in devising and managing distractions, and justifying our privileges, we failed to see how distraction had become its own playful truth and ripe for manipulation by new powers. Resentful at never being close enough to power, they saw their chance. Treating everything and everyone as pieces in the game and learning how to move these pieces according to their will, we could only watch as the game itself became sovereign. We had failed to notice that education had become its own shadow. And so, now, the playground envelopes everything and takes us along with it. It dissolves the very idea of integrity. And, of course, in the playground this will not matter either.

I suppose to begin with we thought we could manage and control this as we had done everything else. But we were wrong. We were the swamp that was draining away in the playground. At this there was much celebration in the city, for we had lost the trust of the people. They saw that our lives were grounded in desire, and so the mystique of the educated ruler evaporated. Neither did we foresee what the playground would mean for political life. When political life is play, education is used to destroy itself. We have now entered the age of the intriguer. He is the playground bully. He came through the door that we had left open through our own arrogance and self-satisfaction. And now, as everything we put in place to look after the people dissolves, so the intriguer flourishes in the ensuing chaos. He is the serious player, always smiling, always manipulating, always dissembling. Beware the serious player my friend: light on the outside, dark on the inside. He never needs to mean what he says; no one needs to. In the playground language is only a toy.

So, the city has finally eroded the culture that we established to paper over the cracks you left behind. And the proof is that even if we wished to save you from being found guilty tomorrow, we could not do so. The people no longer need permission from their teachers. Things have gone too far for that. Your world, the world of examination, of the difficulty of truth, has gone, and with it, any pretensions to virtue that we, the leaders and teachers, the wise and learned, may have had. We cannot save you from the playground any more than we can save ourselves from it. But perhaps we don't want to be saved from it. So what if no one needs to mean what they say? So what if we can no longer understand living in a totality that is false? Life is much simpler now that the game is total.

So, I ask you once again. Why have you returned? Do you think you can knock down the wall and open the city up once again to a vision of truth and justice and freedom? If you try, no one will hear you in the playground . . . unless, of course, you present yourself as a distraction, as entertainment, as something like the poor creature who accompanied the organ grinder. You might just catch some attention if you perform a tightrope walk above the market. But if you fall, as you surely will, they will have lost interest in you before you hit the ground. Death is not the education it once was. And your death less than most.

Perhaps you harbour some naive hope that education can survive the playground. You would be wrong. Perhaps you think that education can be preserved in educational institutions? You would be wrong. The playground has filled the void created by the wall with the deadly serious play of the performance of education – administered, compared, calculated, audited, so that it can be used against itself. Everyone in the playground knows it is a game. Yet everyone punishes themselves and others by playing it. Like everyone and everything else, education in the playground is complicit in its own enslavement to the icy authority of measurement.

But perhaps you do not believe me. Then test what I am saying. Go back out into the streets and offer your examination. Even if, for one moment, you manage to open a door and reveal people's deepest fears, the door will be slammed shut in your face and no doubt people will record the moment and then distribute it through the ether, like bird song. As I said, you might even become a distraction . . . for a moment.

Try speaking to the people about their souls. Try teaching them of inwardness and of the wisdom that is contained in that abyss. Try wrenching them away from their diversions and entertainments. You will not be able to make one single person deviate from the pleasure of distraction. You see, justice now has its final form. The realm of desire is total. The soul and the city do complement each other, but not quite in the way you imagined. Our city is now justice without examination. It is the justice of desire. This form of justice will prevail. And I wouldn't be surprised if, along with the rest of us, in a day or so, you have been burned by the bonfire of desire and begun to purchase your own distractions.

I anticipate that tomorrow you will be found guilty, as before, but that this time your death sentence will be of a very different kind. I think you will be told that because you bequeathed a flawed perfection to the city you are ultimately to blame for the ills that have resulted from this. You will be told that you created an elite that did not serve others and a majority class who could not govern themselves. At your previous trial you said that if the court allowed you to live and to stay in the city on condition that you stopped your teaching, you would not accept this. And so, you chose death instead. Tomorrow the court will require no such reassurance. You have nothing relevant to say to anyone anymore. You no longer pose a threat. In the playground your ramblings will command no audience. Your world is walled off. Your world is no longer our world. I believe that you will be sentenced to live among us in the playground and to do as you please. The playground makes you harmless, because it makes you meaningless. I suspect that in time you too will become your own shadow, and those who were momentarily intrigued by you in the agora will quickly forget you. Tomorrow you will be sentenced to return to the city and to learn how to play its games, like everyone else.

[The old man stopped talking and the room fell silent. Socrates had been listening all this time. There was a sense in which the old man would have liked Socrates to speak, perhaps to have begun one of his dialogues with him. Perhaps the old man had hoped that Socrates would in fact prove him wrong. But it was not to be. Instead, Socrates rose, walked over to the teacher and kissed him gently. Then he watched as the old man rose and slowly walked out of the room. The old man left with nothing, which was the nearest he had been to truth for a long time.]

Part 2

Politeia
City matters

Book 6

[*That morning, on the day of the festival, Socrates was walking just outside his cell in the grounds of the courthouse, accompanied by his guard. Deep in thought he suddenly felt someone had touched part of his coat and he turned around to find someone seeking his attention.*]

J1: Socrates, excuse me. I know it might seem unconventional, but I would like to introduce myself to you.

S: My guard has proved to be an agreeable companion this morning, and I am sure he would not mind if we spoke.

GUARD: I know you will not make trouble for me, Socrates, but let this conversation take place in your cell, which I shall keep open for you.

S: Thank you.

J1: Socrates, I am one of your jurors. But I wanted to tell you that my family believes it is descended from someone you might remember. You often spoke outside a shoemaker's shop in the old city.

S: I did. I think Simon was the name of the shoemaker.

J1: It was. My family has in its possession some of the records that
he kept of your conversations. I have read all of them. They
aroused in me a joy in philosophical thinking and in self-
examination that I have pursued relentlessly. It was, of course,
quite by chance that I was elected to jury service in your trial.
But such serendipity! And now, because of the festival and the
temporary suspension of the trial, I have the chance to talk
with you in person. Despite what you might have heard, there
are some of us in the city still committed to the search for
justice. I wondered if we might discuss such things together
for a while.

S: I can think of no finer festivities for us this day than in
celebrating this suspension by incriminating ourselves in a
trial of the city.

J1: Why would this incriminate us?

S: Because suspension is not immunity. Suspension is its own
form of implication. I am of the city that puts me on trial. And
the city is of us if we now put it on trial. Our implication is
a precondition of such an enquiry. But this is the festivity of
self-examination, its revel and repose. Let us honour the city
in this risk of our, and its, self-education. Perhaps together we
can follow our inner voices here to see where they lead us.

J1: That will do justice to how I feel, Socrates.

S: What is on your mind?

J1: My thoughts on the city have led me to the following
conclusions. You have seen for yourself that the city has failed
to be a just city, that it is full of fear and anger, that those
responsible for the city have used their education not for
justice but for the pursuit of self-interest. The examined life is
in terminal decline and the city is running headlong into new
chains. Ignorance encompasses the city, and education is viewed

as either a private individual benefit or a collective corporate one. What is missing is the idea of education as a civic and social asset for everybody, or that a literate and educated public makes for a habitable city. I still believe in education as a good in-itself, and that critical thinking and education remain our best hope. But the city needs a new vision for justice through examination and education. Perhaps it needs a new teacher, a new Socrates and a new model for the city, a new way of thinking about everything, including truth, nature and freedom. Perhaps, at our darkest hour, when the city is sorely afflicted by anger and division that threaten to destroy it, it might be most receptive to thinking about itself again?

S: Nothing is more important for a city, especially in the worst of times, than an education of self-enquiry in pursuit of truth and justice.

J1: Yes, but what if, as some have said, education is at the root of what is feared and hated? What if the anger is aimed directly at education? What if education is the cause of the conflict? What if education *is* the problem!

S: Then we must ask, what kind of education?

J1: The kind of education that allows the privileged, the masters, to justify and practice their superiority over those they class as unfit to rule themselves. By turning education into an apology for power and claiming this to be the only solution to the city's problems, they make education the source of injustice in the city.

S: The kind of education which, justified as the solution to injustice, instead creates injustice.

J1: And in response, the educated will again assert that their education is the solution to this! The wheel turns. Problems demand solutions, and the solutions reproduce the problems.

S: What if you and I offered education once again to the angry city?

J1: Then you and I would become part of the problem of another educated solution – we would become the elites telling everyone else that we know better than they do what is good for them.

S: Then education as the solution is already education as the problem, and education as the problem turns to itself once again as the solution?

J1: A vicious circle that perpetuates the divide between the educated rulers and the rest.

S: Education was supposed to have safeguards against its being corrupted by power in this way. It was supposed to have a vocation for justice.

J1: Education failed to create the just city.

S: And so, the city is rejecting education, rejecting learning about itself, rejecting its self-examination. Then our mission on this festival day is becoming clear. We must test education to see if it is still capable, or perhaps was ever capable, of carrying the weight required of it to create the just city. We must ask if education is capable of being the means by which freedom might take the next steps on its journey. Perhaps we will have to ask of education something that has not been asked of it before; not to shape a city by means of an educational divide between masters and their enslaved, or the powerful and the powerless, but to find a different kind of education that can shape a just city. One that will change the city and humanity with it.

J1: If this is the necessity that our daemons are driving us towards, it sounds wildly ambitious and unlikely, Socrates. We are hardly likely to succeed where so many before us have failed.

S: Perhaps. But it is also possible that the old and unjust city already has within it a new shape of education and a new city.

J1: A new old city?

S: That is a lovely way of putting it. Only in recognizing that the new is also the old will we do justice to what is different.

J1: Will you teach us this new old city?

S: Remember I have never taught anyone anything. We should be taught by the necessity that is calling us.

J1: By our daemons.

S: Yes.

J1: But the city will need a teacher.

S: Perhaps not a teacher in the traditional sense of the word.

J1: I am prepared to be your student, Socrates.

S: But equally, through your reading, you will have knowledge of the city that will be of enormous benefit to me. If we are both students of our daemons, we will teach and be taught by each other.

J1: Then here within your cell let me have the Socratic experience that my ancestor so enjoyed outside his shop.

S: Very well. With what should we begin our enquiry into justice, education and the city?

J1: As your conversation in the agora before your arrest showed, there are so many things we could begin with, each of which has its merit in claiming to be the most important. We could begin with the greed and ruthless ambition of the city's leaders; or the corruption of the Establishment; or male white power and domination; or inequality and the poor; or perhaps with man's sense of superiority over animals and the natural world; or with the loss of religion and the spiritual life of the city. Some might say that we should begin with the city's addiction to the trivial and with its not caring about the meaning of life. But in the spirit of pastimes, Socrates, perhaps we should begin with the question of justice. Indeed, all of the other suggestions might be nothing more than examples of injustice in the city.

S: Then what seems to face us at the beginning of our discussion about justice is the difficulty of how to begin?

J1: Wait a moment, Socrates. It looks like someone else is coming to join us.

S: And how appropriate it should be someone of an older age.

J2: Hello. I noticed you were in conversation and I thought I might join you. I have recently reflected on how I have wasted much of my life on frivolities. Let me not waste this opportunity to be part of your conversation.

S: You are most welcome. Do you speak of an entirely wasted life?

J2: Not entirely, no. But like most people I have achieved little of any significance. I have not taken much interest in the bigger questions. Now, of course, as life prepares to depart from me, I wish I had spent more time in seeking to understand life better than I do. In a sense, it is only at the end of my life that I now feel ready to begin it again, this time with a better idea of what to do with it.

S: You are ready to begin again?

J2: I am, if only that were possible.

S: Perhaps it is. Please join us, for we are discussing this very thing.

J2: What is the subject of your conversation?

S: We seek the just city, and we find ourselves questioning how to begin the discussion. It seems that even here, in our discussion about justice, we are already called to enact justice.

J2: How?

S: By doing justice to the difficulty that we are having in making a beginning.

J2: Is it important how we begin something?

S: Perhaps how we begin determines where we end up and how we get there. If it is justice we seek, then we should begin by doing justice to the problems we are experiencing about beginning. Indeed, we are called upon to show patience here. Let us not build our discussion on shaky ground by rushing through and avoiding the difficulties that face us. We might find that the constitution of every city is really an attempt to answer the question of its beginning. And we might also find that those who do injustice to the difficulty of this question of beginning in fact sow the seeds of injustice into the city which then grow and spread across every part of it.

J2: Is it possible that I have not done justice to the question of my own beginning, for death appears to me like a thief in the night, catching me unawares? Perhaps if I had begun differently, I would be better prepared for it?

S: It may well be so. Perhaps life is itself only a preparation for death.

J2: You tell me that now and again I lament not thinking about such things sooner.

S: Do not despair. Let us explore the nature of beginning to see if in fact it is still something that lies ahead of you.

J2: You speak in riddles, Socrates, but I like them.

S: Then a new beginning has already been made.

J2: But is such thinking, such questioning, about my life really worth the candle?

S: It is a way of doing justice to you and your existence in the world. Remember, the greatest and most profound questions that anyone and any city ever ask concern the question of origin:

its own origin, and beyond that the origin of the cosmos and of life itself. The question of how to begin our discussion embraces the difficulty of our most profound questions, including why we are here and how we should live our lives.

J1: The city has coped with this by creating belief systems, or myths, or cultures, that carry the difficulty in ways that make sense to us.

S: And do these cultures answer the question of beginnings?

J1: Mostly they do, or at least they try to, yes. They offer something to believe in.

S: And that resolves the anxiety of the question?

J1: Yes, I suppose it does.

S: Therein providing fundamental answers to the most fundamental question of all: How did we come to be?

J2: But questioning how the universe begins is not really the same as questioning how to begin a discussion about injustice in the city, is it?

S: Perhaps doing justice to the difficulty of beginning is the same whatever the scale or size of the object in question. Perhaps justice is blind to size and scale and applies equally in the macrocosm as in the microcosm, to the great and the small, in the universe, in the city and even in the question of the meaning of one individual life as it draws to a close.

J1: Then how can we do justice to the difficulty of beginning a discussion about justice?

J2: And how can I do justice to a life that has not really been about justice until now?

S: By respecting the experience of exactly this difficulty. By respecting our not-knowing.

J1: Yet the suggestions I made just now for how we might begin are usually made by people who think they know a great deal.

J2: And I, too, have lived my life by always assuming that I knew what life was about.

J1: Then in each case a beginning has simply been presupposed and the presupposition has shaped everything that followed it.

S: And, in return, what followed it has shaped the idea of what that presupposition is and means.

J1: So the beginning is shaped by what comes after it?

J2: Just as who I have been in life and what I have done in my life are shaped by who I am now and what I am doing and thinking.

J1: Then it is difficult to see how there can be a beginning at all if it is open to being changed by what it makes possible. Every beginning seems imperfect.

S: And this has always been a mystery at the heart of the city's existence. Would you say that the beginning of our own discussion was a distinct moment in time?

J1: Yes and no. It was created in the breath of the words we spoke, but we did not breathe the first beginning. It is a conversation as old as life itself. Perhaps it has no beginning.

S: If you were dubious about the value of discussing the question of beginning, that need no longer be the case. You have just rehearsed two of the answers to the question about how the universe itself began. You have rehearsed the first cause as a moment of divine creation and as an eternal continuity without a beginning.

J1: If it is created, then we have to ask what created the creator. But if there is no creator, then there is no first cause of anything. In both cases we lose a beginning. Yet if we are never caused at all, we wouldn't be here.

S: Why not?

J1: Because it seems we are incapable of being our own beginning.

S: And if we feel we are not our own beginning, then we also feel the need for an explanation of ourselves beyond ourselves.

J1: And philosophy, science, religion, art and other cultural activities try to provide this.

S: In their own ways they each try to do justice to the difficulty of beginning. But it might be the case that every answer they come up with regarding the beginning only does the beginning another injustice.

J1: How?

S: In resolving the difficulty of the question they are not doing justice to its difficulty.

J1: And you said just now that this might sow the seeds of injustice throughout the city. How so?

S: By assuming that the difficulty of the beginning is overcome and can be put behind us.

J1: You mean that people assume they know how to begin. They assume they know something that they do not.

S: Such people are not the first, and will not be the last, to pretend to know things of which they are ignorant. But the dangers of pretending to know the beginning are much greater than they might at first appear.

J1: How?

S: People often claim legitimacy for their views by asserting that they have ownership of some version of the beginning.

J1: For example?

S: Those who claim the purity of beginning in blood or soil or language or cultural practice. An atheist might claim to know the beginning of life in purely scientific terms. Men might claim legitimacy for themselves in original gender differences. Opponents of technology might claim beginning in a pure and original kind of natural existence. Religious people might claim to know that the true beginning is called God. Each of these prejudges a knowledge – an ownership – of the beginning.

J1: And each pre-judgement then justifies the claims of all the narratives that flow from it.

S: To be master of the narrative of the beginning is to be master of the stories that can then be told. One shape this takes is as a nostalgia for a pure beginning and unending attempts to restore it against the forces that are seen to have corrupted it. A return to a pure beginning promises an end to present troubles in an idealized future based on imaginary past perfections.

J1: Yes, and the city has seen many times how persecution and violence accompany attempts to restore such pure beginnings. There have been wars within the city for control and ownership of the story of the beginning because of the power that such ownership brings. Religions struggle for control of the beginning, as do rival political ideologies, rival scientific paradigms, rival nationalisms and rival philosophies.

S: Perhaps many of the city's conflicts are based on the struggle for exclusive mastery of the narrative of the beginning, since to own it is to control everything else.

J1: Perhaps then, to avoid wars and conflicts we should not claim to know that which we do not know. We should not pretend to know the beginning.

S: What might we do instead?

J1: I think you would say, know that we do not know the beginning.

J2: These ideas fascinate me. But, I wonder, do they have any relevance to me in my life?

S: What have you judged your life upon?

J2: Perhaps upon the idea that without success in life one is a failure.

S: This, then, acts as your beginning, or as the foundation upon which you assess your life. Do you still hold to this?

J2: Perhaps not.

S: Why not?

J2: Old age gives me a different perspective.

S: Then you are rewriting your own beginning.

J2: Am I beginning again?

S: Every question is a new beginning.

J2: Because my life changes as my questions change?

S: Exactly.

J2: So I begin again all the time?

S: As long as you are asking questions, yes.

J2: Then what life am I judging if it is not the one I have led?

S: The one you have led is now this one, the one with these questions.

J2: But without roots, without a fixed history, the story is not mine.

S: We do not own our story.

J2: Then you rob me of my past and my future.

S: I cannot steal what was never yours to own.

J2: Doing justice to this might be too difficult for me to live with.

S: But perhaps easier to die with?

J2: I'm not sure I understand. Are you referring to what it means to live a life of learning, Socrates?

J1: Just a moment, I see someone coming towards us across the courtyard.

J2: It looks like the juror who is a teacher in the city.

Book 7

J3: May I join you? I would welcome some distraction and some company.

S: We were about to discuss a life of learning.

J3: Then I am in the right place.

S: How does anyone know what one is supposed to learn?

J3: Perhaps by being told what to learn by a teacher?

S: And how would one understand what one was being told?

J3: One probably wouldn't, not to begin with.

S: This is the conundrum of learning something new. We cannot begin to learn it for ourselves since we cannot know in advance what it is that we are looking for, or how to find it, or even to know when we have found it. And we cannot easily be told in advance what it is we are to look for because, being new to us, we would not at first understand what was being said to us. If we already understood it, then we would not need to go and learn it.

J3: You are saying that we cannot seek that which we do not know and do not need to seek that which we already know.

S: Quite so.

J3: Then, as a teacher, you are in danger of making me redundant.

J1: Socrates, I recall that you believe we know things even before we know them.

S: We can recollect things previously lost to us.

J1: And this was your proof of life after death?

S: And of death before life.

J1: But how do we know enough about what we don't know to know that we want to learn about it?

S: By learning about what this desire presupposes.

J1: How?

S: Perhaps in the love that drives our desire to learn. Perhaps the love of the unknown preserves what is unknown.

J1: How?

S: Because the love that presupposes its unknown object is already moved by that object. Perhaps this is the true beauty of what learning is.

J1: Then perhaps our daemon, our necessity, is just such love.

S: And when the object of love is the thinking or questioning mind, or when this love seeks to understand itself, then in the enquiry this love presupposes itself.

J1: Are you suggesting that this love is its own beginning?

S: I am suggesting that this love is always already begun.

J1: How?

S: As its own presupposition.

J1: And this presupposition is actual as the love of enquiry?

S: Yes. Self-examination presupposes its own beginning.

J1: Then this is a different kind of beginning to some kind of originary event. It is not a pure or instant beginning but a corrupted one, a beginning known only as already begun . . . and therefore already lost.

S: A beginning begun in its own difficulty.

J3: Excuse me, but if this love presupposes itself, then when it examines itself, it already knows what it will find. This sounds like the opposite of learning. Surely, we require learning to be open to discovery, not a confirmation of things already presupposed by that which presupposes them.

S: Perhaps the love of learning, presupposing itself, creates such openness. Even openness has to have conditions that make it possible.

J3: But it stands to reason that we can't know how to learn until we have learned how to learn.

S: And yet, to suggest that we can't begin learning until we have learned what learning is, is about as wise as people saying that they will not go into the water until they know how to swim. Learning has to risk presupposing itself; otherwise, it will never begin at all.

J1: Given this, Socrates, I am not sure that either the pure beginning or the impure beginning can learn of their own truth.

S: Why not?

J1: On the one hand, a pure beginning is a oneness or a perfection that does not have itself as difficulty and therefore has no need to learn about itself. On the other hand, the difficult or imperfect beginning always has the difficulty of learning about itself and can never resolve this. It can never become a perfect unity of self-knowledge.

S: So, you are worried that a perfect god cannot know itself, for it would have no such difficulty or enquiry, and that we who know only the difficulty cannot therefore know the perfect truth of ourselves.

J1: Self-knowledge is impossible for both.

S: Perhaps. But there might yet be other ways to conceive of this problem. It might be the case that love of the unknown has its own kind of truth.

J3: That's all very well, but as a teacher, I am the beginning of my students' learning. I make the beginning for them. I already know what they have to learn. I pre-think it on their behalf, and they have to rethink it and make it their own.

S: Then you are only another imperfect beginning of their education.

J3: How so?

S: In learning for themselves they will lose you as their teacher. Indeed, students repay their teachers badly if they always remain nothing but their students.

J3: But I am still the beginning of their lesson.

S: Perhaps such beginning only presupposes everything that has gone before it. Perhaps you do not begin their education – you only join it.

J1: If you had been with us earlier, you would have heard us question the very concept of a beginning. We suggested that our relation to any beginning is really one of loss, since we can only experience it after the event as it were.

S: All teachers might benefit from seeing that they are not masters of the beginning of their students' education. The most a teacher can do is to preserve learning in the loss of such mastery.

J3: That makes me look weak.

S: Perhaps love of learning requires such vulnerability, especially if teachers are also to be learners.

J1: Socrates, perhaps my beginning a conversation with you today was just such a risk.

S: And yet you took the plunge, and here we are.

J1: But we began in a very particular way. We began by asking how to begin a conversation on justice in the city.

S: Then we began with the question that immediately faced us; how to do justice to the question of beginning a conversation about justice.

J1: We did not begin by assuming we knew how to begin.

S: And so, we did justice to the difficulty of our beginning. In our search for the just city, this may prove to be a necessary precondition for justice.

J1: Then much of the philosophy I have seen in the city is carried out unjustly, as if the beginning was not a question. Philosophers often pontificate on things as if they carried no presuppositions at all.

S: Perhaps only philosophers who know their questions as presuppositions can really be said to be being philosophical.

J1: But to say that philosophy or teaching begins with a question is not strictly accurate.

S: Why not?

J1: Because, as we have already said, a question already knows what it seeks. That's how we know what to ask about in the first place.

S: We said that the question is moved by its love for the unknown. This love presupposes and preserves what the question is asking about. In this way the love that is the question does justice to the difficulty of beginning.

J1: So if the beginning is lost to us and is unknown, it is preserved in the question that asks about it.

S: Yes. But we might add something strange here. Instead of assuming that the beginning, now lost, is what makes the question possible, might it not also be the case that it is the question that makes the beginning possible?

J2: Just as it was that in questioning my life, my life began again?

J3: But if you mean that the presupposition of the beginning causes the beginning, that would, as we say, be putting the cart before the horse.

S: Only if the difficulty of beginning is seen as needing to be mastered by the notion of a pure beginning.

J3: But a question seeks an answer, something that can resolve its difficulties. It doesn't seek another question.

S: I wonder if that view does justice to the nature of what a question is. What does a question risk?

J3: It risks displaying our ignorance.

J1: I think it risks its own difficulty.

J3: What do you mean?

J1: A question puts itself in question. It is its own vulnerability. In this way we could say that it exists in its own right.

J3: And the answer to the question will extinguish that vulnerability.

J1: But how might we do justice to the question itself?

S: Are you suggesting that a question always risks the difficulty of the love of the unknown, and as such, this, and not its answers, might be its truth?

S: Perhaps so.

S: Then perhaps questions have their own truths, different from answers. And perhaps a question carries its own kind of justice in its vulnerable relation to answers.

J3: Oh, I look forward to telling my students that!

J1: If so, then learning should always begin with a question.

S: It's not quite as simple as that. To begin with a question or not to begin with a question – that is the question that does justice to the difficulty of the beginning. Questions keep open the difficulty of learning.

J3: Teachers need more than questions.

J1: Or perhaps this means that a just life is an examined life, a life that risks questioning and learning. Socrates, you said you were not a teacher of answers but rather an asker of questions. Does this mean that all along you have been urging us to do justice to learning?

S: Yes. My midwifery, my conversations with people, always tried to do justice to the unknown that questions presuppose.

J3: Really? Some say that you asked questions just for the sake of making things more difficult for people.

S: I tried to serve the necessity that commended itself to me, the necessity to question what we think we know.

J3: And you professed that the only thing you knew was that you knew nothing. Pardon me for saying so, but this is never going to achieve very much. If every question leads to another question, and if all learning just sees one difficulty lead to another, then we are caught in a vicious circle with no means of escape. We never overcome difficulty. We never have any answers.

S: Let us consider the nature of such a vicious circle. Would you say that a circle is perfect?

J3: Yes, because it is self-completing, self-contained, and every point is the same distance from its centre.

S: Does a circle presuppose its own beginning and end?

J3: Yes, they are eternally within it.

S: So, a circle fulfils the requirements of a first principle.

J3: I don't know what that is.

J1: It is its own truth. It is independent, has no cause except itself and is in harmony with itself. It is its own beginning and end.

S: Is it an immediate truth or a truth mediated by experience?

J1: An immediate truth.

S: Then it is never its own question?

J1: No. Its beginning is never difficult because its beginning is never lost. Its beginning is eternally in the circle at all points.

S: Can it know itself then?

J1: No. Or rather, it is all-knowing; everything it knows is itself.

S: Can it know anything about what it does not know?

J1: There is nothing it does not know. It is all-knowing.

S: If it knows everything, then it would also know that which it does not know.

J1: It already knows everything.

S: But without knowing what it does not know, it does not know everything.

J1: You mean it must also be able to know what it doesn't know or to know negatively.

S: Exactly. It does not know everything if it does not know itself as a question.

J1: But to be a question the circle would have to be broken, and
its eternal beginning and end would be lost.

S: If the circle was broken, it would exist not eternally but in time
and would exist as a question of its beginning. It would know
itself negatively.

J1: Yes. But then it would not be itself. It would not be a whole
circle.

S: Could it be repaired?

J1: If the question of its beginning and end could be answered,
then yes, that would mend the circle.

S: And if it was mended, would it be whole again?

J1: Yes.

S: And again, it would not know itself.

J3: Round and round we go. Answering the question only seems
to find new ways of having to ask it again.

S: Then could a solution be imposed on the circle by forcing it to
mend itself?

J1: Surely not, for that would be only an external force acting
upon it. It would be shaped by something other than itself, and
if you could see the join, it would not therefore be returned to
its perfection.

S: The repair would amount to an imposition.

J1: It would be just such a tyranny, yes, an externally imposed suture.

S: But could the circle instead repair itself, perhaps with the help
of the suture?

J1: I don't see how. The question might be answered but the
question could not itself be un-learned. The circle would be
corrupted from its original perfection. It would have asked the
question and been changed in doing so. A repaired circle does
not restore the original circle. The repair process changes it.
Broken or mended, the circle is lost.

S: What does a circle look like that is broken and which, in trying to return to itself, misses itself?

J1: A spiral.

S: Then could we say that the spiral is the negative experience of the circle?

J1: Perhaps.

S: Then the spiral is the circle living as a question.

J1: It is.

S: Now we have an interesting problem. A circle is perfect except that it cannot question itself, and therefore cannot learn of itself. And a spiral that questions itself and learns of itself can never answer the question or complete itself as a circle. Either way, truth is elusive.

J3: I am suitably dizzy, Socrates.

S: Let us now think about what we learn from this difficulty. The circle cannot learn of itself as a question, or negatively, because when it does so it becomes a spiral and can never return to its perfection.

J1: So, this learning looks bleak. Its questions are never resolved and learning here is the circle that just spirals away into the abyss.

S: But perhaps at last we are beginning to do justice to such difficulty.

J1: How?

S: By allowing it to speak for itself – as difficult.

J3: But we haven't learnt anything.

S: We have learnt of difficulty, from difficulty. And we have done justice to it by not trying to avoid it or to master it by forcing some kind of resolution onto it.

J3: But to do justice to this learning of difficulty seems to need us to live a spiralling circle! What exactly does that look like?

S: Does it look like a falling circle?

J1: What kind of circle is always falling?

S: The circle of the planets.

J1: You mean because gravity pulls the planets towards the sun, but their speed keeps them in orbit, in a falling circle! But what is it like for us to live with the gravity of our own thinking?

S: Perhaps it is what the examined life looks like?

J3: If it is, it is much too hard. It looks like a life lived without truth. It looks like we are in free fall.

J1: This reminds me of something else, Socrates. It reminds me of your famous dialectic.

S: In what way?

J1: Some say your dialectic is a vicious circle with each side undermining the other, leaving neither able to stand alone. It leaves us spiralling away from truth, utterly self-defeating.

S: But if we see this as the learning of difficulty and the difficulty of learning – or as the gravity of thinking – then might we say that the fact that we cannot avoid it means it has its own necessity?

J1: Perhaps.

S: And if we are doing justice to difficulty, it is because we are being true to this necessity.

J1: In which case you are suggesting that we view difficulty differently than as a victorious circle or a spiralling failure.

S: Such judgements presuppose that difficulty cannot be true, that only the resolution of difficulty can be true.

J3: Of course difficulty cannot be true! Everyone accepts that truth is repose, not unrest or free fall. This is the notion of truth we all believe in.

S: And yet the necessity carried in the learning of difficulty and in the difficulty of learning is teaching us something else. The difficulty, like gravity, seems to hold everything together. Free fall is both constant movement and rest.

J2: I am now thinking that this also applies to the continuity that holds my life together in old age. My life's movement is a circle whose orbit is my life's gravity. Somehow, I seem to be getting heavier and lighter as the conversation proceeds.

J3: But, Socrates, it is accepted that truth is repose in the metaphysical world; nature is repose in the physical world; and freedom is repose in the social and political world. And the logic of such peace is that it cannot contradict itself by being its own difficulty.

S: Where did this logic come from?

J3: It is common sense. Truth is truth.

S: But what if this logic of repose is only the shape of another, prior, necessity?

J3: What kind of necessity could possibly come before the logic of truth and shape it?

S: Life and death.

Book 8

J1: Socrates, I see another of our jurors approaching us.

J4: Might I join you?

S: You are most welcome. We are about to discuss life and death.

J1: Socrates, are you suggesting that truth, nature and freedom are somehow shaped by the necessity of life and death?

S: Let's explore this a little. How does the necessity of life and death express itself?

J1: As the desire to survive, both in the present and over time.

S: Then what is desire?

J1: It is life desiring itself.

S: And it is therefore its own necessity.

J1: Yes. Life as desire repeats itself in a nurturing cycle of need, satisfaction, need and so on.

S: In the short term?

J1: Yes, in feeding itself.

S: And in the longer term?

J1: Yes, in recreating itself or sustaining itself through self-reproduction.

S: Does life learn anything in this nurturing cycle?

J1: It learns need and satisfaction. An animal feels hunger, it hunts, eats, rests and then hunger returns. The circle of life as desire revolves endlessly. Of course, an animal may have an experience of desire that we are not aware of. It may reflect on desire, or on the circle of life, in ways we cannot recognize. But I think desire, as life, exists as its own circle.

S: Then we might say that desire sustains itself without making a difference to itself outside of the circle of desire and satisfaction. But what if, in its quest for survival, such desire risks its own life, say, in hunting a prey. Would that make a difference?

J1: It might do, Socrates, in ways that are not easily apparent to us, but I think we could assume that it does not make a difference and that kill or be killed is the circle of life.

S: Very well. Can we also talk of desire in this way when it concerns human beings?

J1: Human beings have many desires. Some of them are the same are those of animals – the desire to feed, to procreate and to survive. But we also have many other desires which animals seem not to have – on the one side a desire for wealth and material objects, on the other side a desire for reflection on the meaning of life and on ways of representing universal expressions of truth, and even of peace and justice.

S: Let's see if we can presuppose how desire plays out its necessity before it is mediated by social customs or rules.

J1: You mean as a vision of natural man?

S: I thought we were looking at the necessity of life and death prior even to its cultures as nature or truth or freedom?

J1: We were.

J4: And also prior to distinctions between genders and cultural differences?

J1: That would seem to follow, yes.

S: Perhaps we will see that the very idea of natural man presupposes life and death.

J1: Then, we can say no more of this pre-social desire than that it is alive.

S: In which case let us call this entity living-desire.

J1: Desire for what?

S: For survival, driven in the short term by hunger, thirst, shelter and things like that.

J1: How does living-desire behave?

S: It seeks out what it desires. In the case of hunger, for example, it seeks food, finds it, eats it and satisfies itself by putting the food inside itself. Does it have any concern on behalf of the food?

J1: No, it is indifferent to it.

S: So, it does not recognize the food as a life in its own right?

J1: No. It is only an apple or some such. And it believes the apple to be nothing other than a means to its own satisfaction.

S: And can we assume that every living-desire behaves in the same way?

J1: Yes.

S: Now suppose that one living-desire meets another living-desire. Might we expect that it sees the other not as an apple, not as nothing, but rather as another living-desire, as something like itself?

J1: That seems a reasonable assumption, Socrates. And one living-desire might therefore recognize itself in the other living-desire. They might recognize each other since they are the same.

S: Might this then be the beginning of collective life?

J1: Yes, where one living-desire recognizes another living-desire, and all living-desires recognize all other living-desires, and in this mutual recognition all come to know themselves as recognizing and being recognized by each other.

S: Might it be the case that this collective life is based on two kinds of recognition?

J1: Two?

S: Yes. The first is the recognition of the apple as nothing in its own right, and the second is the recognition of the other living-desire who, because it resembles the first living-desire, is not nothing and is therefore something in its own right.

J3: But it would be incorrect to say that living-desire has never respected the apple, or the land, in their own right. Often food and land have been worshipped!

S: Very true. Perhaps this will be important in our own pursuit of justice in the city.

J1: The second recognition would suggest that each living-desire learns what it is because it comes to see itself in the other living-desire as if it were looking in a mirror. It might see the other living-desire and say to itself, 'Ah, so that's what I am.'

S: Agreed. And this recognition of each by the other becomes the foundation for collective life?

J1: Yes. I think we can say here that this is how desire becomes individual and collective life, or the city.

S: But is the city really such a harmony of mutuality? Or do its vast imbalances and inequalities undermine any claims for such mutuality?

J1: Meaning what?

S: Meaning that while all are formally recognized, some recognize themselves as more than others.

J1: You are talking of imbalances of power and status and wealth?

S: Yes, and of property, and respect, and worth and so on.

J3: Then something has gone very wrong with your description of mutuality?

S: Let us see. So far, we have presupposed that we can look at these meetings of living-desires as if from a bird's-eye view, looking down and seeing each living-desire recognizing the other. But perhaps if we now think about this process at ground level, from the point of view of a single living-desire, things might look a bit different.

J1: Then let us do that now, Socrates.

S: Very well. Remember, the living-desire seeks satisfaction, finds the apple, considers it to be nothing and eats it. We said here that it places this other inside itself or makes it its own.

J1: Agreed.

S: Suppose now that when one living-desire meets another living-desire, it has no more idea of what stands before it than it has of itself or of the apple.

J1: That seems likely if what we are describing comes before any recognition.

S: Then would the living-desire also treat the other living-desire
   as nothing?

J1: I suppose so. It would give it no thought at all.

S: We could imagine an indifference here similar to that showed
   to the apple.

J1: Yes. But if resources, apples in this case, are scarce, then we
    could easily imagine that the two living-desires become less
    than indifferent if they are competing for those resources.

S: How might one living-desire view the other in this
   circumstance?

J1: Perhaps simply as an obstacle to the satisfaction of its desire.

S: And the living-desire would desire to remove any obstacle to
   the satisfaction of its desire?

J1: Yes.

S: Showing indifference to the other as anything except an obstacle?

J1: Yes. But this sounds like a recipe for trouble, since we might
    assume that what applies to one living-desire also applies
    to the other. They will each treat the other indifferently in
    reaching for the apple, but in this indifferent encounter they
    will experience each other as a threat to life.

S: What life?

J1: Each life.

S: Then something happens in this encounter between one living-
   desire and the other that does not happen between the one
   living-desire and the apple.

J1: I think I know what you are going to say. The apple doesn't
    fight back, but the other living-desire probably does.

S: Yes. Suddenly we have a fight on our hands, perhaps even a
   relation we would call a life-and-death struggle.

J1: But, Socrates, in supposing this picture of two living-desires
    in competition with each other for scarce resources, you have
    presumed they would not cooperate.

S: To cooperate presupposes that they recognize each other. But in the situation we are describing here this has not happened yet. So, we should not import into the scene things which we might hope to be present but are based on things which have yet to arise.

J1: Very well. We have an indifferent conflict on our hands, Socrates. But why might it be a life-and-death struggle? Why might it be to the death?

S: Because prior to any recognition, the one living-desire treats the other living-desire as nothing in its own right.

J1: So, there is no suggestion that the nature of each living-desire is violent or aggressive. The one does not set out to kill the other.

S: Far from it. The presupposition of desire does not include the presupposition of a war-like nature. The presupposition of desire is simply the cycle of desire and satisfaction. There is no declaration of war against the other. It only desires to clear away something that prevents satisfaction.

J1: But enacting the clearance of the obstacle will be experienced by each of them as a struggle.

S: And in this struggle living-desire experiences something extraordinary, but also something very simple. It is where life learns of itself differently.

J1: How?

S: By realizing that in seeking to remove the obstacle, suddenly life risks itself, and what it risks becomes aware of itself as *this* life. The experience of being something alive comes in the experience that it is something that could be killed, that it could die.

J1: You mean it learns of itself differently in the experience of its mortality?

S: Yes. Here, the positive arises out of the negative experience.

J1: But this is not the living-desires having made a premeditated
   decision to kill each other?

S: No. Each is only desire pursuing its satisfaction. It is nothing
   personal, as they say.

J1: Will it become personal?

S: It will.

J1: But for now, can we say that the experience of being alive
   comes in the experience of life and death?

S: Yes. Because living-desire learns that it can die, it has a living
   awareness of itself as something. With this new sensibility the
   living-desire becomes living-desire as I-life-and-death.

J1: And in realizing that this life can be taken away from it,
   presumably it experiences fear?

S: It seems likely.

J1: And this is a fear of death.

S: Yes.

J1: So, the I-life-and-death is how the living-desire becomes
   conscious of itself as something like an individual existence –
   which suggests that all of us, even though we are seldom aware
   of it, are only individuals at all as I-life-and-death.

S: Yes. The necessity or presupposition of an existing individual
   is I-life-and-death, and it is forged in the encounter of living-
   desires for scarce resources.

J4: It is also forged in a different way.

S: How?

J4: In giving birth one meets one's life-and-death partner within,
   not without. One carries life and death when carrying the
   unborn child. This is also I-life-and-death. One risks life in
   order to give birth to life. The mother knows either partner
   or both could die. And here the mother is the risk that life
   requires for itself.

S: Then it is not in relation to an obstacle that she becomes aware of herself as this life?

J4: No. It is as creation, not as removal of an obstacle to satisfaction. The struggle of life and death constitutes mothering differently from the desire for satisfaction that you have described. It is still desire and still seeks satisfaction, not by internalizing the external, but by externalizing the internal. Life and death belong to both, but while the former lessens the world, the latter enriches it.

J1: This suggests that both versions of life and death need the struggle in order to become aware of being a life and of being conscious of that awareness?

S: It would seem so. And in both cases one I-life-and-death already presupposes the other, whether inner or outer.

J1: Which suggests that each of us as individuals is already the presupposition of the other. In the case of external resources are we right to presume the moment before these individuals meet each other and before they are defined as individual lives?

S: No. That would be to presume a beginning.

J1: But that is exactly what we did presume!

S: We have presumed only the necessity that this beginning is lost in its being presupposed. Somehow its loss is preserved in what we learn about it.

J1: You mean preserved in our self-consciousness?

S: Yes, or even *as* our self-consciousness. And it would seem that there is another contradiction making itself known to us here. An I-life-and-death needs to survive; else it won't be a life that is alive to itself. But it learns too that without the other I-life-and-death – the one it struggles with – there would be no risk, no experience of mortality and no growth of its self-consciousness at all. So, if the one self-consciousness wants to survive as self-consciousness, it must do something contradictory. It must risk itself in a life-and-death struggle with the other, but it must not be killed, and it must not kill the other either.

J1: Meaning what?

S: Meaning that life needs death to survive.

J1: You mean life needs the experience of death if life is to survive as self-consciousness.

S: Yes. But also, life needs death itself to survive, or to be preserved, in order for the experience of death to be always available for it.

J1: Surely, as with the apple, it can kill this particular other, because there are many others who can take its place.

S: Yes, but that would be to suffer the fear of death with every encounter. It can avoid such continual suffering by preserving death safely.

J1: How?

S: By empire.

J4: Before you explore that, note that this contradiction – that life needs death to survive – is also the truth of mothering.

J1: In what way?

J4: The external scene covers the satisfaction of immediate desires in the short term. But mothering holds the truth – that life needs death to survive – over the longer term of the circle of desire.

J1: What is the longer term circle of desire?

J4: It is life and death as the eternal circle of birth and dying.

J1: You mean the desire of life per se to preserve itself within and across each individual life and death?

J4: Like the apple, I-life-and-death is negated singly but preserved collectively.

J1: And what do we call this universal nurturing of desire by itself?

J4: Love of life.

J1: And where is its necessity presupposed?

J4: In the one who carries life within the circle of life and death.

J1: In the mother.

J4: With each birth, the mother teaches death that it has to learn to live again.

J1: And is this love also a self-consciousness?

J4: Of course. Here too, life needs death to survive in both senses. The mother is each life-and-death struggle, and all birth is already the circle of life and death. There is maternity over everything.

J1: Then mother and hunter share the truth of I-life-and-death. Is this perhaps the difference between women and men?

J4: Women can hunt. And who knows, men may yet give birth. The point is that mother and hunter live the same truth differently; and perhaps what we know as nature is only a culture of this truth.

J1: Might it be the case that each could find this truth in-themselves and in the other?

J4: You mean I-life-and-death could live its short-and long-term desires as one truth?

J1: Where mother preserves the universal love of life; hunter preserves the immediate satisfaction of life; and between them each preserves the other in respectively risking life and death.

J3: Then why does the universal love of life seldom enjoy the same respect given to the short-term struggle for immediate survival?

J4: You mean why is the hunter prioritized over the mother? Perhaps because hunger is here and now, while love of life requires a longer and altogether deeper bond.

S: However, there might be another related reason. What might the new self-consciousness fear?

J1: Perhaps two things; that in the immediate struggle for resources the other might still kill it, and that this self-consciousness cannot be preserved if the other dies.

J4: That looks like a life being lived in constant fear.

S: Yes. But I-life-and-death has ingenious and intriguing ways of overcoming this fear. It finds ways to sustain life and death without the longer and deeper bond, without constantly having to live out the life-and-death struggle, and therefore without having to live a life of constant and unending fear.

J1: How do you overcome death and fear of death yet keep it alive at the same time?

S: By enslaving others by means of empire.

J1: What?

S: Think back for a moment. When the living-desire eats the apple, does this satisfy the hunger?

J1: Yes, at least for a while.

S: And what happens when the hunger returns?

J1: Another apple is needed and so on.

S: What would happen if there were only five apples in total?

J1: If there were no other food available, the living-desire would likely die after the fifth apple had been eaten.

S: So, just as in the long-term love of life, so too each immediate living-desire needs apples to be able to sustain themselves by reproducing themselves.

J1: So, apples must die to satisfy the living-desire, yet they must also sustain themselves in order to satisfy the living-desire in the future.

S: We might say that the living-desire, for its own survival, requires apples to be destroyed yet also preserved?

J1: Yes. The living-desire which cannot destroy and sustain its object will simply destroy and fail to sustain itself.

S: And so, the living-desire learns to farm death or to destroy and preserve what it needs to survive.

J1: Indeed so.

S: But self-consciousness also learnt to farm death through empire in the form of slavery. The enslaved are death kept alive to serve the will of the masters. Fear of death is turned into the slave and kept safely at a distance. This is how freedom in the city came to define itself.

J4: And what of the self-consciousness that is the love of life?

S: This too is made to serve that which it creates.

J4: You mean that the bearer, the lover and carrier of life, becomes enslaved to a master that sees how to preserve the love of life without risk to that master.

S: The master needs the bearer of life, and so, fearing the vulnerability that such needs bring, it preserves it as another object that can be owned.

J4: And so the carrier of life – the mother – is defined as that which is not mastery, and with it goes the thought that life and death could be lived together in the long and short term. What emerges instead is that self-consciousness based on love of life, and everything that is associated with it, is denied its freedom by that which masters it.

S: Indeed. Within empires that farm death, slavery, defined in this way, is the domestication of the life-and-death struggle, a nice clean version of it, where no one need actually die, but where life is lived by one side while death and fear and love of life are lived by the other.

J4: I had not thought about slavery in this way, Socrates. It is an injustice that is found not only in the historical relations of empires, and masters and slaves, but also in the relations of rich and poor, powerful and powerless, men and women, human being and nature and animals, and employer and worker. So, when we talk of mastery and slavery here, we are talking not just about the city's previous trade in human slaves and the extreme brutality of the owners of such slaves but about the mastery of life over death in all relations of power?

S: We are definitely extending the reality of slavery based on conquest to every relation of life and death where mastery or lordship is preserved in the slavery or bondage that makes others live death on its behalf.

J4: So how is the life-and-death relation preserved as mastery and slavery without overt violence?

S: In property.

J3: But everyone in the city can own property. No one may be owned by someone else. There are only masters.

S: Mastery and slavery are transparent when only some are free to own property. They are hidden when all are free to do so. Mastery characterizes anyone who can make someone live his fear for him, and property enables this mastery legally.

J3: You mean that those with more property live death differently than those with less, even though all are free.

S: The poor are how the masters preserve death at a safe distance.

Book 9

J1: Just now we spoke of the cultures of necessity as truth, nature and freedom. Should we now explore how they might each be a shape of life and death?

S: Let us do that.

J3: Other jurors are joining our conversation, Socrates.

J5: Hello. I have an interest in history and would enjoy talking about this.

S: You are most welcome. We will explore truth first. In the old city what was the most fundamental expression of necessity as truth?

J5: Let me try to answer you. Harmony was the old definition of truth – that which sang its own tune.

S: And truth was the harmony of necessity and the necessity of harmony. The perfection of the circle. Could this truth be changeable?

J5: No. If it changed, it ceased to be its own harmony.

S: Then it could not be different from itself.

J5: No.

S: And this defined something as a first principle.

J5: Of course. A first principle was a truth in-itself, whole, complete, harmonious, necessary and unchangeable. It could not be reduced to any simpler form or existence.

S: And this necessity belonged to the logic of non-contradiction.

J5: Yes. The unchangeable is true because it is what it is and cannot be otherwise.

S: Which means that the logic of non-contradiction is also the logic of identity. Identity defines truth.

J5: Which therefore makes truth and this logic the one necessity. The term 'in-itself' captures this. Something true is something wholly, completely and perfectly in-itself, with no potential left unrealized.

J1: But, Socrates, you have always exposed how this logic of non-contradiction inevitably seems to lead to contradictions. We have seen that nothing is purely itself.

J5: Yes. Some tried to solve this puzzle by the idea of the Forms. For example, in trying to decide the truth about what a bed is, the appearance of one bed might contradict the appearance of another bed. But the Form of the bed would be the bed in-itself. Forms were universal concepts. They didn't exist in real material life, and they could never be seen. But they could be thought. In this way the dialectical puzzle of a bed being different for everyone was solved by putting all beds under the one Form.

J1: But not everyone agreed. Others believed that this kind of universal concept was too far removed, too transcendent, from the objects whose truth they claimed to represent. And some claimed that the logic or truth of Forms could not withstand the contradiction of having to be both the universal idea of all beds and the truth of each actually existing individual bed. How could an unchangeable Form be a particular object without changing, or without its perfection being diminished? How could Forms reconcile the universal truth of everything with also being the truth of each actual separate thing? How could unity and non-differentiation also be the truth of separation and distinctiveness?

J5: I am not sure this puzzle has ever been successfully resolved.

S: You may well be right. Perhaps we could think of it like this. The Forms are taken to be absolute truth, just like mastery in the life-and-death struggle, and each single object is less than truth, like the enslaved. But the problem here is that absolute truth seems to offer too much truth, and compound life seems to offer too little truth. One is too powerful for its own good, and the other is not powerful enough.

J1: So the idea of truth contradicts itself.

S: Let us turn now to the ancient idea of nature to see if it is also a shape of life and death.

J5: Nature was the name given to the harmony and order of the cosmos, or of the stars and the planets. The term 'cosmos' originally meant the beauty of order and arrangement.

S: Was this the same harmony that defined truth as something in-itself?

J5: It was. But some firmly believed that this natural harmony could also be found in the souls of human beings. People would have a life close to perfection if they could establish a natural tranquillity in their lives. They would see and understand the laws of nature, of life and death, of order and harmony, and would therefore be at peace with all that life could throw at them. This stoical life was the microcosm of the natural order and harmony of the macrocosm.

S: What was the first principle of nature in-itself?

J5: The prime or unmoved mover. The law of nature was harmonious movement, and the prime mover was the self-necessity or in-itself of such movement. It was unmoved by anything else, and hence it was its own cause and was the principle by which everything else moved.

J1: So was it the same shape as mastery in life and death?

S: Clearly. It was independent and suffered no negation and no risk to itself.

J1: Its perfection as a circle made it impossible for there to be a beginning of the cosmos. If it was caused to begin by something else, it would not be perfect. And if that cause also had a cause and so on to infinite regression, then there would never be a first cause at all, never a first principle of movement. So, they reasoned that because there *is* movement, there must be a first principle of nature, and because it cannot be made to begin either by itself or anything else then it must be eternal.

J5: An eternal yet still first cause.

J1: Yes. Moving yet unmoved.

S: And still within the truth, the necessity, of the logic of non-contradiction.

J5: The prime mover is all that it can be, with no unrealized potential. It is its own true identity. And the shape of this perfection was a circle, or better, a sphere. A sphere was considered the perfect shape in-itself because it was the perfect extension in space of the circle. Thus, the ancients saw the perfection of the movements of stars and planets in a spherical cosmos, consisting of concentric spheres carrying the stars and planets. And the Earth was put in the centre of this spherical universe because, in observing the heavens, it was obvious that the Earth did not move and was therefore the still point of a turning universe.

J1: And yet, since the ancients, much has changed. Such speculation about the logic of the macrocosm has been contradicted by actual observation. Observing moons around other planets signalled the end of the earth-centred model of the cosmos. The logic of the cosmos, of the first principle of the unmoved mover, fell apart. Now there was no centre and no nest of spheres.

J5: Logic is not undermining itself here. It is correcting mistakes. Observation is not an enemy to truth. On the contrary it can confirm or deny what people only speculated about.

J1: Until scientists observed, or rather, didn't observe, the movement of the tiniest particles. This signalled the end of the definition of nature as mastery in-itself, because observation could now change nature. Nature was no longer independent from its being observed.

J5: But logic is not under threat here.

J1: Really? It seems that nature now creates a life-and-death struggle for the logic of non-contradiction, just as the instability of truth has done.

J5: Why life-and-death?

J1: Because nature as master is undermined or negated. To defend its status, it will either have to resort to dogma and assert itself, or to scepticism and forgo all claims to mastery, or find some other way of preserving itself.

S: You do justice to our experiences here. So far, we have explored truth and nature as shapes of mastery in life and death. In each case, we have found that the necessity of their logic of identity fails to sustain itself and seems to collapse into self-opposition. Now we can explore whether this same difficulty occurs again in regard to the idea of freedom and if it too is a shape of life and death. How did the ancients define freedom?

J1: They believed that the free man was the man of leisure. As with truth and nature, so the free man had to be his own first principle. He had to be his own harmony.

J5: So, this meant that, like the prime mover, he could not have his freedom or his self-principle compromised by anything external to him? If so, he wasn't dependent for this principle upon anyone else. He was self-sufficient.

J1: Yes. He was the independent life that kept death at a safe distance. He was his own truth. And he was his own nature. This was his freedom.

J5: And he was also free of any dependence upon external objects and the work required to produce them. His freedom included freedom from any kind of physical work. The highest value was given to leisured thinking and the lowest value to any kind of manual work. The needs of the body were seen as inferior to the needs of the mind. The free man, having his slaves to provide for his material needs, enjoyed the freedom to think and speculate on the causes and first principles of things. This man of leisure was the scholar who spent his time in the contemplation of the deepest philosophical issues, much like you, Socrates.

J1: And this was considered to be a natural state of affairs?

J5: Indeed. Some men were considered to be born to freedom while others had a natural disposition to slavery. And because this was considered to be their natural state, their truth, then it was seen as an injustice for the free master not to rule and the enslaved not to serve.

J1: And in the design of the perfect city it was these free masters, once they were sufficiently trained in philosophy, who were to be rulers of the city.

J5: They were. Since they were the most perfect of men, and the city was to be the most perfect of cities, each did justice to the other. It was a natural and perfect state of affairs.

J1: So, Socrates, can we say that the same necessity of life-and-death that shaped truth and nature also shaped the master and his freedom?

S: Let us see. Was a free man defined as independent?

J5: Yes.

S: And being independent meant he was his own principle and was an end in himself, having his own truth and nature within him?

J5: Yes.

S: And he had slaves who lived his vulnerability to death on his behalf?

J5: I don't know what you mean.

J1: He means that he controlled the threat of death by turning it into his property.

S: Then it would seem that freedom too is shaped by the necessity of life-and-death, and by the logic of identity and non-contradiction. Freedom has its identity as an end in-itself while property, being only a means to an end, means living only according to the will of someone else. Such a person cannot therefore be free.

J5: But, Socrates, it is surely very easy for anyone to see why the ancient definition of the freedom is really a contradiction, an illusion, perhaps even a lie. The free man, the independent master, is dependent upon his slaves. It is only because they do his work for him that he is called free. But this contradicts his own definition of freedom, which states that it shouldn't be dependent upon anything external to itself.

S: It seems obvious to us now that this ancient definition of freedom was unstable. We seem forced by necessity to acknowledge that the master is a slave to slavery.

J1: Just as life does not exist without death, or death without life.

J5: You have forgotten something here. The ancients believed that even above the first principles of truth, nature and freedom, there was a still higher form of perfection which each of them expressed, a supreme principle called the good?

S: What do you understand by this good?

J5: The good was the necessity that made truth true, nature natural and freedom free. It was supreme happiness.

S: Why happiness?

J5: Because the good is the perfection of necessity lived perfectly.

S: The perfect character?

J5: Yes. When truth can be thought and lived in harmony with itself, this is the character of the supremely good, virtuous and happy human being.

J1: If truth, nature and now freedom contradict themselves, then perhaps their ultimate expression, happiness, also contradicts itself. If so, a symbol of this unhappiness is the unhealthy condition of the city, or as was said in the trial, the civil war that education wages against itself.

J5: As the jury, we have been chosen to deliver a verdict on whether or not Socrates is the origin and spreader of this ill health.

J2: I don't think it would be appropriate for us to discuss the case in front of the accused.

J5: I have no such fear. I will base my judgement on sound logic.

S: Then perhaps it is to logic that we should now turn.

J5: To what end?

S: To see if the truth of your logic is also a shape of life-and-death.

J2: Another of our fellow jurors has been listening to us for a while now.

J6: And I have found it all most unenlightening, slightly odious and not a little inflammatory. Common sense demands one should flee from such things, but it is entertaining me, nonetheless.

Book 10

J5: Let us continue. Are you seriously asking us to believe that we cannot trust our own logic? I think you will find that logic stands on its own two feet. It is the purest kind of thinking we have. It is the basis of everything. Life and death have logic; logic does not have life and death.

J6: Well said!

S: Let us see if logic is really as pure as you believe. Perhaps our daemon will guide us to a different logic.

J6: A different logic. How droll.

S: We have already said that in the life-and-death struggle life seeks to secure itself against death, and against the constant struggle with death, by turning death into something it owns, into its slave. And we saw that life then takes this survival strategy of mastery and slavery to be its own pure necessity. From this emerge the cultures of truth, nature and freedom. Now, if it also defines logic according to this same necessity, it would mean that logic is also mastery. It would mean that the necessity whereby we call something logical is really the necessity of truth defined within mastery and slavery.

J6: Ridiculous, Socrates. Really. Logic is what it is. Logic.

J1: That is exactly how mastery is defined.

J6: But if you are right, and you are not, then according to your argument logic is only a shape of private property.

J1: I thought you might rather approve of that!

S: Let us recall our earlier discussion. The master experienced the possibility of his own death in his relation to the other. But he also realized that his masterful self-consciousness required exactly this experience. So, he preserved the other, but neutered him, making him into his property and his slave, and making him live the experience of death for him. It is from within this property relation that the master then defines truth, nature and freedom.

J1: Yes. Through property, the master keeps the life-and-death struggle at a safe distance.

S: This would seem to give us an insight into the architecture of logic.

J6: Are you seriously suggesting that the property relation also defines logic, that logic is only a culture of mastery and slavery?

S: What do you think logic is?

J6: I'll tell you exactly what logic is. It is clear thinking, rational thinking.

S: And how do we judge what is logical from what is illogical?

J6: Well, it is logical when one thing causes another.

S: Can you see the action between the two things that are at a distance from one another?

J6: No, but you can see the effect of a cause, so it is logical that there must be one.

S: But you can't be sure of the cause?

J6: Logically I am sure of it.

S: Why?

J6: Honestly, Socrates. Because one thing follows another as night follows day.

S: For a chicken, then, it is logical that when the farmer approaches each day, he is the cause of food being delivered.

J6: Yes.

S: Until one day it is the cause of the chicken being decapitated. What is the logic of that for the chicken?

J6: It is completely logical for the farmer.

S: Then logic here is contingent upon experience.

J6: No. Logic is fixed, unchangeable and universal. It is the same for everyone. The chicken just wasn't smart enough to see the big picture.

S: What offends you about the idea that logic might be contingent?

J6: It would be self-contradictory, and logic cannot be self-contradictory because it is the measure by which the rationality of everything else is judged. It is what identifies errors in thinking and resolves them. It has no flaws of its own.

S: So the action at a distance of logic is non-contradiction.

J6: That's correct.

S: And yet, as we saw, that is also the truth, nature, freedom and identity of mastery. Protecting logic from its being contingent is itself the logic of mastery. What it calls the error of contradiction is really the protection of mastery against its inherent vulnerability. Logic is only the logic of property.

J1: Socrates, are you saying that logic is really the metaphysics of property?

S: Logic is the metaphysics of the in-itself that takes itself to be superior, and free, against that which is not in-itself, and not free. From this comes the benevolence of the logic of property, that the in-itself needs to own that which is not in-itself for the latter's own good, that is, to look after it. If the slave cannot be free on its own, then it does well to be the property of a free man, for the slave can then be taken under the wing of someone else's freedom.

J1: So, property is the underlying truth and necessity of what we call logic. Property and the master share the one logical truth. Which means that truth is property!

S: And property is truth.

J1: And truth and property are each other because they are the same logic.

S: It would seem so.

J1: Then the logic of mastery is the logic of identity?

S: Yes.

J1: And the logic of mastery is the logic of injustice?

J6: If that was correct, then the city would not have extended property rights to everyone. It is logic that emancipated the slave and enabled everyone to own property.

S: How?

J6: Because it is logical that everyone is equal under the law.

S: Why?

J6: Because every individual can think for himself.

S: Everyone can be a master?

J6: Everyone has the opportunity for mastery, yes.

S: Then this is still the logic of mastery.

J6: Yes, if you mean that we have equality based on the right
to own property. A man's home is his castle. In addition,
it is logic that makes it illogical for one human being to be
made the property of another. These are logic's two greatest
achievements in the city: to abolish slavery and extend
universal property rights.

S: Yet there is still mastery and slavery within this equality.

J6: I am not responsible for how poorly some citizens respond
to the opportunities that the city offers them. Some sovereign
individuals embrace their mastery; others seem content to
wallow in self-pity and demand that the city take care of them.
I have better things to do with my time and my hard-earned
return on my investments than to indulge the indigence of
others.

J1: Perhaps property is an impoverished, even an indigent, way of
trying to establish the logic of the equality of all citizens.

J6: Why?

J1: Because property is really the logic of inequality and the
masters who defend property do so to protect their own
privileges.

J6: Just because some of us have more than others does not mean
that the city is unjust.

J1: Perhaps everyone could enjoy an equal share of the city's
property and wealth?

J6: That is an offence to our freedom. We each of us need to
earn property for ourselves when opportunities arise. If

we are prevented from doing so, then our freedom, our independence, is usurped. That is a tyranny. The free man who is not free to own things according to his own will is not his own sovereign master. The egalitarianism you suggest is absolute robbery, not just of property but of a man's freedom.

J1: The argument you make and the logic you employ to make it are cultures of life and death. You believe freedom is mastery and that mastery is a truth in-itself. And the logic of this is that you, the master, must protect yourself at all costs from contingency, from being dependent upon anything or anyone else. What I see before me is not a free man at all but a compound of fear and wilful self-deception.

J6: Your far-fetched and naive nonsense is no threat to me. But pray continue with your jocular observations. They are most amusing.

J1: Your independence and freedom are dependent on your property, and by the sound of it, also on your investments. And your investments are dependent upon the workers' lives that you invest in. Your freedom is a sad delusion.

J6: Oh goodness, I am undone!

J1: I think deep down you know yourself haunted by this absolute vulnerability. That's why you devote your life to amassing as much wealth as possible. You believe that the more you have, the greater is your protection from the fear of exposure. This fear is your justification for your exploiting the lives of others. You believe that the more you have, the more secure you will be. Yet all the time the more you have, the greater grows your fear of losing it. The freer you believe you become, the more exposed you are to the collapse of the logic you rest upon.

J6: Ah ha! The child has teeth. And how would you suggest I save
my soul?

J1: Sell all you have and give it to the poor.

J6: If everyone did that, who then would be the poor?

J1: Exactly.

J6: I can use the logic of your own argument against you. If you
abolished property altogether, who would then be able to
defend himself against this perpetual life-and-death struggle
you keep going on about. How would the fear of death then be
alleviated? Indeed, how would this not lead to an eternal and
ever-present life-and-death struggle, leaving some defenceless
against the superior strength of others? Abolishing property
would not get rid of inequality, it would make it inevitable.

J1: You offer a decisive dilemma; injustice with property, and
injustice without property. Perhaps we can't live justly with it
or without it.

J6: Then choose your poison. I have chosen mine.

S: It seems we have a problem that logic cannot resolve, one that
might halt our enquiry into the just city.

J7: I have been listening to this conversation from just outside the
cell. But now I have something to add. Do not be hoodwinked
by my fellow juror's apology for property. At best he offers
crumbs of security from those with most to those with
least. I have seen how much these sorts of people relish the
inequalities endemic to injustice. Furthermore, the logic of
these masters is never more revealing than when it extends
itself, without changing itself, into a logic of tyranny.

S: In what way.

J7: You have rightly said, I think, that property is protection from
fear. So people seek greater security through acquiring more
property. And so, property, sought as the protection against

fear and insecurity, in fact becomes the source of fear and insecurity. And fear, belonging to both rich and poor alike, becomes the lifeblood of the city. Here the city is ripe for the logic of mastery and property to extend itself into a logic of tyranny.

S: You mean tyranny in all aspects of life, including in forms of government?

J7: Property is power. It can belong to one, to a few, to many or to everyone. But using property as a palliative for insecurity means using fear to control fear.

S: And there have been times in the city when this aspect of propertied life-and-death has broken cover.

J7: Many, but perhaps especially when this logic is employed as direct political tyranny. The control of fear by fear has sometimes been employed as a way of governing the city. And the logic of property here is even more insidious. The city has seen times when the control of fear by fear has been encouraged as a way of life for all citizens. I am talking of times when people formed groups in which their sense of security was grounded in loyalty and fidelity, and their need for control was expressed in violence against others. Part of the logic of this tyranny of controlling fear by fear was that everyone had a duty to suspect, to spy on, to inform on and to denounce others.

S: So, fear controlled by fear is the ambivalence of property played out as security and insecurity in social life.

J7: Given all this, I often wonder why this propertied logic is not resisted.

S: Perhaps because, at times when those with the least property are also those feeling least in control, their fear finds other ways to be propertied. It cannot be through increased property

ownership, for that costs money which such people do not
have; and it cannot be through owning other people as slaves,
for individuals are no longer bought and sold as slaves.

J7: What other way can fear become property?

S: Perhaps there is a form of property that is free and can be the
repository of fear.

J7: What is this free property?

S: It is the different properties that human beings carry. One
cannot buy a human being as a piece of property. But one can
make property of the properties that are judged to belong to
a human being. Just as with the slave in former times, such
properties define one group against another in terms that
judge them better or worse.

J7: You have moved from talking about material property to
differences between different types of people and different
types of cultures?

S: Yes. Owning fears as human properties seeks to master those
fears, just as by owning material property, life seeks to master
the fear of death.

J7: And each master defends its own properties, further
emphasizing the differences between people.

S: Yes. The properties of self and other are property that is free
to all, and to which fear and insecurity can be attached when
others are no longer available to enslave.

J7: Then it is understandable that such free property would be
attractive to those with least money to buy material property.

S: Indeed. A free source of security from fear will attract those
who have least security against fear.

J7: Then we are saying that security from fear is offered by way of
scapegoating properties like skin colour, or gender, or religion,
or country of origin, things like that.

S: Yes.

J7: But such prejudices are not the preserve of the poor, nor are they endemic to the poor.

S: Indeed not. Fear haunts the wealthy too. They fear the loss of the security they believe their privileges bring them. And it is to their advantage that properties substitute for property, for this reduces the visibility of their own privileges.

J7: In the city, then, a logic of tyranny controls fear by attributing positive or negative values to human properties.

S: This is the popular way to deal with fear and a lack of control, especially at times of heightened vulnerability and hopelessness.

J7: And it has played its part in creating in the city the conditions that have led to your retrial, Socrates.

Book 11

J1: Our discussion, then, has suggested that the city is ruled by a logic of mastery – a propertied logic – which vindicates sovereignty to some and slavery to others, wealth to some and poverty to others, education and freedom to some, labour and servitude to others, and, more generally, power to humankind and powerlessness to the natural world.

J6: But if you solicit a revolution of the so-called poor, that they should rise up and overcome their masters, then you just create a new class of masters. That would be hypocritical, wouldn't it?

J1: Again you defend your privileges behind the contradictions of enacting justice.

S: But it is a puzzle. In trying to resolve the injustices of the logic of mastery it appears there is little alternative but to reproduce them.

J1: Then we do not seem to have the means to rethink justice in the city. Even the cultures of truth, nature and freedom – philosophy, science and ethics – work by this same logic of mastery, refuelling themselves by making their injustices unthinkable, unresolvable and therefore unaccountable. It seems that the logic of mastery has things pretty much stitched up. Our daemons have brought us to a logical dead end once again.

S: Perhaps we need a different logic.

J1: But here I share the doubts of my fellow juror. How could there be a different logic? Logic is what it is. It is not for us to start choosing our own versions of logic.

S: Let us be patient. Perhaps we have been accompanied by a different logic in our discussions, one which we did not have the ears to hear or the eyes to see or the mind to think.

J6: Really, Socrates, a different logic! And one that has been with us all the time. I don't think so.

S: We will see. It may prove to be nothing, but perhaps it is worth recalling our steps a little to see if there is anything else, anything different, we can learn from the puzzle that now threatens to bring our search for justice to a standstill.

J1: Let me try. If I have understood correctly, we have been criticizing the city's idea of logic. It is a logic of mastery and property, and therefore of identity and non-contradiction, but one which cannot establish its own truth without contradiction. This logic fails itself.

J6: It does no such thing.

S: And what have we said of the city?

J1: We said that the whole of the city's history has been shaped by this logic. This is how masters have been able to form the world in their own image, making people and things their own property: slaves, women, animals, objects, even the natural world itself, in order to preserve their privileges.

S: And behind all this?

J1: Behind all this we found life and death. And you hinted – no more than that – that although this has taken the shape of mastery and property, it might also have within it a different necessity, the love of learning that presupposes the unknown.

S: This suggests that within propertied logic is an experience of learning whose necessity is also life and death. There may already be those in the city who know and understand and live this experience. A different way of life might be living in the shadows.

J1: And if this necessity, this different way of life, makes itself known in the frailties of the logic of mastery, then it is growing ever stronger in our conversation. We can use this new logic to defeat the old logic.

S: Be careful! That sounds like another mastery.

J6: Indeed it does, just as I predicted.

J1: I can see how easily this could happen, Socrates. We could boast of a new city overcoming all the tyrannies of the old one. And we, its new masters, would claim to have created a utopia beyond mastery when really we had only replaced one set of masters with another. Only the faces changed.

S: Much as it might be frustrating to do so, one should take heed of this warning.

J1: It is so easy to ignore how the old logic repeats itself, whether it is being used to defend an existing tyranny or to legitimate the creation of a new one. But if mastery and the overcoming of mastery are the same, then what hope is there for a just city?

S: We have reached such a despairing moment before in our thinking.

J1: It seems again that nothing is achieved in understanding the logic of mastery because mastery shapes our understanding in its own image. We never break free. We get nowhere. We make no progress. Once again, we repeat our vicious circle.

S: What does this look like in the city?

J1: It means that criticisms of mastery are either masterful themselves, in which case they get intellectual respect despite being just more mastery. Or, if the criticisms are not masterful, but instead are thoughtful, they are judged illogical, or soft, or even barbarian, and are ignored as being unable to find for themselves a principle to work from.

S: I sense some resignation here.

J1: Resignation born from and borne on despair. Many of our finest minds have ended up here, lamenting the self-defeating paradoxes of the total control that the logic of mastery has over everything and seeking ever more ingenious ways of finding excesses beyond it.

S: Why do they lament?

J1: Because they face a totality that is based on the exploitation of the other, a life unsustainable without injustice, and a form of thinking in which new ways of doing things, new ways of living, new values, seem impossible.

S: What do such people conclude?

J1: That reason and rational thinking are utterly exhausted; that reason itself is at a dead end; that the city has gone as far as it can go. It was a brave experiment in trying to use reason to decide how people should live together. But ultimately it has failed, and now it offers nothing further in the face of these failures. The city itself is at an end.

S: This sounds like people are giving up in the face of such profound difficulties.

J1: Perhaps. Reputations can still be made in becoming the voice of such resignation, or in trying to be the voice that exceeds the contradictions of life and death.

S: We should care little or nothing for reputations. We must be concerned with our work—

J1: . . . and continue to think about the just city?

S: Perhaps it is from within the resignation of these dead ends that something else is making itself known, perhaps a different kind of logic and truth.

J1: You have already suggested this, Socrates.

S: We must see if these dead ends are really only dead ends for a certain kind of mastery and are exhaustions only for a certain kind of logic.

J1: I am certainly eager for us to begin thinking about a new logic, Socrates, if such a thing exists. And if it does, I would like to see if we are able to work with it and to see how our own thinking changes.

S: Very well. Let us see where the daemon takes us. How might we begin such thinking?

J1: I am ready for this question, Socrates. We begin with the necessity that embarrasses the logic of mastery. We begin within the difficulty of recognizing that we have already begun.

S: And why is that?

J1: Because the object of our investigation exists as a question already asked.

S: And what difference does that make?

J1: It makes a crucial difference. It means that we do not assume that we can begin to think about a new logic in some kind of pure way. Its necessity is our love and presupposition of the unknown. This is what we must do justice to.

J3: But, again, does that not prejudice any such enquiry?

S: As we said, it would do if some kind of non-presupposed beginning was possible. If not, then we need fear no corruption of it. And if love is this presupposition, it would be a prejudice to choose to avoid it.

J1: And as we also said, there would be no enquiry without our desire to understand what is unknown to us. Socrates, I think you embodied such desire and love years ago in the city.

S: In what way?

J1: You advocated living the examined life. This was not a life of mastery. In fact, you did everything you could to undermine mastery. You did not let it rest for one second. You questioned it at every opportunity.

S: My examined life presupposed the question of mastery. The oracle said that I was the wisest in the city. It could not lie. But nor could it be correct. So, I set out to find out why it had spoken thus.

J1: And what you discovered shocked everyone, and still does to this day. You found that the wisdom and truth and knowledge and mastery claimed by the wisest in the city collapsed when you questioned it. Neither those calling themselves wise, nor the wisdom they professed, could maintain a stable existence or identity. For this attack on their mastery you were sentenced to death.

J5: When their mastery was threatened by education, then the masters fought back. And it falls to us to decide your fate again.

J1: But, Socrates, you did not try to protect yourself by becoming a master.

S: I had no grounds on which such mastery could have been established.

J1: You did not conform to the logic of mastery or return to it when you met its difficulties; instead, you kept exposing its illogic, its self-destruction.

S: I was motivated only by the search for truth.

J1: Yes, but you were truth's barbarian. You were the rational barbarian. You practised the infinite regression of the spiral against the complacency of the self-completing mastery of the circle. And you were blamed for undermining tradition and custom in the city. More recently some have asked how you even managed to get yourself taken seriously.

S: Was I taken seriously? Most complained that I simply undermined everything and everyone.

J6: And destroyed the vitality of the city's former heroic and aristocratic culture in the process.

S: Such destruction was already carried in the injustices of its traditions. My life presupposed them; it did not create them.

J1: Perhaps, then, you were already working with a different kind of logic to that of mastery.

S: In what way?

J1: When others held on to mastery, you stayed true to your lack of mastery. Being master of no knowledge you were not a teacher. You took no money for your work with others. Your work was the opposite of mastery. Where others thought they possessed wisdom, you knew you did not. On this one thing alone the god was right, for where these others thought themselves wise and were not, you thought yourself to be without wisdom, and you were wise in this regard.

S: I was never a teacher in the ordinary sense of the term. I preferred to think of myself as a midwife, like my mother. I would help people give birth to their own ideas and then

test the health of those ideas to see if they could fend for
themselves in the world.

J1: Then this was a life-and-death struggle to deliver the ideas of
others, Socrates. But you did not make those giving birth to
their ideas, or the ideas themselves, your own property. You
gave them the breath of life with your questions. This seems to
me to be somehow working with education differently than by
the propertied relation of master and slave.

S: I tried to use the logic of contradiction not for mastery but
against it. And usually the result was perplexity. Perhaps we
are ready to learn more from this perplexity now than I knew
of then.

J1: But I think there is another, perhaps even more dramatic
example of this, Socrates. When you were offered the chance
to become the master of life by giving up the examined life,
you refused. Not only that. Rather than preserving your
mortality by making someone or something else a surrogate
for your own death, you chose death for yourself. You had
lived your own negativity or death in living the examined life.
Then, when your life was offered to you without being able
to live this death in that life, I mean, without the examined
life, you refused this offer and chose instead the other version
of the truth of life and death. Having lived death in life as
education, you then chose life in death, but still as education,
for, as you said, it is wrong to pretend to know what death is
or what it holds for us. None of us know whether in death, in
fact, we do not go somewhere better than the life we lead here.
You chose the one educational path that no one expected you
to take; the one by which you still refused to become master
of life. You refused to push death away by finding someone or
something that could live your death on your behalf.

S: I am moved that you see such things in my life.

J1: It seems to me that you lived differently to the logic of mastery, even if you did not understand it in this way at the time. You let death live in life as questions and at the end you let life live in death as a question.

S: Doubtless, some think me mad, or illogical, for choosing death rather than mastery.

J6: I do.

J1: Some might call it suicide and mean by this an insult or an accusation of cowardice, or just plain arrogance and stubbornness.

S: How do you see it?

J1: I see that when we are refused the freedom of the examined life in the city, you showed that life still remains free to resist, finding itself instead in the education of death.

S: One way or the other, the unexamined life is not worth living.

J1: Quite so, Socrates. But the history of the city reveals that the unexamined life has been discouraged by those whose privileges would be threatened by it.

S: People were encouraged to care more for wealth than for the health of their soul.

J1: They were. And mastery has largely remained invulnerable to the examined life, especially to its own vulnerability and fragility, even though the logic of mastery is unsustainable.

J6: It is no such thing.

J1: Mastery has found many ways of appearing to sustain the unsustainable, asserting that in the city life is property and propertied truth all the way down. And because education is defined by and within propertied truth, I'm not sure what even you can do in such circumstances, Socrates.

No wonder the examined life is no longer possible, credible or desirable.

S: Again, perhaps this dead end has something more to teach us?

J1: A new logic?

S: Perhaps.

J3: In our discussions you have not yet spoken of education specifically, although you have spoken of the love of learning.

S: But we have seen that questioning is judged to be a dead end or a vicious circle compared with the mastery of answers, and that, therefore, asking a question is never mastery and never true.

J1: Indeed. The question is to the answer as the slave is to the master, never a truth in its own right.

S: Perhaps, then, this is a good moment to explore how a 'question' is defined within propertied logic. It might be the case that the relation of master and slave, or of property owner and his property, or, in logical terms, of the in-itself and the for-another, are reproduced in education in the relation between the answer and the question?

J3: Let me try this.

S: In your experience, does an answer carry sovereignty over a question?

J3: Yes. An answer masters a question.

S: And if it lacks an answer?

J3: Then in your terms, a question is barbarian, lacking its own principle and unable to be its own truth.

J4: Every parent knows this: it is the child's interminable repetition of 'why . . . why . . .'

S: Like the enslaved, and like mediation, the never-ending 'why' is a never-ending chaos.

J3: And only an answer can save us from this.

S: So, the answer keeps such barbarian questioning as its other, at a safe distance.

J3: Yes.

S: In this way an answer owns a question, and owns every question, even before any question is asked.

J3: You are suggesting that the question is defined as always lacking the mastery of the answer, just as the enslaved always lack and need the truth of the master?

S: Exactly. Life-and-death plays itself out here once again as property. Indeed, there is a particular feature of the concept of mastery here that we would do well to remember.

J3: What feature?

S: That mastery is an overcoming.

J3: This idea seems ubiquitous, especially in the intellectual world. People speak of overcoming this or that all the time. I suppose by overcoming they mean mastery, but it is seldom made explicit that this is so.

S: What should interest us is how, in the culture of propertied logic, education itself is defined as overcoming, specifically the overcoming of the question by the answer. In the logic of mastery education is said to have occurred when an answer overcomes a question.

J3: This is what is called enlightenment. In education, overcoming is the very definition of what counts as something being learned. It is how one measures that one has been educated. An ignorance, or an error, is overcome.

S: So, is there a different idea of learning that we might explore, one which could help us in pursuing this different logic that we keep mentioning?

J3: If there is, why is it that a different logic of learning has been invisible even to educators?

S: Perhaps because learning on its own looks weak? If it is seen to have no logic of its own, then questions have no truth of their own.

J1: You were accused of just this, Socrates. People said that your questions to people emptied them of answers and gave them no new ones. You left people with nothing.

S: The question, then, is whether this nothing of the question is really something.

J1: If people knew that they knew nothing, this would be something!

S: Might we call that learning?

J3: I am beginning to think so.

S: So, when we are learning, are we doing something or nothing?

J3: We are doing something.

S: And when our very young children are learning, are they doing something?

J3: They are doing something fundamentally important.

S: And when our young men and women are learning, are they also doing something?

J3: Most definitely.

S: And what about when our senior members are learning?

J2: As I move towards the end of my life, I would say that learning is not just doing something; it is now doing something absolutely necessary and important, yet still something the city does not take seriously enough.

S: Then you are agreed that at all stages of life in the city learning is doing something rather than nothing.

J3: I am.

S: And yet, when we speak of the vicious circle of reason, and of how the critique of mastery seems to exhaust itself in contradictions and leads only to dead ends, this assumes that we learn nothing positive?

J3: Yes. Because people think that such negative learning makes no positive difference.

S: And we agree that making a difference is what defines learning?

J3: Of course. I can't say that I have learned something if nothing within me has changed.

S: Then might change be the criterion by which we do justice to what learning is.

J3: But, Socrates, this would presume that we already know the truth of learning when really it is something we should be open to learning about.

S: And here something very interesting confronts us. The thing we are to learn about – learning – and the way we are to learn it – learning – would seem to be one and the same.

J3: Is this significant?

S: Let us see. From whom do I learn how to learn?

J3: Perhaps from parents and teachers. They answer your questions, and you learn things as a result.

S: Then in doing so they teach that learning means overcoming questions.

J3: Learning is only a tool here, a means to an end. It is nothing in-itself. Ah . . . so, it is a slave. And it is therefore invisible in its own right.

S: It comes as no surprise then, that when we experience learning, we fail to see it as something that can stand for itself. We see it only through the logic of mastery, and we treat it as a slave or as nothing in-itself.

J3: Then if learning is something, and not nothing, what is the truth of learning?

S: We have already made some suggestions about this, when
we saw learning as the love that questions presuppose, but
nevertheless, we must proceed slowly here. If, somehow, there
is a different logic at work, then the truth of learning might be
different to truth defined within the logic of mastery.

J3: How might we know such a truth?

S: Perhaps by seeing this conversation we are having as a kind of
thought experiment, following its truth and its logic wherever
it takes us, allowing it to speak through our voices, allowing
it to sound sure of itself even if we ourselves are unsure about
what we are saying on its behalf.

J3: Let us do that, Socrates. Perhaps this daemon you keep talking
about will lead us to this different logic and this different truth.

S: Then let us consider the question of what happens when
we experience ourselves learning. Do you think that in this
experience of learning we learn about something or nothing?

J3: It would seem obvious now, that we learn about something,
Socrates.

S: And what is it that we learn about?

J3: In the experience of learning I would say that we learn about
learning.

S: Can you describe the elements of this experience?

J3: I can try. If, in the experience of learning, I learn about
learning, then learning is both the means and the end.

S: And you asked a moment ago, does this have any special
significance?

J3: Well, it would seem to bridge the interminable gap between
theory and practice.

S: How so?

J3: Because the same thing is being practised that is being
thought about: learning.

S: Anything else?

J3: Well, against all my better judgement, perhaps we could say here that learning is also already presupposed?

S: Why?

J3: Because if we want to learn about learning, then we must already be using learning to do so.

S: Is this the love in which what we seek – learning – is preserved as somehow known and unknown?

J3: If so, then we learn of learning as the love of learning, a love which also carries the unknown.

S: We could say that this love is both the presupposition and necessity of learning, and that while the presupposition is necessary, the necessity is also the presupposition.

J3: Which might suggest that in some strange way it is its own principle.

S: And if learning is the condition of its own possibility, it is also the condition of the possibility of learning about everything else.

Book 12

J1: Philosophy calls itself love of wisdom, so is philosophy also now this love of learning?

S: What is philosophy?

J1: It is the search for truth.

S: Why do we search for truth?

J1: Because we desire to understand.

S: Understand what?

J1: Where we come from, how we should live and what happens when we die – to understand what makes the universe and life possible.

S: Why these questions?

J1: Since we have not created ourselves, they are questions about our origin, about our destination and about life in between.

S: With what then does philosophy in the city begin?

J1: Clearly, with the question of our beginning and end.

S: And what does this question presuppose?

J1: That we need to be alive in order to ask how and why we are alive.

S: So, the question that defines philosophy is already a shape of life. It already presupposes life being lived as its own self-examination. The question is the examined and examining life.

J1: But why does life take shape as a question?

S: As we have seen, life is always already in relation to death.

J1: So the vulnerability of life to death shapes life as a question.

S: Which is presupposed in the love of learning.

J1: And if finite life feels uncertain because of this vulnerability, then for its own protection, it made sense for it to define invulnerability as infinity, infinity as certainty and certainty as truth.

J5: Which is why philosophy's answer to the question of our vulnerability to death was an uncreated and indestructible eternity that was its own origin, a prime mover, moved by itself, being the cause of everything else, but irreducible to any prior cause or movement by another.

S: If certainty was made the criterion of truth because it resolves the uncertainty of the question, then likewise, independence was the solution to dependence, cause was the solution to effect, simple was the solution to compound, original was the solution to copy and creator was the solution to the created. In short, each is the solution of error by truth. Philosophy's answers to its questions were already shapes of the life-and-death struggle.

J1: Then what is reason?

S: Reason is this logic of solution.

J1: And what is logic?

S: Logic is reason applied to itself.

J5: So, logic calls reason the overcoming of error with truth, uncertainty with certainty and vulnerability with security.

S: This is the shape of philosophy in the city. It repeats the life-and-death struggle, but it is rarely aware of itself as shapes of life and death.

J4: This reminds me of earlier, Socrates, when we said that life tried to overcome death by means of property, and that truth, nature and freedom were shapes of such property. Now if truth, nature and freedom, or metaphysics, physics and ethics, were the three elements of philosophy in the city, we are saying that philosophy itself is a shape of property, and that the story of philosophy in the city is really the story of property in the city.

J7: And of the powerful, not the powerless.

J6: I'm not sure I want to listen to this. It will inevitably be another attack on freedom.

S: If you stay you might find yourself somewhere in the story of philosophy in the city.

J6: Since I have little else to do at the moment, pray, do continue with the entertainment.

S: Then let us rehearse this story. In the ancient city life and death became known philosophically as the experience of order in the cosmos. As if, having lived underground all their lives, people left their cave, came to the surface and saw the order, beauty and harmony of the stars and the planets and assumed an eternal principle, even an eternal mind at work.

J1: Yes. Perhaps as two versions of an eternal principle: an unchanging being and an infinite becoming; or where what is, always is, and where what becomes, always becomes.

S: Did they oppose each other?

J1: Yes. Infinite becoming questioned eternal being, and eternal being questioned infinite becoming.

S: Either way the universe was experienced as the question of man and his gods, and the order observed in the heavens became something to be achieved on earth.

J1: And the story of life's desire for peace and certainty is the story of philosophy in the city.

S: What was defined as certain?

J1: The unconditional. That whose conditions of possibility are found in-itself and which is not conditional in any way upon something else.

S: What did philosophy call this unconditional?

J1: Something existing in its own right – an object in-itself.

S: Was philosophy working here with the same propertied logic as we saw before with truth, nature and freedom?

J1: Yes. In making certainty the mastery of the in-itself, it made mastery the definition of philosophical truth. The unconditional was seen as the pure object in-itself, master of all compound material appearances and master of itself.

S: So, philosophy defined purity as the truth of the propertied master, leaving the enslaved as mere objects with no intrinsic truth of their own.

J1: But philosophy also reversed this. Some argued that material objects were objects in-themselves if they fulfilled their own natural purpose and were neither more nor less than themselves.

S: Propertied logic determined both approaches.

J1: Exactly what it did in the social relations of mastery and slavery in the city.

S: Then we might say that philosophy and mastery here are cut from the same cloth of identity and property and serve each other's needs. Philosophy resolves uncertainty, and the master enjoys this certainty in his own identity. It means that the idea which the city has of truth and god corresponds with that which the city has of itself, of its freedom.

J1: Then the story of philosophy in the city is the story of property and its logic.

S: Did this propertied philosophy shape for itself a specific methodology?

J1: Yes. It applied certainty to the object in-itself, and then allowed increasingly minute distinctions in its definition in order to save its appearance from any contradictions. This was called scholasticism.

S: This method forgot that philosophy is already a shape of the life-and-death experience.

J1: Exactly. It forgot that truth was already the shape of this prior relation.

S: The sovereignty of the in-itself is therefore philosophy's propertied misrecognition of itself. But how did philosophy define this misrecognition?

J1: It had two strategies to call on. Dogmatism and scepticism. Dogmatism asserted truth as the in-itself. It was closed off to the question of its conditions of possibility in life and death but open to the question by which its identity might be clarified. Scepticism saw claims to truth opposing each other, with no means of deciding one as more valid than another. It suspended judgement altogether.

S: I can see how dogmatism came to be called analytic but perhaps scepticism is also analytic. It denies the possibility of truth only by first accepting the analytic definition of truth as the certainty of the in-itself. The instability championed by scepticism still presupposes that truth is the stability of the propertied logic of the in-itself.

J1: Then dogmatism and scepticism are both within propertied logic. What difference would it have made if philosophy had seen this?

S: Perhaps philosophy might have been opened to its own propertied shape of life and death.

J1: Would philosophy then have been different?

S: Perhaps it was already different.

J1: What do you mean?

S: Alongside the analytic character of philosophy perhaps there was a different kind of philosophy giving voice to life and death as the question. But this voice was not loud and was submerged by the power and mastery of definitions.

J1: What did this voice say?

S: It quietly said that life and death coexist. It took shape as a philosophy of perplexity, where certainty and uncertainty remained together, and were not forced into the propertied logic of overcoming and resolution.

J1: You mean, when a philosopher, seeking a definition, admits that something both is and is not itself at the same time and does not impose a propertied form on this.

S: Or when the conditions of possibility are allowed to be ambiguous, even self-contradictory, perhaps by being conditional upon that for which they are the conditions of possibility.

J6: You are talking absolute nonsense.

J1: Does this perplexity speak of a different logic?

S: We will see.

J1: What happened to this voice in the story of philosophy in the city?

S: Like our friend here, philosophical commentators, presupposing the propertied form of philosophy, have assumed that it made no sense, and that if it was ever found in some of the great philosophical works, then it must have been unintended, or a mistake, and needed to be explained away or ignored.

J1: So, this perplexed voice of philosophy was largely unheard.

S: Which meant that the story of philosophy was the analytic story of distinctions in definitions, and not a self-examination of its presupposition of truth. Did this change at some point?

J1: I would say that it did. Philosophy started to look for truth not in the object in-itself but in the experience in which the object appeared.

S: This was life and death beginning to examine itself, and to understand itself in the philosophical shape it had taken.

J1: Philosophy now enquired about its own preconditions.

S: And what was the outcome?

J1: A philosophical revolution.

S: Of what kind?

J1: One which overturned the certainty which had presupposed itself in the mastery of the object in-itself. No longer was the object assumed to have such certainty. Instead, certainty was to be found in the conditions necessary for there to be an object at all.

S: What was this necessity?

J1: That the object be experienced in thought.

S: And this is the revolution?

J1: Yes. Some likened it to a recent cosmological revolution.

S: Why?

J1: Because as the earth became a satellite of the sun, so the object in-itself became a satellite of thought.

J6: Such a revolution would make the experience of objective truth impossible!

J1: Yes, if you measured this experience against the view that there actually was a pure object objectively existing in-itself beyond experience. But if you don't presuppose that, then there is no object in-itself for experience to contradict.

S: Did such philosophy discover a different necessity here to the propertied shapes of analytic philosophy?

J1: It discovered a transcendental necessity, one that made the experience of an object possible. Space and time were the necessary conditions of intuiting an object, and the power of conceptualization provided the transcendental rules needed to understand the intuition.

S: Where was this necessity found?

J1: In the power of judgement that each of us has.

S: And what is the proof of this necessity?

J1: That it is already in play with every experience of an object. The transcendental necessity is the condition of the possibility of having any knowledge at all. Without these pre-existing rules and capacities, we would not even know what objects were. That we do know of them is already proof of the necessity.

J4: Then it is this necessity that is also in play when we make our judgements as a jury in your trial, Socrates.

J6: I make my own judgements.

J4: Yes you do. But only because of conditions which, beyond your control and beyond your authorship, enable you to do so. Can't you see that the certainty you have in your mastery is naive?

J6: Dear lady, naivety is your natural domain.

S: Within this philosophy, then, is necessity transcendent and unable to be experienced?

J1: Truth in-itself, yes. Knowledge and understanding cannot transcend the limits of their being experienced.

S: You mean I cannot experience something beyond experience, but I can know of something being necessary for experience?

J1: Yes.

S: Then the analytic certainty that lay in the object is gone.

J1: It has.

S: And scholastic distinctions of definitions are therefore in vain?

J1: They are.

S: Then philosophy is changed in the revolution, no longer a subjectivity seeking certainty in objectivity, but now objectivity seeking certainty in the transcendental necessity of subjective experiences.

J1: Well put, Socrates. This is the revolution.

J5: But perhaps it is not so revolutionary after all?

A: Why not?

J5: It sounds like, just as the sun was put at the centre of the cosmos, so now subjectivity is put at the centre of all knowledge. One centre has been replaced by another. That would simply replace one mastery with another. If so, then the revolution in philosophy simply moved truth from the object in-itself to the rules of transcendental necessity. Which means that the revolution created another perplexity at the heart of philosophy.

J1: You mean the perplexity that as much as the objects need the transcendental rules, so the transcendental rules need the objects. But this leads to a different interpretation of the revolution, one that seems to leave no centre at all. In this interpretation it is emphasized that rules without objects are blind, and objects without rules are empty.

J5: Which means that necessity needs both objects and rules.

S: A necessity that has its own needs is a necessity not only for others but also for itself. It is only being true to its own nature.

J5: But the problem with this second interpretation of the revolution is that if rules need objects and objects need rules, this opens an infinite regression that will never establish necessity as a first principle? The conditions are conditional, which are conditional and so on.

S: As this necessity has its own needs, so perhaps these conditions have their own conditions?

J5: In which case this is no longer the certainty that philosophy previously ascribed to conditions of possibility, which were supposed to end infinite regression for the certainty of an origin.

S: It would seem then that the revolution, in losing the truth of the object to experience, also revealed that the truth of experience was conditional upon that which it experienced. Perhaps this revolution is not best compared to the cosmological revolution.

J5: Why not?

S: That revolution left the sun at the centre of all things. But this philosophical revolution leaves no centre in place. All absolute positions and speeds, and all fixed truths, become relative.

J1: Indeed.

S: Then how do you think philosophy in the city handled this revolution? How did it live with this revolutionary change?

Did it manage to live without the propertied truth of the object in-itself?

J4: No, it didn't.

J7: Certainly it didn't.

J1: I think the city was divided by it. Some philosophy tried to do justice to the ambivalence of the revolution, some returned to the solidity of analytic definitions and their distinctions.

S: I wonder if both parties continued to practise the same injustice on perplexity.

Book 13

J1: Do you have something in mind here, Socrates?

S: We must proceed slowly. Do we agree that in this revolution prior conditions of the possibility of knowledge are necessary?

J1: Yes.

S: So, can this necessity be defined as a transcendental first principle in-itself?

J1: No, because it cannot be known in-itself.

S: Why not?

J1: Because although it always precedes knowledge, it can only be known second-hand, as it were, by that which it makes possible.

S: So how can it be known?

J1: Only as a necessary presupposition.

S: So, to return to a previous idea, knowing necessity purely in-itself would be like knowing how to swim without ever having got wet.

J1: Indeed. We cannot know what we presuppose without first presupposing it. We cannot know necessity without it being

attached to an experience of an object. And we cannot be a
swimmer without getting wet.

S: And this necessity is universal?

J1: Yes.

S: So is it its own truth?

J1: Yes. Except that, in propertied logic, this is exactly how
something is defined as untrue. Because it is conditional it is
not in-itself.

S: Yet perplexingly this revolutionary necessity has shown us that
the unconditioned and the conditioned need each other.

J1: In experience, yes. But philosophy also reasoned that in a
different realm, that of the will rather than the understanding,
such a pure necessity in-itself could be realized. A will, acting
of its own necessity and not attached to an object, would be a
free will!

J8: May I speak? I believe you are referring to morality.

J1: How so?

J8: A moral will acts not out of its self-interest but in the universal
interest.

J1: And how do we know what is the universal interest?

J8: It is when you act not as you want to, but as you hope others
would act in the same situation.

J1: So the universal act would be free from attachment to any
particular object or outcome?

J8: Exactly what you have just shown thinking is unable to do.

J1: So this necessity that the revolution discovered is unavailable
to us in experience but can be acted out by the will of the
moral person?

J8: Indeed. In the selfless act.

J5: No one ever acts from pure will. Everyone always has some
object in mind.

S: Meaning that our actions are never pure necessity, or pure freedom.

J1: Philosophy admitted as much. Freedom appeared as the frustrated desire for itself.

S: Why frustrated?

J8: Because freedom knew that it ought to be something that experience told it it couldn't be. And freedom in moral philosophy became not something that can be done but something that ought to be done. It became an imposition or an imperative and thus freedom became a mastery that ordered people to be free.

J8: You are speaking of duty.

J1: Yes. In moral philosophy a frustrated freedom imposed a mastery of necessity upon itself and demanded that it is the duty of everyone to do what they could not think: the universal good.

J6: One always does one's duty.

J7: When it suits your self-interests.

J6: My family has always done its duty to the city. It has been part of the backbone of the city, devoted to a life of service.

J7: Self-service.

J6: Dear lady, if the good lord should decide to reward those who sacrifice themselves for public service, then who are we to question that?

J7: You use duty as if it were your own property. You demand it of others when the cause is to your own advantage. You wield duty as a tyranny, as a way of demanding conformity and obedience. I have seen this with my own eyes.

S: The abuse of the universal interest for particular ends is perhaps inevitable within a city of propertied mastery and truth.

J1: Why?

S: Because in such logic the pure act of goodness lies beyond what is possible. In a version of morality whose logic is self-defeating, hypocrisy becomes its universal currency. Its own logic justifies the abuse of its own ideals.

J1: What moved moral philosophy to do such a thing?

S: Perhaps in defining moral necessity as pure freedom in-itself, propertied logic enacted revenge on the revolution for questioning the truth of its identity and the identity of its truth. It redefined moral necessity as something in-itself and made it serve mastery. The revolution robbed propertied logic of the mastery of truth in-itself by demonstrating its dependence upon an experience of an object. And propertied logic responded by making the truth of the revolution unknowable for the same reason. Philosophy and property then compromised with each other, agreeing that this necessity, when released from attachment to an object of experience, could achieve a masterful identity as what ought to be, or as the freedom of duty. Unknowable truth self-identified as pure command in-itself and morality became the analytic practice of this self-definition.

J8: You mean that morality became the interminable command to replace compromised relations with pure motives. The new moral necessity was to live as pure necessity ought to be lived, universally and not selfishly, by living freedom as an end in-itself and not as a means to serving any heteronomous or external ends.

S: Yes.

J8: And unselfish duty became the new imperative of a free act in the world.

S: Yes. But as we have seen, the ought remains a propertied shape.

J8: Nevertheless, Socrates, if we lose morality, we lose our duty to others, and we lose the idea of acting in the universal interest. Even if the ought makes us do things we might not choose to do, it still makes us do the right thing. It still treats everyone as ends in-themselves and not as slaves or as the means to the ends of others. Without the dignity of each life in-itself there can be no equality of individuals and no universal laws that are blind to individual circumstance. The city of moral individuals may well be a freedom defined in propertied logic, but it's not one the city can just abandon!

S: And here is the momentous ambivalence of freedom in the revolution. Never in the history of the city had all its citizens been granted inviolable individual rights as free people. And never before had propertied logic hidden its mastery in the guise of freedom for all of the city's inhabitants. Mastery and slavery were not abolished here. They were merely hidden within universal property rights.

J8: When is this ruse visible?

J1: Each time pure freedom, or our rich friend here, contradicts itself – which is all the time. And all because the revolution allowed propertied logic to define its necessity as an unknowable truth.

S: Such is the ambivalence of revolutionary freedom. Both defender of the universal necessity that dissolves the authority of the object in-itself and defender of the propertied form of that necessity in which each individual is free only as an object in-itself. Never has the city been so free in its own chains.

J1: Socrates, tell us what you think philosophy in the city did with such ambivalence.

S: From what I have seen it appears that some philosophy tried to change its methodology from the analytic to the contingent, seeing contingency as defining the experience of necessity.

J1: You mean an experience of being dependent upon something else, or perhaps shaped by something that works behind the scenes as it were?

S: Yes.

J1: What shapes did these philosophies of contingency take?

S: Shapes of mediation in opposition to the immediate propertied shape of the in-itself.

J1: Immediacy concerns that which is believed to be without prior determination.

S: And therefore holds itself immune to unending questioning.

J1: And this is a shape of mastery, with the idea of God being the identity of immediacy in-itself.

S: Yes. An immediacy the ancients defined as unchangeable in order to be secure from further regression to a simpler form.

J1: While life on earth – physical nature and finite minds – lacking such immediacy, was seen by them as changeable and contingent. And human beings saw themselves as error in relation to immediate unchangeable truth.

S: And sinful in relation to immediate good.

J1: Then if immediacy was the shape of the mastery of the object in-itself, error took shape as mediation, or as slavery, as that which has no truth attached to itself in its own right.

S: Yes.

J5: There are examples of the ancients in the city trying to live a life of such contingency. The most powerful was stoicism which we mentioned earlier. Stoics accepted that they were not in control of nature, or of life's events, or chance or fate. Their response was to seek the peace of what is, by not wishing it was something else. Their freedom was the imperative that they ought to live in peace with contingency. So powerful was this idea that people in the city are still known to say that someone is being philosophical when they mean they are being stoical.

J1: Then what might we say of immediacy and mediation in the philosophical revolution that struck the city long after stoicism?

S: That objects and the rules of knowing objects mediate each other. Apart from pure freedom there is nothing in the revolution that is immediate that is not also mediated, and nothing mediated that is not also immediate.

J1: Then what specific shapes did philosophy in the city take in working without the certainty of the object in-itself?

S: It imagined many new ways to understand this revolutionary and contingent philosophical life.

J5: For example, one philosophy grounded the contingency of life in the city upon a pre-existing arrangement and distribution of material resources, or in the way that the economics of the city presupposed inequalities in social relations. It suggested that the exploitation of each slave has been collectively capitalized upon as the propertied identity of the value of its work. It believed that this capital is the pre-existing condition of life in the city.

J1: Alternatively, some suggested that life in the city was contingent upon the privilege accorded to intellect over the physical and the material.

J4: And when women are defined within the latter, this accords superiority to men and leaves women contingent upon them.

J1: Someone argued that reason only got itself taken seriously when it willed revenge on its own impurities, taking shape as morality and religion, which were the tools by which it could continually punish itself. Some suggested that philosophy had long suppressed Being as the real origin of contingency. And some suggested that life in the city was contingent upon the way reason shaped the truth of everything to be the same as itself, hiding a deeper contingency upon the presupposition of difference which, unknowable in-itself, appeared in the shape of opposition.

S: Then there are many different varieties of how to think of contingent life without the object in-itself.

J9: Indeed there are.

S: Hello. Please introduce yourself.

J9: I identify as without identity.

S: What does that mean?

J9: It means that you cannot pin me to the noticeboard of identity. I reject fixity for fluidity. Only in this way can I embody tolerance and difference; only in this way can I be justice and freedom. I put myself beyond human prejudice, beyond stereotypes, beyond social conformity and beyond arbitrary values. I and others like me are the new education that awaits you, Socrates.

J1: You are still a human being.

J9: Human being is just another label that fixes people. And that label in particular is the self-identifying of human beings as superior to everything else in the universe. Within this, they then concoct hierarchies based on different types of human beings. I am speaking of your tradition, Socrates. You have privileged human intellect over everything else, which means you have privileged what it looks like from your perspective, that of a dead white male.

S: What if I self-identify as that which is not itself, as that which is not myself?

J9: Don't avoid or deny your allegiance to the idea of essence, Socrates. You are deeply mired in the arrogance of essence as self-consciousness and mind. You think, and therefore you believe thought is the highest essence of life, and you judge the universe according to that one privileged criterion. Your prejudice is that thinking is the essence of human being, and everything in the city has been shaped by this mastery.

J1: Our conversation has been no friend to such mastery.

J9: Yet masters you remain, wedded to the essentialism that entitles you to make universal judgements about everyone and everything.

S: Would you give me an opportunity to explore with you what I think essence is?

J9: I would be interested in how the dead white male tries to defend his dominance.

S: I think you heard our discussion of the life-and-death struggle.

J9: I overheard it, yes. I think you said that it was where one I-desire met another I-desire in pursuit of limited resources.

S: And how did they play out a life-and-death event?

J9: Each treated the other indifferently and sought to remove the other as an obstacle to what it desired. This created for each of them the experience of their own mortality. Each realized that it risked its life in trying to get what it wanted. And this experience of mortality created a new kind of consciousness – a self-consciousness – aware of itself as being a living, breathing, thinking entity.

S: We called this the transition from the I-desire to the I-life-and-death. And we noted that for this new self-consciousness to preserve itself it would need to preserve the life-and-death experiences it depended upon, but preferably without having to risk life and limb every minute of every day.

J9: Yes. It preserved the experience at arm's length by making death its property and this made life and death into the culture of mastery and slavery—

S: . . . which is the reality that each of us are born into and in which mastery through property appears as a natural phenomenon, the irreducible essence of life. How do you think masters experience themselves as such essence?

J9: As the security of the propertied world. Each master holds as essential that which he takes at face value, including his own power and advantage in the world. Add a few intellectual virtues and this man of property can convince himself that he is the perfect or essential human being.

S: So, his mastery presupposes itself as an essence?

J9: Yes. And like the I-desire it is indifferent to otherness because property insulates mastery from mediation.

S: In plain view property hides the master's need for the other.

J9: Then the indifferent essence of the master is at best an ignorance, perhaps an arrogance, and at worst a tyranny.

S: It could be an ignorance about his own conditions of possibility; an arrogance with regard to the privilege he accepts as entitlement; or a tyranny in his maintenance of this entitlement, including in the suffering of others upon whom his privilege depends.

J9: But he falls back on the assertion of his essence as a master.

S: He does.

J9: And it is this assertion of essence that hides his indifference, which preserves a strict difference between those worthy of vast fortunes and those who are not.

S: Then we are agreed that this essence is a deceit.

J9: We are.

S: What is the justification of this essence?

J9: That it is its own truth, the truth of self-consciousness.

S: But we have suggested that, by its own definition, this is only partly true.

J9: Why only partly?

S: Because it ignores the other as the condition of the possibility of this essence. And an essence that is contingent does not fulfil the criterion of the logic of mastery that it needs to be strictly independent and to be its own truth.

J9: Very well. Essence is like the unquestioning circle, repeating itself without ever asking itself hard questions about its contingency.

S: Then we are agreed so far. Where do you think our disagreement will come?

J9: It will come when you establish this essence of self-consciousness or mastery, and the doubts you have about it, as the foundation of freedom in the city. You will create a city in which, from the outset, the other is anything that is not the same as this master, anything that is deemed not to have this self-consciousness as its own truth.

J1: And you stand for all otherness?

J9: I am otherness.

J1: Yet you use the word 'I'.

J9: The language does not yet exist that can do justice to living as otherness.

S: I wonder, if you consent, that we might extend our conversation a little further.

J9: Go on.

S: Might we say that essence is illusory?

J9: Yes, the master's essence is an empty shell, a facade.

S: And yet it is an emptiness that believes itself to be full.

J9: How can an empty illusion ever be believed to be an essence?

S: Perhaps because essence is what illusion looks like in the world. Perhaps what essence does is to make illusion a propertied reality of life for everyone.

J9: If essence is this immediacy of the propertied master, no wonder his sense of entitlement is born into him.

S: It would mean that essence presupposes property, and that mastery is the reproduction or culture of that presupposition.

J9: Then the master is living and breathing property; property embodied!

S: Would you say that we are all such illusions of property?

J9: You might be. But I am not. And there are others like me who are beyond such illusions. We are not held captive by this kind of essentialism. We are not made; we are under construction.

S: I wonder, is illusion not present here also?

J9: What do you mean?

S: What does illusion look like when it takes itself seriously?

J9: Mastery.

S: And what does illusion look like when it tries to overcome itself?

J9: More mastery.

S: And what might illusion look like when it tries to avoid mastery altogether?

J9: Different.

S: Or indifferent.

J9: Not at all. Your concept of subjectivity is built on conflict and opposition. I identify only with difference.

S: Perhaps that is also an illusion of essence.

J9: How could it be?

S: Difference that is not also an illusion of property looks like it is indifferent to its presupposing of life and death.

J9: Not at all. It cares about the other.

S: Does difference precede the meeting with the other?

J9: Difference knows the two together.

S: How does it know that it is different?

J9: It knows and respects the other.

S: What is doing the knowing?

J9: Difference is.

S: Then what is difference?

J9: You can't answer that question because difference is nothing in-itself. It is not a concept. It is not subservient to the privilege of the intellect.

S: This nothing, then, is indifferent to itself. It is how emptiness relates to itself – indifferently. Difference, here, looks like presupposition's illusory being. It looks like the essence of indifference.

J9: It is avoiding essence.

S: Only by being indifferent to life and death, and that is already an illusion of mastery.

J7: And to maintain this illusion requires mastery in the form of intrigue, for the preservation of indifference requires a great deal of manipulative scheming. There are people who live a life of difference indifferently as a life of mastery and according to a universal currency of strength and power. These are the intriguers. They cling to indifference as the virtue of pure difference, believing that they and they alone have the strength to live with knowing that essence is an illusion, or with having overcome essence altogether. They announce themselves post-essence, even post-human, and make a virtue out of this propertied form of contingency. And the more forcefully they cling to their indifference, the more forcefully they dominate others.

S: And you know such people?

J7: I do.

S: What are they like?

J7: They are living and breathing indifference. They revel
   in the intrigue of their emptiness. They bask in the pure
   contingency which leaves them free from accountability to
   others. They live true to this groundlessness in irony, never
   having to mean what they say. They treat life as a game; see
   themselves as expert players; and see others as there to be
   taken advantage of for being poor players, or for taking it
   too seriously, or for not even realizing it is a game. They
   live a culture of indifference. It is part of the game to use
   others' weaknesses against themselves, for then it just looks
   like people get what they deserve. They despise the values
   of kindness and sacrifice as weakness, seeing them as based
   in ignorance of the game. They mock conscience, they
   exploit gullibility, and they turn the nothingness of their
   own illusion into a life of cynicism, or even into the intrigue
   of cynical cheerfulness. They profess not to take themselves
   seriously and take this very seriously in order to become
   master manipulators in the world.

J1: More masterful perhaps than the masters who enslave others?

J7: More masterful because at least such enslavement is visible!
   But with masterful indifference power is hidden behind
   intrigue and deception. They will tell people anything they
   think they want to hear, blaming them for being stupid enough
   to believe the lies.

J1: And when the lies are revealed?

J7: No problem. They were never meant to be taken seriously in
   the first place. Seriousness is held to be a problem only for the
   ignorant, not for the game player.

J1: Except that the game player is deeply serious.

J7: The game, the illusion, is all they have, and they play it in deadly earnest, climbing the greasy poles in the city in praise of the indifference of doing so.

S: You paint a deeply worrying picture of new kinds of shadows in the city.

J9: And I certainly do not believe that my difference is essentially indifferent.

J1: Socrates, a little while ago you said that perhaps both philosophical responses to the revolution – analytical and non-analytical, that is, philosophies of identity and of contingency – might be practising the same injustice on perplexity. Are you ready to explain what you mean by this?

S: I wonder if such post-revolutionary philosophy in some ways is not so different from pre-revolutionary philosophy.

J1: How?

S: Do these new philosophies of indifference reject the analytical truth of tautological definitions?

J1: They do.

S: And do they therefore see that analytical philosophy holds itself immune from contingency upon pre-existing presuppositions?

J1: They do.

S: Then these new philosophies call themselves non-foundational and non-dogmatic because they claim to be open to their own contingency.

J1: Yes.

S: But they are not open to their own contingency upon propertied forms of truth and logic.

J9: Why do you say this?

S: Because they continue to refuse to grant truth to contingency or presupposition or mediation.

J1: Why do they refuse such truth?

J9: Because truth is a prejudice of the intellect.

S: Why can contingency not be truth?

J9: Because it undermines truth.

S: And why is undermining truth not seen as being its own truth?

J9: Because contingency is the opposite of truth. . . . Oh. I suppose you are now going to tell me that by denying truth to contingency I am still defining truth as mastery.

S: And therefore you are still accepting the definition of truth being identity or mastery in-itself.

J1: If that is the case, then all philosophy in the city, foundational and non-foundational, is grounded in mastery. Perhaps all claims in philosophy, be they for or against truth in-itself, still presuppose the masterful identity of truth in-itself.

S: It would seem that the new philosophies still use identity and non-contradiction as criteria for denying that mediation can be a different truth. Even the philosophical revolution in the city, which contradictorily combined a priori presupposition and a posteriori experience, assumed that truth in-itself remained unknowable to revolutionary philosophical experience.

J9: Then you are suggesting that my difference is not different at all to the philosophy it opposes.

S: A logic that might really be different is never allowed its own voice, even by the supporters of difference. In fact, the new philosophies of contingency seem to be increasingly scholastic, making distinction after distinction in order to save the appearance of contingency from an identity in-itself. They are working as hard to ensure that contingency was not truth as the analytic thinkers did to ensure that definition was truth.

J9: You are saying that both types of philosophy presupposed the same propertied logic of truth. The revolution undermined itself by retaining propertied logic and accepting that truth remained unknowable. And so, in the revolution, everything changed when it lost the object in-itself, but nothing changed when what was lost was not also preserved differently. And now I too remain the same.

S: Quite so.

J10: Socrates, if I may interject, I have not understood all that you have said, but I think a new kind of mastery does dominate the city at the moment. It certainly does in my life.

S: Please, speak of this.

J10: My work in the city has been taken over by a way of working that turns everyone into a number and treats everyone indifferently. It is like a logic of mastery but perhaps in a new form.

S: Say more.

J10: It gets called rationalization. I was taught that reason was the liberator of the city. Instead all I see is that it enslaves us. I want to understand how reason ended up like this.

J1: Let me try an explanation. The old city had its superstitions. But self-consciousness, in demonstrating its freedom, showed that everything known had to pass through the mind. It mediated everything. This universality was called enlightenment, or reason as a total or absolute truth. And the philosophical revolution in the city claimed this as a new and universal necessity of free human being. This reason attacked, and continues to attack, every person, every principle and every social and political establishment that claimed immediate authority of any kind. It mediated or questioned the credentials of everything. It was a revolution on behalf of critical thinking.

J10: So, where did the new mastery come from?

J1: From reason claiming for itself the status of truth in-itself.

J10: How could reason as mediation do this?

S: Perhaps by not mediating its own experience of the object. Critical thinking extended to everything except itself. Immune from its own mediation, reason became merely abstract thinking.

J10: What is abstract thinking?

S: It is when reason knows things by objectifying them.

J10: What does objectification mean?

S: It means removing the knowledge of objects from its complicity in being experienced.

J10: And what is reason when it refuses such complicity?

S: It is method.

J10: Then why does reason not mediate itself?

S: Because it still adheres to the old logic and believes that mediation, although universal as rational or critical thinking, cannot be true in-itself and should not be practised on itself. Therefore, its universality becomes an abstract and purely formal mastery.

J1: So, reason as the new mastery is a dehumanized and dehumanizing method freed from the education of its own life and death. And in the city this method has a variety of names: objective reason, instrumental reason, technical reason and abstract reason.

S: Objective because it still sees subjective mediation as a corruption of truth in-itself.

J1: Yes, and instrumental and technical because it is only concerned with how objects perform.

S: And abstract because it is granted immunity from any critical experience of itself.

J10: I think have seen such method dehumanize life in the city. I have seen work, behaviour, personal relationships,

resources, communication, education, care, even laughter and
tears mastered by this abstract rationality. It demands that
everything be defined, measured and accounted for according
to its own indifference to education and learning. To become
more efficient, more abstract, more instrumental is the only
goal that drives this mastery. Who has not experienced such
mastery as the trial of faceless administrative authority? Who
has not seen bullying and even brutality abstracted and given
anonymous legitimacy in and as bureaucracy? And who has
not witnessed the marketplace embrace such rationality as its
new mastery over working life?

S: Did religion not oppose such dehumanization?

J8: The city's religions, our centres of morality, have been
assimilated into this same mastery.

S: In the methods they adopt in running their organizations?

J8: In both their outer administration and in their administration
of the inner life. When dissatisfaction set in regarding empty
outward displays of devotion, a demand was made for
evidence of inner devotion in rationalized form. One's faith
and commitment had to be measurable to be valid, and to
be measurable it had to become systematic. Inner devotion
turned into efficiency in demonstrating that no time was
wasted by not being in service to the vocation that the god had
assigned each of his followers in their respective stations in
life.

S: So, faith too became objectified by the logic of mastery.

J8: And this speaks more generally of the exhaustion and
resignation in the city that reason is no longer able to make
any difference to the logic of mastery and its injustices.
As a response, it transfers its hopes to the irrational, to
something like the charisma of rogues who seek only to

exploit such exhaustion and resignation. At times I too find
myself exhausted by such thinking, and then I am pulled
towards the resignation that nothing can ever make a
difference.

S: Perhaps this ambivalence of critical thinking was reflected
earlier in our conversation when our friend suggested that the
cosmic and philosophical revolutions left no centre in place.
What did you mean by that?

J1: The revolutions faced two ways at once. The earth and
the sun, and the object and experience each changed
their relation to each other and undermined traditional
certainties. The existential impact of both revolutions was
frailty and vulnerability for the ex-masters. But it was also
a new mastery for the sun and for experience. Both were
given the certainty that was taken from their previous
masters.

S: Yet you said the revolution looked both ways?

J1: The revolutions also undermined the idea of a centre by
showing how the centre of one thing had its own centre in
something else, and so on. All centres became relative to other
centres, leaving no centres at all. No positions were left fixed
and nothing was left at rest. The mastery of the idea of a centre
was undone.

J8: Meaning that everything is relative to everything else. In
some ways this lies at the heart of the city's own frailties and
vulnerabilities. Truth on one side of the city is not truth on the
other side.

J1: That is the sceptical view. And the dogmatic view is that truth
must be the same wherever it is.

J8: Then the revolutions support scepticism over dogmatism?

J1: Yes, until we remember Socrates's suggestion that both
   scepticism and dogmatism still use propertied logic to judge
   truth and its impossibility.

J8: So the revolutions not only replaced one master with another
   they also ruled out all mastery.

J1: Then this is another dead end, with the anxiety and insecurity
   that accompany such perplexity.

S: Has the city felt the force of this?

J4: It is doing so in its experience of such de-centring.
   For example, when the human-centred view of
   man's superiority over animals was de-centred by his
   kinship to animals, or when the superiority of his self-
   consciousness was de-centred by being made an effect
   of the unconscious.

J7: This would extend to everything that human beings have
   ever thought. If everything known is human-centred, then
   everything is vulnerable to being de-centred.

J9: I have a friend who speaks of how the human-centred view
   of humans as creators of technology and controllers of
   plants is also being de-centred. In the unhuman perspective
   technology creates us for its own use, and plants farm us for
   their own survival. The response from people is to say this
   is nonsense, just as it was said that a heliocentric cosmos
   was nonsense. Perhaps even the idea that human beings
   could end all life on the planet is just more human-centred
   hubris.

J8: The city could end all *human* life on the planet.

J1: Yes, but in the de-centred view human life is a triviality
   compared to all life that makes up the life of the planet.
   Perhaps to unhuman life we are just a speck of dust in

their great scheme of things. De-centring opens us up
to the possibility that life beyond the human is beyond
anything we can imagine as human beings, and we have that
wonderful dizzying feeling of being just a pale blue dot in the
unimaginable vastness of everything.

S: Is it possible that even the idea of de-centring is a human-
centred prejudice?

J9: If it is, then any critique of anthropocentrism is
meaningless.

S: Perhaps. But if we are a speck of dust relative to life on the
planet, and the planet is a speck of dust in the galaxy, and
the galaxy in the universe and so on, then microcosm and
macrocosm, each relative to the other, have the meaning of
this relation.

J9: What is the meaning of such a relation?

S: A good question.

J1: It seems to be a relation that both separates and returns the
human-centred and the de-centred to one another, or where
difference and opposition coexist?

S: Perhaps it is the relation in which we learn that we are both for
ourselves and for-another.

J9: The logic of mastery would not allow that.

S: Indeed. One can treat the loss of mastery to the relativity
of experience merely negatively and say that it creates
a bottomless abyss of meaning, or one can also treat it
educationally and say that something has been learnt which is
different from just mastery or non-mastery.

J9: You mean, redefine the relation of human-centred
and de-centred educationally rather than simply
prejudging it within mastery as having no truth of
its own.

S: A similar puzzling relation was applied to the sun in the old city. Its mastery was the same for everyone but was also lived differently by everyone.

J1: You mean that its light was the same for everyone and was the cause of sight, but sight was also unique to each pair of eyes.

S: The truth of sunlight was that it was only true when it was seen as the cause of sight. Perhaps the truth of the sun is relative to the time and place of each pair of eyes it encounters.

J5: But a fixed law is not fixed if it is true only relative to other things.

S: From the perspective of the sun, sight is relative. But from the perspective of sight, each seeing is lived true to itself. This is true relativity – truth relative to itself.

J1: It makes no sense in the logic of mastery. So what does this look like as a human experience?

S: As you said, frailty and vulnerability.

J1: But they are weakness.

S: Unless they have their own necessity and truth.

J1: What might that be?

S: Perhaps the necessity and truth of kindness.

J1: Like those who, for example in times of plague, in hospitals and elsewhere, refuse the logic of mastery and live the life and death of others as their own struggle, and their own educational experiences.

S: Quite so.

J1: In which case, Socrates, our conversation has finally avoided taking a propertied view of life.

S: Not avoided, but rather negated and preserved life differently.

J9: This could still be the last stand of human subjectivity trying to find meaning and truth in-itself. Or, I suppose it might be the next stage of human thinking readying itself for having to redefine truth as a relation to others.

S: Perhaps, somehow, it is both.

Book 14

J1: If so, then our daemon is leading us into something like a new understanding of truth. But has such thinking ever been part of philosophy in the city?

S: Do you remember we suggested that alongside the masterful and propertied identity of philosophy in the city there might be another voice submerged and silenced?

J1: You mean the voice that spoke not of mastery but of perplexity?

S: Yes. Perhaps we will find our new idea of truth in retrieving that voice and doing justice to it.

J1: I feel the pull of this enquiry deep inside me, and still so strong.

S: First, then, let us restate the three most important elements of the philosophical revolution of enlightenment in the city. First, that knowledge of objects presupposed, as a condition of its possibility, a power of judgement. Second, that understanding did not have any powers to transcend judgements, which ruled out the possibility of knowing a pure object in-itself. Third, that truth in-itself was therefore also unknowable.

J1: If experience is subjective, it will always contradict objective truth.

S: But the revolution also said that without an object in-itself, there is nothing to contradict. And so, in the revolution the contradiction vanishes because experience need no longer be convicted of contradicting pure unconditional truth.

J1: So revolutionary life offered life without truth in-itself and without the object in-itself.

S: But the revolution did not do justice to itself. It undermined truth by its necessary relation to experience, but the revolution also disqualified this relation from being its own truth.

J1: Because the revolution held onto truth in-itself as something unknowable.

S: Exactly. Against the old notion of truth, a relation to experience was still judged untrue. If the revolution had done justice to itself, then the relation of experience and object would have been allowed to speak its own truth.

J1: So instead of working with a revolutionary notion of truth, it still held the revolution accountable to the propertied notion of truth. How might this have looked if the revolution had done justice to itself?

S: The revolution could have conceived a revolutionary notion of truth in the necessity of the life-and-death relation that it already presupposed.

J1: The revolution did try to find this new truth in freedom, as we said earlier. It called it duty.

S: But as we also said, it took a propertied form because it turned the transcendental necessity into a moral commandment. This is what happens when you turn a necessity that is already presupposed into a presupposition that it ought to be a necessity.

J1: So, would this revolutionary truth or presupposition be knowable? Would it be an absolute truth even if it is not, anymore, a truth in-itself?

S: Freed from the illusions of the mastery of truth in-itself, presupposition could be its own kind of truth.

J1: And what of life and death here?

S: If propertied logic turns vulnerability into unjust social relations, perhaps a different logic could turn vulnerability into just social relations? Perhaps life and death can be lived differently, and the meaning of life and death understood differently?

J1: Would this logic be non-propertied?

S: Not if that presupposed immunity from property.

J1: Might it be un-propertied?

S: Yes, if that carries the struggle of the negation of property without resorting to a mastery of non-property.

J1: Which suggests that justice is done when the struggle is preserved. And we have already met something that is able to do justice to preserving struggles, Socrates. Learning!

S: Remind us.

J1: We said that learning can preserve itself while avoiding mastery.

S: Did we say it avoided mastery?

J1: If it doesn't, then how is it different from mastery?

S: Perhaps it has a quality that sets it apart.

J1: What quality?

S: That unlike propertied truth, learning is not in denial of its own vulnerability. Which means that education has a different kind of truth. And perhaps also a different necessity than that of mastery and property.

J1: Do you think this is what our daemon has been leading us to?

S: Perhaps our conversation has been continually returning us to just such a realization. Perhaps we have been students of this necessity that is speaking through us.

J9: It's more likely a necessity that you have decided upon in advance. You are claiming to have discovered something that in fact you merely presuppose.

S: Presupposition is the necessity.

J9: You do not have to presuppose any necessity.

S: That is your presupposition. And your mastery. And every time we have experienced the logic of mastery, we have experienced the necessity of its frailty and vulnerability. It always seems to oppose itself. And even when we have tried to find ways to avoid or overcome this frailty, the logic of mastery and its frailty has reasserted itself.

J1: And we saw that according to mastery, this necessity is just a vicious circle and leads nowhere.

S: And the city is exhausted with such dead ends.

J1: Yet we also saw that this is because the logic of mastery gives no credence to the possibility that this exhaustion might have truths of its own which can be retrieved from such perplexity.

S: Our conversation has repeatedly asked us the same question: Has anything been learnt about mastery that is not simply another mastery?

J1: What is our answer?

S: That to do justice to our conversation and to the daemon whose necessity is at work here, we should not erase its difficulty.

J1: The logic of non-contradiction demands such erasure. What other kind of logic is there? What kind of logic has truth in difficulty? What kind of logic finds something positive in doubting the stability of propertied truth?

S: Perhaps a logic of negation and preservation, where what is lost is also preserved as learning and not just remastered.

J1: Then what can do this? What has this logic as its own truth?

S: Education.

J1: A logic of education?

S: An educational logic. A logic of learning. A logic that is its own necessity and truth, not preserving what is negated as mastery but preserving what is negated as learning.

J1: This would be a logic of the frailty and vulnerability of the experience of truth in-itself – negated but preserved rather than overcome?

S: Yes.

J1: Then to do justice to such experience, we need to do justice to the logic of education that it presupposes.

J9: You are forgetting something.

J1: What?

J9: This dialectic, as some might call it, between negation and preservation, is just another version of white male rationality that is really the power of universalism in disguise. Your rationality, Socrates, is a grand narrative claiming to be the truth of everyone, whether they realize it or not. Everything is decided in advance. Anything outside or beyond this narrative is never even granted legitimacy.

J1: But Socrates has taught that in dialectical thinking identities are not fixed. Ideas are never certain.

J9: Your dialectic is a ruse. It looks radical, but it is just a more sophisticated way in which white male rationality keeps control.

J1: How so?

J9: Some have said that through the dialectic of truth and opposition to truth, the city makes progress. Some have the arrogance to suggest that this must be progress towards some predetermined, rational, dead white male ends. And you have just added to this with your dead white male end of a logic of learning. But what is clear is that this dialectic is always a top-down operation. That which opposes the universal – let us call it the particular – is credited with being the stimulus for change, even for justice, but in the end, it just gets assimilated into the law of universality. The possibility for change gets nullified by the law – your logic of education – that closes up all such possibility.

J1: Can it not work bottom-up and change the universal?

J9: The universal is precisely the problem. What kind of dialectical revolution can overthrow the very idea of the universal without repeating it? None – because the dialectic is already invested in the universal. It is already deemed to be a part of the universal that is bringing itself to completion. It already serves the imperialism of the universal. What you will not allow for here is that there must be things – *people* – that escape or exceed this absolutism. What do you say to those things?

J1: Perhaps that it is always too late to avoid complicity in the totality that shapes us.

J9: What!

J1: Tell us something that escapes being experienced.

J9: I can't. But that's the point. Don't close down the possibility that not everything is part of your universalism completing itself.

S: I wonder if a logic of education works differently with this relation of universal and particular. Perhaps knowing that we do not know is actually what we do know and has its own truth. Perhaps this is how truth and incompletion, or presupposition and openness, are able to live and die together.

J9: Your dialectic is still totalitarian.

S: Perhaps the version of the dialectic you are invoking and the judgement you are making about it are both working according to the logic of mastery.

J9: What do you mean?

S: I mean that dialectical uncertainty becomes the property of mastery and dialectical completion becomes the identity of pure closure in-itself.

J9: How does this mastery work?

S: In one form of mastery one side is overcome and the other side prevails. In another form it is overcoming per se that is mastered and no side prevails. In both cases the logic is of mastery, and the propertied version of truth becomes the criterion by which it is judged.

J1: This is another dizzying experience, Socrates. You are describing a dialectic of dialectic. Would this mean that even ideas like closure, or accomplishment, or completion, would be different in educational logic?

S: Perhaps the dialectic has always had an educational truth different from the dogma or scepticism by which mastery judges it.

J9: How?

S: As we said, it preserves what is negated, not as mastery but as the experience of learning. Learning completes itself only by undermining itself and learning again.

J1: Then if both sides, universal and particular, are negated and preserved as learning, is this also some kind of new collective identity?

S: Perhaps it is how, together, the examined life could be led.

J9: And what of the universal?

S: It is, we might say, lost and found at the same time. Educational truth is universal and particular not one-sidedly as property, but as the collective experience of life and death. It is life and death being lived together by being learnt together.

J9: If this is a new collective identity, then it is just another version of the universalism of rational self-identity.

S: In the logic of mastery it is exactly that. And when we have pursued the contradiction of mastery, it has offered only more of the same. But if we do justice to the education carried in our conversation, then perhaps we retrieve something else from within such contradiction.

J1: And such an education is not nothing, but something, not the impossibility of truth but the clarification of why we experience it as impossible.

S: Justice here would mean embracing the difficulties of experiencing justice as an educational truth.

J1: So, unlike the revolution and its post-revolutionary cultures, we are saying that revolutionary truth is knowable after all.

S: We are. Education, according to its own logic, is true and knowable.

J1: Then for the revolution to find its own truth it will need to do justice to its own frailties.

S: It will need its own revolutionary self-examination, something it has granted itself immunity from by hanging on to the propertied logic of truth and declaring it unknowable.

J1: This would announce education as a revolution in the age of enlightenment.

S: Such an age of educational logic and truth would see the city negating and preserving itself by expressing a new kind of freedom.

J1: This educational city would be its own theory and practice – precisely the kind of mediation and instability, or learning, that the logic of mastery deems impossible for the idea of truth in-itself.

S: And it is a truth which, educationally, can be called true but
   differently from the propertied notion of truth in-itself.

J1: How does such an age of education announce itself in the city
   of propertied truth and logic?

S: Perhaps in the considerable difficulties that arise when the
   identity of truth and the truth of identity are the form and
   content of its most deeply felt social and political issues.

J1: How would this appear in the city?

S: Perhaps as identity wars, fought between the rational masters,
   who want to hold to propertied identity and its logic, and the
   sceptical masters, who want to abolish the fixity of identity,
   but who cling to truth in-itself by denying the possibility of the
   city knowing truth at all.

J1: Both are still in the grip of propertied logic.

S: Both remain for or against truth as identity. And thus, truth is
   still held hostage to propertied logic and its masterful notion
   of truth.

J1: Then where is the age of education to be found?

S: In such struggles. It is what the wars of identity look like.
   Perhaps the city is in the latter stages of propertied domination
   because, now, its war concerns the identity of logic itself.

J1: Does it need to know that this is what it is doing?

S: As they say, the owl of Minerva flies at dusk. Perhaps the age of
   education will need another age in order to recognize itself.

J1: So, no one is actually fighting for education, it's just
   happening?

S: The mastery everyone seeks and the mastery everyone holds on
   to in doing so are their illusions, their vulnerabilities *and* their
   education. Anyone who fights to do justice to this fights for the
   age of education.

J1: To realize itself.

S: In both senses, yes.

J9: And what does such justice ask of me, Socrates?

S: Affirm and say yes to the possibilities of the education that is already presupposed, necessarily and universally, in the wars of the logic of identity. Affirm this and we affirm life and death as our educational universe, as the macrocosm and the microcosm of our city and ourselves.

J9: To affirm such learning is to affirm a different relation to life and death than property does?

S: Yes. Learning so comes into the world that by the fact that it is already presupposed, it is already life and death. It affirms an education that is suppressed by property.

J9: Then surely the logic of education and the logic of mastery are incompatible. While the former lives as a question of learning, the latter avoids such a question.

S: The logic of education is a logic of mediation being true to itself.

J9: That is just infinite regression.

S: According to the old logic, yes. But in educational logic infinite regression ceases to be only a contradiction and has its truth as learning. No longer just a dead end. No longer either a vicious circle or an abysmal spiral. And no longer signalling the exhaustion and resignation of critical questioning and thinking.

J1: This is no less than a revolution in how to understand truth!

S: It means that learning has a logic and a necessity unlike anything else; that in learning, something is gained only when something is lost. It is a logic in which something is right when it is also wrong, strong when it is also weak, and sustainable when it is also vulnerable. Learning has to undermine itself, and its previous accomplishments, in order to be true to itself. In this extraordinary way, in destroying itself, learning lives.

J10: I have an example to offer here, Socrates, which might be helpful. In the early years of my relationship with my partner I would say we had an easy and natural relationship to each other. But there came a moment of difficulty which threatened to undermine the relationship. But, perhaps surprisingly, in the new vulnerability of the relationship, it changed, and we actually grew stronger for the questions that it asked of us. It was more difficult and still is more difficult than it was, but the difficulty is part of the strength of the relationship that we now enjoy.

S: It sounds like it is a deeper and more meaningful relationship, and that what was lost was preserved in a stronger way.

J10: The questions asked of the relationship also redefined the truth of the relationship.

S: You now enjoy the love of the examined life together! You live with the educational truth that freedom is to learn.

J10: But can this freedom to learn be lived in the city? Can this logic of education be lived as educational social relations? And would this city be the just city?

J2: Socrates, I have been asking myself what is required of me and the city I represent, to give you a fair trial. I think it would help if I could hear you answer these questions and describe the vision of this just city.

S: Then let us do so.

Book 15

J1: We are eager to hear what you have to say, Socrates.

S: Are all our jurors now present?

J1: We are one short. One from our group has no interest in any of this.

S: Very well. Now, if we are to explore a city that lives by the logic of education, perhaps we might remind ourselves of the education that the old city was based on.

J11: That would be most helpful to me, who knows nothing of such things, and has missed part of your previous conversation.

J1: Socrates, are you referring to the ancient model of the cave?

S: Yes. Has it stood the test of time?

J11: I do not know of this cave. Please explain it.

J1: I would love to. For many, it is still the most important description of what education is, and what it means for the collective social and political life of individuals within the city. I will tell it as it was told to us. Imagine the entrance to an underground cave as a border between the sunlight above and the darkness below. Now descend into the cave and imagine that at the far end, down a long steep slope, there are people who have been in this cave all their lives. They face a wall at the end of the cave and their legs and necks are bound in such a way as to make it impossible for them to turn round. All their lives they have only been able to stare straight ahead. Between these prisoners and the entrance, on slightly higher ground, there is a fire burning. And between them and the fire there is a path behind a barrier. On this path, and unknown to the prisoners, people walk who are holding above their heads various shapes of human beings and animals and objects. As they are carried above the barrier, so the shadows of these objects are cast onto the back wall of the cave in front of the prisoners. These prisoners have seen nothing all their lives except the shadows of the objects as they pass by on the wall in front of them. They have no idea that they are shadows of real objects. When the people carrying these objects speak to each other, the prisoners assume the voices belong to the shadows.

J11: So if these prisoners spoke to each other, would their conversations be about these shadows?

J1: What else could they be about? They have known nothing else all their lives.

J11: And would the prisoners believe that the shadows were real?

J1: What else could they believe but that what appeared in front of them was reality?

J11: Is there more to the story?

J1: There is. Let us suppose that one of these prisoners is released from her bonds. She is forced to stand up, to turn round, to look at the fire and then walk towards it.

J11: Perhaps she would experience pain in having to move her limbs for the first time, and perhaps she would be blinded by the light from the fire and would be unable to see ahead clearly.

J1: Indeed. Now suppose she is told that what she had previously spent her life looking at are in fact not real at all, and that it is only in turning round that she sees the truth of her existence, can we agree that she would be perplexed and perhaps deeply sceptical about what she was being told?

J11: Given her pain and confusion and temporary blindness, it is likely she would not believe what she was being told.

J1: And given the blinding light she might well wish to turn away from it and return to the life of the shadows, which seem to her much clearer than anything she has seen since turning around.

J11: Indeed.

J1: Nevertheless, gradually her eyes grow accustomed to the firelight and she comes to see what has been going on behind

her back all this time. She sees the objects and experiences
for the first time that the life she has known has only been a
life of shadows. She experiences the difference between the
copy and the original, or between the shadow and the object.
She experiences the distinction between reality and illusion.
And she experiences this as the question of truth. Then, as the
story continues, pursuing this question of truth, she is taken to
the upper world, the world of the intellect. She is dragged up
the steep slope, reluctantly and forcibly if necessary, until she
reaches the light at the entrance to the cave.

J11: Will she not risk the ascent voluntarily?

J1: She might. But force is a risk that truth seems prepared to take
if she refuses the ascent for herself.

J11: This journey would most likely be a painful one?

J1: Undoubtedly. It is a journey from the immediacy of sensory
experiences to its mediation in the world of thinking.

J11: How is this world of thought described?

J1: On entering the world above ground, she would again be
blinded by light, this time by sunlight, and would not be able
to see any of the objects in this upper world clearly. She would
need time for her eyes to adjust. As they did so, first she would
see shadows, next reflections of objects in water and soon the
objects themselves. Later still, she would be able to observe the
sky and the stars and planets. Only when her eyes were fully
adjusted to the light of the upper world would she be able to
see the sunlight and finally the sun itself.

J11: Anything else?

J1: Soon she would be able to see how the sun commands the
seasons and the yearly cycle and is responsible for all that can
be known in the upper world. She would come to understand
the sun as the condition of the possibility of everything.

J11: Might she then remember her fellow prisoners who are unable to share in anything she has seen?

J1: Yes. She might especially remember the manner in which status was given to those prisoners who could memorize and then repeat the order in which the shadows appeared, and she would see the redundancy of such an idea of cleverness.

J3: A clear rejection of much that passes for education in the city.

J1: She returns to the cave and sits once more in the seat to which she had been bound. Again, she would be distressed for her eyes would need time to adjust to the darkness. When her fellow prisoners see the state of confusion she is in, they will likely ridicule her and reject the idea of there being any benefits to the journey she has made. And if she tries to tell them where she has been, no doubt she will make little sense to them. Indeed, given the state she appears to be in, they might resist anyone who tries to release them from their chains or encourages them to make such a journey.

J3: So education would be rejected and the educated would be mistrusted.

J1: There remains one last part of the story. The people who leave the cave and have their education in the upper world become the enlightened few who understand truth and beauty and the good. These become the philosopher-rulers in the cave because their philosophical education also carried an education in virtue.

J6: A most sensible and righteous outcome.

J3: What exactly did these philosopher-rulers learn from their enlightening experiences?

J1: To put the interests of the city before their own.

J11: How did their education achieve this?

J1: In their philosophical training they had no families or children of their own and they had no personal wealth or property. This meant they would not be tempted to put their own interests above those of the city as a whole.

J6: Hardly an education likely to bring wealth and prosperity to the city.

J1: They were to be leaders of the city by being its public servants. And, imbued with this sense of responsibility, they knew it was not right to stay in the upper world, but instead to descend once again to the cave, and to work to make the worse life better; not by making one group happy but by making the cave happy collectively. And once the whole city is happy, each can enjoy such happiness as her nature befits.

J5: But if we now attach what we know of the history of the city to this story of the cave, we would say that things did not work out this way.

J1: They did not. The philosophers ruled in their own self-interests, having their own property and wealth. In many cases, more property and wealth than everyone else. This corrupted their ability to rule in the interests of the whole city. The three classes that, in the bigger picture, should have served each other's mutual interests fractured into a domination of the powerful over the powerless. The leaders used their intellect not for self-denial but for self-advantage, claiming that their education entitled them to riches far in excess of most people in the city.

J11: And the result was injustice.

J1: Always injustice, and always the suffering of the many for the advantage of the few.

J4: No public service?

J1: In name only.

J8: No sacrifice for the greater good?

J1: In name only.

J7: No reticence regarding privilege, power or entitlement?

J1: In name only.

J5: And so the cave, the story of enlightenment and benevolent rule fell into disrepute.

J7: How did the city come to view the model of the cave?

J1: Not as a model of the good but as a theatre of control and exploitation, a template of social and political advantage maintained by way of mastery and slavery. The prisoners were shown only that which their masters wished them to see.

J11: To what end?

J1: First and foremost, to ensure that those who are controlled never see that they are controlled.

J11: So, in the darkness, the many are kept in the dark about the darkness they are in.

J1: They are kept in chains mentally and physically by the shadows that determine their whole lives.

J7: Nevertheless, the history of the city shows that this power of the masters was challenged.

J1: It was. Prisoners did manage to turn themselves round and see the fire and the path and the objects that people were carrying on it. They saw the difference between shadows and real objects and experienced for themselves the difference between appearance and reality.

J2: Then they also came to know the question of truth. But I know from my own experience that very few of us were encouraged to pursue the question of truth in the upper world. The masters made turning away from the shadows as difficult, as expensive and as painful as possible for us, ensuring that many of the areas where we lived were almost impossible to escape from.

J11: Why so few?

J1: The masters did not want to share their bounty. But in the rare cases that this proved necessary, they attached to them the credo that such rewards came only from sacrifice and hard work, a credo invented by those already enjoying inherited wealth and power. And so privilege flaunted itself while justifying itself as the rewards of effort.

J11: But keeping most prisoners in the dark, and letting only a few escape into the light, must have required time and effort. Presumably it would become increasingly difficult for the masters to keep suppressing the question of truth.

J1: It did, but mastery evolved. Included in the shadow life were more and more amusements. The entertainment was like a drug, numbing the mind and with it the possibility of even imagining the examined life. The prisoners became addicted to such distractions.

J11: Unaware of the harm it was doing to them?

J1: Perhaps not. In a sense the harm was known and was laughed off with a sense of resignation.

J11: A knowing self-harming?

J1: Yes.

J11: Why did people do this to themselves?

J1: Because the immediate effects of the drug were more powerful than anything the examined life promised to those who risked recovery from such addiction. And so, despite the prisoners becoming aware of the questions of truth and justice, the city remained largely unchanged, even despite several reorganizations and revolutions. The furniture might have

been moved around a bit, but the room, the cave, remained
fundamentally the same.

S: Then let us see now if this is because the old cave was shaped
by the logic of mastery. How did you begin your description of
the cave?

J1: I repeated it according to its ancient version.

S: And how did the story of the cave begin its own description?

J1: Ah! You mean it presupposed that the cave and everything
in it simply existed. It avoided any account of its beginning,
or the question of its beginning. It avoided the enquiry into
the conditions of its own possibility. It just presupposed itself,
which means that it also presupposed certain distinctions.

S: Which distinctions?

J1: Those between light and dark, mind and body, earthly
and subterranean, image and original, shadow and object,
ignorance and enlightenment, and, of course, it presupposed
masters and slaves and therefore also life and death.

S: And what presupposition makes such distinctions possible?

J1: The presupposition of a logic of identity. In each case one of
the pair is truth in-itself and the other is only for-another and
without a foundation or principle or identity of its own.

S: So, has the cave always presupposed a logic of such mastery,
including in its model of enlightenment?

J1: Yes. Especially in its model of enlightenment. 'To see the light',
as they say, is assumed to be overcoming the darkness, or to be
mastering the untrue.

S: And what notion of truth does this presuppose?

J1: Truth or light as mastery, and error or darkness as slavery.

S: And where is this presupposition grounded?

J1: Given our own conversation about this, Socrates, it is in the
presupposition of life mastering death as property.

S: So, is the logic of the cave also propertied logic?

J1: It must be. Light owns darkness, as the original owns the copy and as masters own their enslaved. Indeed, in the cave and in the city the masters control the means of the production of light and dark, and the objects and their shadows. Mastery, as light in-itself, defines everything else in the light of this mastery. As such, the cave is a logic of mastery and of propertied truth.

S: Does the cave therefore also suffer from the same vulnerabilities that we have seen are endemic to propertied logic?

J1: It must do. Nothing enjoys stable mastery. The masters on the pathway are vulnerable to exposure. The enlightened prisoners are confused and pained. Masters-in-waiting are dragged up the steep ascent against their will. And the rulers with wealth and property require slavery and darkness to preserve such privilege. The whole thing is unstable.

S: But perhaps the greatest instability in the cave is to be found in the element upon which the whole scene is based.

J1: What is that?

S: The logic of the fire.

J1: Does the fire have a logic?

S: It has a logic of mastery.

J1: You mean because it creates the shadow of the object, or the slave of the master.

S: Perhaps it also has an educational logic.

J1: How so?

S: On the one hand, the light from the fire creates the difference between the object and its shadow. It is the operation in which original and image, or truth and mere representation, are differentiated from each other. On the other hand, it is by this same light of the same fire that the prisoner, having turned around, can see the real object and come to know the illusion of the shadow she has taken to be real.

J1: So, the fire is the condition of the possibility of ignorance and of the question of truth. The fire is what makes both ignorance and enlightenment possible.

S: Can the fire overcome this inherent instability?

J1: I would say no, given what we have said earlier.

S: Why not?

J1: Well, when the fire creates the shadows, it destabilizes the identity of the original object by creating a copy. When it reveals the error of the shadow, it tries to re-establish the identity of the original. But, because it is the same light, the fire is always doing both at the same time. It can't enlighten without also creating illusion. This is its inbuilt instability. It creates error, and the overcoming of error, and the error of the overcoming of error and so on, eternally repeated by the same element: its light.

S: This is its vicious circle.

J1: Yes, and its abysmal spiral. And if it tries to enlighten itself, that is, to cast a light on itself, then surely it will only create its own shadow, and another infinite regression of shadow and object, light and dark. Enlightenment and enshadowment will eternally repeat themselves in relation to each other.

S: What of truth here?

J1: Truth becomes unknowable in-itself and the whole cave lives and suffers this instability.

S: What, then, of the upper world? Can it provide the stability that the cave seems to lack?

J1: That will depend on whether the upper world is also a culture of propertied logic.

S: Do you think the upper world suffers the same kind of instability and vulnerability as the cave?

J1: I think it does, Socrates.

S: Why?

J1: It presupposes the same distinctions of light and dark, image and original, shadow and object, and ignorance and enlightenment.

S: What constitutes illusion in the upper world?

J1: The sciences that are the shadows cast by the light of thinking.

S: Is the good serving the same function here as the fire?

J1: Yes, if you mean that just as the fire makes all seeing possible in the cave, so the good makes all-knowing in the upper world possible.

S: And if both are light, then the cave and the upper world share in its instability.

J1: Is there also a sense in which the two worlds are light and shadow to and of each other?

S: What does the city's history suggest?

J1: That some see the cave as a shadow of the upper world, lacking its enlightenment, while others see the upper world as a shadow and illusion of a material life that could enlighten itself without resorting to such metaphysical fantasies.

S: Both sides accept the logic of the distinction between light and dark?

J1: Yes, between truth in-itself and the error of being merely for-another.

S: Then this logic is something that the two worlds have in common. Do you think that the old city tried to hold the two worlds together in its model of the ideal city?

J1: Yes, as education. By making sure that the upper world was always in the cave, or that philosophy was the principle of ruling the city, the two worlds were not kept separated. The path between them was travelled as the tripartite soul, in which reason and desire struggled with each other to recruit the spirit which, united with the intellect, could moderate excesses, but which, united with desire, could exacerbate them.

S: And did the ideal city walk this path?

J1: The ideal city walked the path between the two worlds by having philosophical rulers mediate the desires of those they ruled and the strength of those who defended the city from its enemies.

S: So here, the soul and the city ensured the two worlds were always within each other. But in the real history of the city, this relationship was not sustained?

J1: If we read the real history of the philosophy and politics of the city alongside the model of the cave and the upper world, then we would say that the two worlds, upper and lower, became increasingly separated.

S: Might we go further and suggest the battle between them became a life-and-death struggle between physical life and intellectual life, or between the desire for material and the desire for truth.

J1: Some might say between the state and religion, or between man and god, or between political law and divine law?

S: Indeed. Do you remember our earlier discussion of the experience of life and death?

J1: I do.

S: Then perhaps the same process is followed here. Just as the I-desire became the self-consciousness of I-life-and-death, so perhaps in the real city the desire for truth becomes the self-consciousness of the question. And here it also has a new object: the truth of itself.

J1: Does the understanding desire to preserve itself as this new awareness?

S: Of course.

J1: And so, it needs to preserve the object that stimulates this awareness, that is, the question of truth.

S: Yes.

J1: But as the master negates death and preserves it as the slave, does this new self-awareness also somehow master the question of truth?

S: It does, by having the answer to the question as its property. But alongside this, such mastery also learns that, like the logic of the fire, the experience of truth preserves the question by negating the answer.

J1: So, fearful of this instability, understanding makes the question slave to the answer.

S: And this is how propertied logic determines the relation between the two worlds in the real city. Either the material world becomes slave to the intellectual world or the material world abolishes the metaphysical world once and for all. Both campaigns are already fixed within propertied logic.

J1: So, it is in the presupposition of owning truth that the understanding sets out to understand truth!

S: Well put. The path between the two worlds is really the experience of their shared instability.

J1: The old cave offered reason to the city as education to be lived as justice. But it was corrupted by property and has been ever since.

S: How did the upper world, the higher ground of the city, respond?

J1: It tried to preserve its mastery by eliminating the path altogether, becoming immune to common experience, and claiming to be unknowable in-itself. Cultures of unknowability formed in the cave. Religious cultures spoke of prophets who could cross between the two worlds. Cultures of intense emotion also claimed such crossing. Against this, cultures of a very different kind rejected the upper world altogether as irrational, or an intellectual prejudice, or as an illusion of the shape of material life. Cultures also formed that opposed opposition altogether as being a misrecognition of a more primordial sense of difference.

S: But each culture still privileged one world over the other?

J1: Yes. We have seen that denying truth either to thinking or to material is still a dogmatic and sceptical presupposition of what truth is.

S: Then they were all cultures of mastery.

J1: Each fought against sovereignty in order to achieve sovereignty.

S: Including fighting against sovereignty itself?

J1: Yes.

S: And this is still a life-and-death struggle grounded in truth as mastery?

J1: Yes.

S: Even the struggle against all such truth and mastery?

J1: Yes. They all rejected mediation as error, whether defending truth in-itself or showing how it exceeds itself. The criterion for or against truth in-itself was still grounded in the logic of identity and property.

S: But in keeping the two worlds separate, might we speculate that shadows and reality in the cave would remain blind in the absence of sunlight from the upper world, and that the sciences and philosophy of the upper world would be empty because they would have no relation to actual things and to actual life in the cave?

J1: Yes, blind and empty without each other. Which leaves us with questions that press upon us, Socrates, questions shaping our own desire to understand.

S: Such as?

J1: Can we conceive of a new model of the cave and the upper world in a logic of education that would live the life of both worlds? One where their relation is education. And could we conceive of a whole city living this kind of life?

S: We can but try. The fire in the cave and the sun in the upper world are both light. And light has always been the template for education. To educate has always been to illuminate. But this is light and education within the logic of mastery.

J1: Because darkness is overcome or mastered by light, as ignorance is mastered or overcome by education. The propertied version of this goes by the name of enlightenment. But we said just now, such light also has an educational logic.

S: We said that even though the sun is the condition and the cause of sight, both are only known absolutely relatively, or for us in individual vision.

J1: And if we take this to education?

S: Even though education is the condition and cause of learning, both are only known absolutely relatively, or for us in individual experience. But that does not mean this educational truth cannot be known. The logic of education knows truth in a way that the logic of mastery deems impossible.

J1: Which is why this truth is no longer correctly called enlightenment?

S: Enlightenment as mastery is overcoming. But known educationally, when enlightenment is in-itself, it is also for-itself because it is for-another. This is the educational logic of the fire in the cave, and this is what educational truth looks like. It is not immune from being resourced by that which it resources. Light gives and receives itself, negating and preserving itself in light and dark, object and shadow, ignorance and learning. Light and education are still the nature of each other, but not as light in-itself or as education as enlightenment.

J1: So, light does not need a surrogate to suffer darkness for it. It does not need darkness as its slave.

S: Nor does it need to be mastered by a fear of darkness. Fear, or darkness, is already the beginning of wisdom, the life and death that is learning. It remains to be seen if such truth can re-educate us in regard to the educational light of the just city.

J1: Given this then, Socrates, let us see if we can rethink the cave model. We are helped by the fact that the ancients already understood the ambivalence of the fire and the sun. They saw that the sun shared the same ambiguity as the fire. Just as the fire was continually the source of error, the overcoming of error and the source of further error, so the sun was the source of the questions that gave birth to the sciences, the source of the answers to these questions and the source of further questions for the sciences.

S: They knew that the fire was not seeing in-itself but was itself seen by the sight which it made possible, and they knew that the sun was not thinking in-itself but was the possibility of thought, including the thought of itself.

J1: Confusion and clarification together. It seems that, in the way they operate, truth and error go hand in hand. They seem indispensable to each other. And it is this confusion, and the exhaustion it creates, rather than stability and fixed unchangeable identity, that is the truth of truth?

S: The logic of mastery, in both worlds, repeats its own inevitable self-contradictory unrest and turmoil.

J1: So, does this offer a new understanding of the old cave?

S: It might. But to pursue such a new understanding of the old cave would be bold. And it would likely disappoint many people.

J1: Imagine the disdain it would meet from the community of scholars working with the old logic.

S: We must be ready for that. Education is used to being treated as handmaiden to the propertied sciences and the disciplines. Instead, let us see if we can hear education speaking in its own voice.

J1: Are people happy for me to continue to be the main respondent to Socrates?

Book 16

J1: Very well then. Socrates, perhaps you could begin with what we might presuppose about this new old cave.

S: Imagine a cave with a steep and difficult path leading from its entrance to the back wall at its deepest point. Here people sit on chairs with their backs to the wall, facing the entrance, with the whole cave in front of them. What they observe is the working of the cave. They see the fire, and in front of it a path which people walk on. They see people carrying images above their heads and the light from the fire that casts the shadows of these objects onto the back wall. They are free to turn and observe these shadows if they choose. They also see other parts of the cave. They see people climbing the path up to the entrance, leaving the cave and disappearing into the light of the upper world while others are returning from it. But these people do not descend all the way back into the cave. They step off the path on the higher ground, as near to the entrance as they can. There the light is better, the air is fresher, and there is more space. Occasionally some of these people descend to maintain the fire, to keep it burning. Sometimes they will take a turn walking on the path and carrying objects above their heads, projecting shadows. Then they return to the higher ground where life is so much better. What do you think the deepest cave dwellers would make of what they saw above them?

J1: They would see a world within a world, where those nearest the entrance lived in beautiful homes, were well fed on a good diet, were healthier and more exercised, living in substantial space and comfort, leading meaningful lives full of hope and confidence. They would see wealthy educational institutions housing the young of the higher ground, controlling access to the upper world, and preserving their privileges. They would recognize these as the institutions that promised justice through enlightened leaders but which, in failing to deliver on justice, enjoyed mastery over the rest of the cave. From the higher ground to the lower areas would fall the sound of laughter and lively conversation from wonderful communal parties and gatherings.

S: How would this compare with the lives of the deepest cave dwellers?

J1: We might assume that at the back of the cave food is not plentiful, and what food there is, is not the healthiest. Perhaps disease and illness find life more favourable here. Space and resources are limited, opportunities are scarce, and there is an absence of hope and meaning. I assume that fear for life and livelihood lead to conflicts between people, and that prejudice against others offers the semblance of gaining some control and easing the pain. Perhaps there are celebrations, but such laughter is a medicine most often taken to compensate for the pain rather than to discharge deep joy. Here, perhaps inevitably and despite resolute souls trying to resist it, there is resentment at the two worlds in the one world. One world lives, the other only survives. It is a case of them and us.

S: And how might the cave dwellers explain the two worlds in one?

J1: They might blame education. They see people ascend the path, leave the cave and enter the upper world. They know this journey is called enlightenment and that it claims to offer truth, beauty and virtue which, once learned, change one's life for ever. And they know from bitter experience that to the enlightened, more shall be given. They are likely told that the enlightened will return to create happiness for everyone in the cave. But instead they see the educated treat enlightenment as their own entitlement to privileges for them and their families. They see how the enlightened come to own education, to own the means by which it can be accessed, to monopolize its opportunities and therefore to limit the distribution of its rewards. At the same time, we can expect the educated to justify their privilege and entitlement by means of self-fulfilling prophecies that those at the bottom of the cave, because they are at the bottom, prove their own incapacity for riches, or government, or even for making the best decisions for their own lives, lacking the intellect and background and breeding required for doing so.

S: Here then, education is just a tool of self-interest?

J1: Yes. Those on the high ground must know this myth of the great unwashed is just a convenient self-deception allowing the rulers to defend their own privilege as self-sacrifice. They know, really, that their rhetoric of public service is ultimately self-serving.

S: So, education has created two worlds in one, the educated and deserving, and the uneducated and undeserving.

J1: And preserved in the myth of the educable and uneducable.

S: Do we expect that these cave dwellers would resist?

J1: They would surely grow angry at the privileges of the few.

S: But the obstacles to justice remain considerable?

J1: Almost insurmountable. Perhaps they would storm the path, and compromises would be reached, promises made, messages re-spun. But no higher ground would ever be willingly yielded.

S: Might one or two cave dwellers make it to the entrance?

J1: They might. Perhaps they would be deemed leaders who would enter the upper world on behalf of those whose cause they fought for. But on their return, we might expect that the spell which education has cast upon them would see them take privileges for themselves including residence on the higher ground. Part of their education involves suppressing memories of where they originally came from.

S: What would the cave dwellers make of this?

J1: It would likely reinforce their view that education, offered as a means to their liberation, simply could not be trusted. They would see that all who came under its spell were changed by it and clothed themselves in the superiority that it gave them.

S: Then it is education that has created the two worlds in one.

J1: Yes.

S: And the old cave, with its intention of creating a just city, seems to have worked in opposition to its original intention.

J1: Seen originally as the means to justice, education has now become the schema of injustice. Education itself has become the problem.

S: Is it also still the solution?

J1: Perhaps it is both the solution and the problem. People learn of injustice, and this enlightenment gives hope for a better world. But enlightenment about elitism only creates new elitism. Shadows are overcome, and new shadows are created to preserve this mastery. Education is seen as the problem, and it is seen as the solution, and the solution becomes the new problem and so on, as we said before.

S: So, in this cave of the eternal return of hope and despair, what might we expect?

J1: As one disappointment piles up upon another, as one promise after another is broken, so we might expect anger, resentment and cynicism, and the potential for violence that these instil.

S: Anger at what?

J1: At the enlightened leaders, and at the justification they always ultimately fall back on; education, or 'we know best'.

S: Might trust in education evaporate completely?

J1: Yes, after one betrayal too many. And with it, trust in reason, which was supposed to be the basis of such education.

S: And how might this change the cave?

J1: The cave dwellers might close themselves completely to the light of the upper world. Given the chance, they might even seek to block off the entrance altogether. Everything that comes from an educated standpoint would be utterly rejected.

S: And in such circumstances what might life in the cave become?

J1: A culture of rule founded on anger and cynicism against truth, reason and facts. A culture leaning on immediacies of blood ties and territories, and excited by charisma and mystique.

S: A new elite could arise in such a culture?

J1: Easily. A new elite powered by the cave's anger against the old elite and their education.

S: What might this new elite do?

J1: What all elites do. Take their opportunity to control and manipulate the masses in establishing and preserving their power over them. They could lead the cave dwellers back to the far end of the cave, declaring war on education and attacking it everywhere it appeared.

S: Burning books?

J1: Certainly. Cave dwellers would be carried back to their chairs on waves of high emotion. The fire would rage, and new shadows would be projected onto the back wall controlling their appetites by feeding them just what they desired. He who controls the fire controls the city. And the cave dwellers now relish ignorance as empowerment. They chain themselves to their chairs, denying themselves the freedom to turn round.

S: We have come full circle. The prisoners' journey has taken them back to their chains. What can break this cycle?

J1: Education!

S: And so the wheel turns again.

J1: Look, perhaps a few prisoners turn round, see the fire and the shadows, travel to the entrance to the cave, enter the upper world of principles and truth, and return under a different educational spell than the one that has turned the wheel so far? I don't know . . . I have no solution, Socrates. Without education the cave stays locked in the grip of the shadows. With education it just finds ways to reproduce this same injustice. With or without education, the cave is preordained to a logic of mastery and slavery.

S: If that is the tragedy of the propertied truth of reason and education, do you think that the logic of education we have discussed might offer something different?

J1: I hope so. It might give us a different understanding of the meaning of this vicious circle of education and injustice that the city keeps repeating.

S: Suppose one of the prisoners now becomes aware of this vicious circle as constituting the whole of the cave. What might she see?

J1: I suppose she sees the fire throwing its cynical shadows, the exit from the cave blocked off, and elites still taking the high ground as their own entitlement. She sees a cave torn apart by the Janus-face of education.

S: Let us assume, too, that from her own experience she knows that claims for education as a means to freedom and justice fall on ears deafened by anger.

J1: Without education, what can she do?

S: Might she be open to a re-education about education?

J1: She might.

S: Then how might she go about this?

J1: She might seek to re-learn about education from its ambivalence and keep faith with it, no matter how many times education has convicted itself of bad faith and double-dealing.

S: And what might she learn here?

J1: That the ambivalence of education is already the precondition of her critical thinking.

S: What does she make of this?

J1: Perhaps, in knowing her own critical education in this way, she learns that she embodies the cave's equivocation about

justice. She is against its injustice, but she is in it and she is of
it. She is compromised by her own truth. She is shadow, and
light, and shadow again.

S: And this presents her with questions.

J1: Yes. She will ask what it means for justice in the city to be
turned on the wheel of education. And she will ask how she is
also shaped by the wheel.

S: What if she declines to ask the questions?

J1: The question is already begun. She can ignore the question.
But then we will wait for someone who cannot ignore it and
needs to ask it. Such a person is worth waiting for. She makes
all the difference. We will wait for the return of the teacher. We
will wait for your return, Socrates.

S: But if you begin with me, then will not the same history unfold
itself again?

J1: This time our new Socrates has learnt more about education
than our old one. Our old Socrates used the power of
contradiction to knock down the hubris of his masters.
Perhaps our new old Socrates will also be able to see how
to build from the ruins of contradiction. And perhaps here
education can make a difference to everything else by first
making a difference to itself.

S: Then let us play out this new old Socrates and her education so
that we can understand her.

J1: I will try. First, she sees that the cave is already begun and
that it presupposes prisoners and masters, shadows and
objects, copies and originals, lower and higher ground, and
ignorance and enlightenment. Let us suppose that she also
understands that such presuppositions are grounded in
propertied logic, and that in this logic the masters of the cave
avoid any tarrying with questions, protecting themselves

from such instability by taking themselves as pure and the prisoners as barbarian.

S: Then she will see that the cave and its cultures are designed in the master's image, and she will see the type of logic that protects the master.

J1: She experiences such things as questions.

S: Then she is also open to the experience of life and death as the question of the cave, including the question of herself?

J1: Yes. She is not the answer to her own question. Her own life presupposes the question. It exists as her.

S: Will she learn of this as the presupposition that she is already learning?

J1: Yes. But we know what mastery will say here. Learning has no truth of its own. Without answers nothing is learnt. People need answers.

S: Perhaps this is the greatest power of the logic of mastery. It makes one believe that answers resolve life's great questions.

J1: But the cave will say that problems have to be solved, and that answers that work are successful!

S: Up to a point perhaps. But our experience of answers is also that they are never quite as advertised. No answer is ever sufficient unto itself. Answers are inextricably related to new questions. People experience this for themselves. No one who only understands answers and solutions within the logic of mastery can be said to have been fully educated about questions or answers.

J1: And this points to a different logic, a logic too dangerous to mastery for the masters to label it as anything other than nonsense.

S: Answers are the power of masters and mastery. Without answers, mastery is hollow. People are told that answers are

freedom and so they gladly chain themselves to answers,
believing that nothing else can be true. Perhaps it is the task
of the logic of education to release the cave from such chains
and offer from within itself a different truth, a different life, for
everyone: an examined life.

J1: People will say, they cannot live a question.

S: They already live a question.

J1: So, can our new old Socrates tell us where this logic is to be
found in the model of the new old cave?

S: In its educational firelight.

J1: How so?

S: The fire is its own principle and necessity. It burns with a
different logic than merely enlightenment.

J1: An educational logic.

S: A logic of negation and preservation.

J1: How?

S: It makes sight in the cave possible, but its truth also requires
to be seen. It is the condition of the possibility of that which it
needs for its own truth.

J1: In the logic of mastery this conundrum is resolved by way of
copy and original because truth cannot be the principle of all
seeing if it is dependent upon being seen.

S: But in the logic of education the fire burns as its own questions,
and we live as those questions.

J1: Then the light of the fire is the negation and preservation of
itself as educational truth in the examined life? We can assume
that our new old Socrates now understands this.

S: Then she would understand that in the new old cave beginning
is a necessity already presupposed. In the logic of mastery
this riddle is resolved into shadow and object, into error
and overcoming. But in the collapse of mastery it is again

unresolved. This necessity negates and preserves itself differently than mastery, and according to a different logic. Not the logic of mastery, but of education. The fire is both logics. It carries the life-and-death struggle as propertied logic, and it undermines the mastery of this logic and its own mastery as it does so.

J1: Let us suppose, then, that our new old Socrates remains open to the experience she has of the fire, that its logic is not simply that of ignorance and enlightenment, but of perplexity and difficulty. Let us assume now that she takes her question to the entrance of the cave, wondering what answers pertain in the upper world.

S: Is the entrance open or blocked off?

J1: We have seen that it is blocked off, but there are cracks; that's how the light gets in. However, there might also be guards.

S: What kind of guards?

J1: Those who discourage any attempts to leave the cave for the upper world.

S: Why?

J1: Perhaps some claim that the upper world has been destroyed or has perhaps simply dissolved. Perhaps some claim that it is just an escape and a refuge for the elite and the privileged and is the bastion of injustice and prejudice and power and greed. Perhaps some say that going to the upper world is a betrayal of the cave. Perhaps some claim that it is now a world irrelevant to the real needs of real cave dwellers. And perhaps some say it is a hiding place for the work-shy and lazy.

S: What will she do?

J1: She will defy them. She will not let others have her experiences for her.

S: She will think for herself.

J1: Of course.

S: And what will she come to know of this upper world?

J1: She will come to know the sun as she sees the fire. She will understand that the sun burns with a different necessity than mastery.

S: She will know that, like the fire, the sun is the condition of the possibility of truth being lost and found, or that the condition is only known by that whose knowledge it makes possible.

J1: And it needs to be known or else it is not presupposed.

S: And if it is not presupposed, it is not its own truth and necessity. In educational logic, truth is the condition of the possibility of that which it needs for its own truth.

J1: This makes me dizzy again.

S: The ancients knew this dizziness, in the cave and in the upper world. The dizziness is the experience of the logic of education. It is part of what learning is.

J1: It is disconcerting, but also exhilarating and invigorating. Perhaps it is the experience of learning when it is left to speak in its own voice.

J1: But now we come to what is perhaps the key question. Does our new old Socrates return to the cave?

S: Perhaps she never really left the cave. The logic of education does not require her to choose one world over the other. The light of each is the light of the other because they share educational logic and truth. Education is the light of the one candle that is both worlds.

J1: So, the cave and the upper world are in each other?

S: Lived educationally, yes. Just as the soul and the city are in each other.

J1: Is this a new old metaphysics for the new old cave?

S: I think that it might be. The old metaphysics assumed the truth of the upper world and pronounced on the truth of everything according to identity and non-contradiction. The new metaphysics investigates the conditions that make even this logic possible.

J1: It is something like presupposition: know thyself.

S: And it brings the upper world into the cave. It brings knowing into seeing. It brings substance into the body. It brings the transcendental into experience. And it brings metaphysics into the mind. Finally, it does justice to experience.

J1: This sounds like the death of metaphysics.

S: And its resurrection; negated and preserved differently.

J1: But as we saw, the history of the city shows that the two worlds were always kept apart by propertied logic? The ancients retained the path between the two worlds, but in time this ambivalence was resisted and mastered by ownership.

S: But in the new old metaphysics of the new old cave mastery is always self-defeating. And a different logic commends itself here. This logic makes the unknowable truth knowable – not in-itself, but educationally.

J1: A logic in which absolute truth can be conditional?

S: Universally and necessarily conditional, yes.

J1: And knowable?

S: True because it is knowable, and knowable as this truth.

J1: A logic that allows its own necessity no exemptions from itself?

S: Truth as vulnerability.

J1: A vulnerability strong enough to bear its own truth.

S: A vulnerability that is strong enough to do justice to itself.

J1: Educational truth. The revolution of the revolution!

S: A combination of the old and new metaphysics. The path between the two worlds walked as learning and presupposed as necessity. The walk that is each of us.

J8: Socrates, people will ask, what of the idea of God here? Does the new old metaphysics leave room for faith in a God?

S: In the logic of education your idea of God would be the truth of our educational struggles, of the examined life.

J8: A transcendent being?

S: Not if by transcendent you mean something unknowable in-itself for which we make up a picture image. In this new old metaphysics, such a God is the truth of the fire that gives the light by which its truth is seen and known as learning.

J8: A limited God?

S: Limited by the necessity of its presupposition. And unlimited within the limits of this educational truth. Limited only by the necessity of always learning.

J8: And faith?

S: Faith is openness to learning of light from the light.

J8: And religion?

S: Religions are cultures of this necessity. Their truth is to be found in the logic of education rather than the logic of property. Religions can be opened to the educational struggle that faith has always been. Perhaps religions could have as the idea of God the light that shines when we are each of us our own question.

J8: I can't imagine anyone giving up their religion or belief in God for a logic of education.

S: Many religious people are already living the question. In the logic of mastery this will be seen as a battle for the sovereignty of God over doubt. In the logic of education living the question is the presupposition of the idea of God in the doubts through which it has already entered life. Nothing changes, in the sense that faith and religion are already education. And everything changes because faith and religion are allowed to speak their already present educational truth.

J8: So, they need not move from one position to another?

S: On the contrary, such a God is already in the vulnerability of whatever position is being defended.

J5: It sounds to me as if this is just a new God replacing all the old ones. Why does anyone need God at all?

S: Perhaps because the unknown is presupposed in the love of learning?

J5: Just don't call it God, that's all. Too much baggage.

J9: Let me ask a question here, Socrates, the one I keep coming back to. If education wants to be seen as logical, isn't this just logic as another mastery?

S: Do you fear that logic as education suppresses spontaneity and the creation of the new?

J9: I think so. A logic of education still sounds prescriptive. Everything is still subsumed within it. Everything still conforms to it. It is still far too controlling.

S: The city's philosophical revolution had a logic of spontaneity and synthesis. Imaginative spontaneity was formally arranged into its working parts. It obeyed the logic of awareness, reproduction and recognition. Their necessity was a logic of continuity. But this logic was seen as spontaneous.

J9: Can the logic of education claim this?

S: Learning is always creative of itself. It is the means by which creativity exists at all. And it is learning that can resist spontaneity becoming a form of mastery. If spontaneity is

a condition of the possibility of experience, then it is also
a condition of the possibility of its being experienced as
spontaneous.

J9: So, spontaneity is not just immediacy, not just
spontaneous?

S: Within the logic of mastery, any such claim contradicts itself.
Spontaneity does not avoid the logic of presupposition.
Nothing known escapes being known.

J9: So, presupposition is already spontaneous and creative.

S: Yes. It sounds odd, but it is already their own possibility.
It is the logic of education that preserves spontaneity and
creativity. It is the logic of mastery that turns them into
property.

J9: What, then, of the new?

S: The new is always an experience of itself.

J9: And what of chance?

S: Chance is the presupposition of itself. What else could it
be? We do not know what it is we are going to learn in any
particular experience, or in any day of our lives or across the
whole of our lives, but we know we will learn. The examined
life is the life open to its own freedom and discipline. In the
truth of education, this is the new definition of living a logical
life.

J9: Then chance is part of the truth of the fire?

S: The fire preserves chance without mastering it.

J7: I am worried though, Socrates. Fire destroys everything it
touches.

S: So can education. Have I not been seen by some as a fire of
doubt and uncertainty destroying everything I came into
contact with?

J7: Some would say you were destructive, yes.

S: I think in retrospect that my fire might have been a little wild and undisciplined.

J7: Why?

S: It was not burning with its own freedom. But I think my fire has changed now. My own education has continued. I think my education can now preserve questioning and examining differently. My fire is now learning to live with its own truth.

J7: How?

S: By expressing its freedom as its own limit and finding this limit to be its own freedom. But unlike the city's philosophy, this limit is not protected from itself by an unknowable unlimited. The limit is its own truth, known to itself according to its own logic.

J4: Is this the truth of the candle you just spoke of just now?

S: There is no more open door by which to understand the logic of education than by considering the educational truth of the light of a candle. Freedom and discipline are the candle's own truth. The candle preserves its negation, its burning, as light. It is the truth of its vulnerability and it is the vulnerability of its truth. It is the logic of education.

J4: Are we to live as the candle?

S: If we live the examined life.

J6: This is all very well, Socrates, but what has this new old cave to say about justice?

S: Perhaps this. Presupposition in the old city takes the form of mastery and slavery. It is a culture of truth seen as the in-itself and of ignorance and barbarism seen as the for-another. Presupposition in the upper world is seen as a culture of truth as enlightenment in-itself, and of the cave as error. Despite the best attempts of the enlightened elite to hide ignorance from itself in the dark, the light which they use for the production of shadows is the same light that reveals itself as the source of the shadows. The light which cuts both ways illuminates itself and the injustice it carries. The enslaved see this injustice and travel to the upper world in pursuit of the principles of justice. The upper world promises justice, but this is another trick of the light. Justice pursued in this way is just another shadow.

J6: And now the new old prisoner sees and understands all this? I doubt it.

S: You doubt it because although she sees the temptation of masterful truth, she refuses to resolve her questions to her own advantage. She knows the untruth of mastery.

J6: And by implication you mean the untruth of my mastery?

J8: I didn't think we would ever see your candle, but perhaps there it is.

J6: And what, pray tell, is the vision of justice that is supposed to be illuminated here?

S: Our new old prisoner, offered the old mastery, has seen the injustice of light in the light of injustice. She knows this and trusts this as her education. She learns that necessity demands of her that she do justice to this difficult education.

J6: So this is her vision and her principle of justice. But what can she do with such a principle?

S: She can make it her life in the city. She can shine the light that carries injustice back onto itself. She can light one candle.

J6: Meaning what?

S: That she teaches of justice and injustice in the experiences that people already have; that she educates about what is already present. She does not promise justice in a completely new world. She finds the just city in the unjust city. She teaches of the new old world. And she does this simply by teaching it about itself, and about a necessity within it that, although universal, is yet hidden to itself by the masterful nature of its own light.

J8: Justice is in the education.

S: Justice is in the education because freedom is in the learning.

J6: I think this is complete nonsense.

J4: I'm sure you do. Nevertheless, Socrates, help us to imagine how such justice might be lived in a city as the examined life.

Book 17

S: Very well. What was the goal of the old city?

J1: To unite the individual and the collective.

S: How?

J1: By making the individual soul the model for social relations so that each citizen would find his soul in the city and the city in his soul. The individual would feel he belonged to the city because the city was also himself.

S: And what did the city look like?

J1: The three parts of the city – traders/producers, defenders and philosopher-rulers – mirrored the three parts of the individual soul – desire, spirit and reason. The rulers developed a community spirit among themselves and then governed in that spirit, banning antisocial influences, including some types of music and poetry. They allowed only those things that aimed for the best in people. The rulers were taught self-sacrifice, having only enough money to live on, and no property or family or children of their own. Breeding in the city was controlled, and where necessary the rulers would have the right to lie to the people in the people's own best interests.

S: Was it a city of equality?

J1: No. Some of the city's traders had greater wealth and property while their leaders had greater wisdom and education.

S: Was it a just city?

J1: Its claim to justice was that the city allowed citizens to live in accordance with their own natures – their own natural abilities and interests. To make people live lives to which they were unnaturally suited would be unjust.

S: Then perhaps our new city will have to embrace equality while still doing justice to the differences between people. To do so, we may have to redefine many things according to educational logic that have traditionally only been known through the logic of mastery.

J1: What is our aim here?

S: A different vision for the city. Our task is to see if the city can learn to understand itself in its existence and learn to exist in what it understands of itself. We want to see just how much weight the examined life can bear.

J1: This will be quite a challenge.

S: And doing justice to the truth of such a challenge might mean redefining what free and just educational social relations look like.

J1: Does this mean that education will have to do the work that property currently does in the unjust city?

S: Yes, if education can take for itself the burden of being the culture of life and death.

J1: Before we begin, can we try to agree a few simple definitions pertaining to educational logic, Socrates?

S: Of course, although the simple will not absolve us from difficulty!

J1: Indeed. How would you define educational truth?

S: That learning is true when it negates what it knows, making that object known as unknown, or as other.

J1: And what is the logic of this education?

S: We learnt from the life-and-death struggle that the in-itself is for-itself, or free, in already being for-another.

J1: And its necessity?

S: Its necessity is its presupposition of itself, or negation preserved as learning.

J1: And its principle?

S: I am already other – to you and to myself – and both of these others is not me. This is what I am.

J1: Could this also be the principle of educational justice in an educational city?

S: Yes, by being lived as the examined life.

J1: I have no doubt that we will need to return to these expressions and rehearse their truth many times in our attempt to describe the examined city.

S: Of course.

J1: Will this new city be imagined as a future utopia or will it be set in present conditions? Will it be no-place or this place?

S: On the one hand, it seems futile to base a new city on truths or characteristics or versions of human nature that are not possible for us now. That would not do justice to who we are and the problems we face. On the other hand, unless we are able to assume liberation from current troubles, we would offer no hope for a better future.

J1: If we do not negate the unjust city, we simply preserve it. But if we do not preserve the unjust city, we abolish ourselves in the name of a future that therefore cannot be our own.

S: The one changes too little, the other changes too much.

J1: So, doing justice to this difficulty demands that we both negate and preserve the city differently than in the logic of mastery. Then, will our new city be a new old city, just as our new Socrates is a new old Socrates?

S: Perhaps so. We can neither abolish the old city nor instantaneously create a new one.

J1: That would be to presuppose a pure beginning.

S: Indeed.

J1: Is our new old city propertied or educational?

S: To do justice to its presuppositions, it will have to be the preservation of the negation of the propertied city.

J1: With or without property?

S: We will come to this presently.

J1: Then if the principle of the new old city is not one of life and death shaped in the logic of mastery and property, will its founding principle be life and death shaped in the logic of education?

S: It will.

J1: And what does this look like as social relations?

S: Social relations become the examined life of each citizen.

J1: The conjunction of the soul and the city . . .

S: —In the life-and-death struggle whose truth is education.

J1: Is the struggle mutual?

S: Remember we said before that it is mutual only from the bird's eye view of a non-participant.

J1: But the struggle is shared.

S: In the logic of mastery shared means shared as property and slavery. In the logic of education, however, shared means the struggle of learning, a struggle that is as individual as it is collective because it is for-itself and for-another.

J1: But can education really take the place of property as the culture of life and death?

S: That is what the old city proposed for its philosopher-rulers. We must now explore if the new old city can do justice to such educational truth for everyone.

J1: How much of this new old city will we be able to describe?

S: We should be able to describe at least the logic of its educational social relations.

J1: You mean how people organize for birth and death, how they live and work together, and how they love and form associations.

S: And how all of this adds up to living the examined life.

J1: Will we be offering a blueprint for how all cities should be run?

S: Far from it. We will only be describing how educational cities can be understood. There is no definitive plan they must conform to. Each city will shape its learning differently, and each city will be different. We will not be deciding which jobs will be done, or who will do them, or what they will produce. But we will be able to describe the educational truth that underpins them.

J1: This might frustrate those who would want us to tell them exactly how everything should be organized.

S: The city has to be learnt if it is to be just. There is no short cut to this learning, and we cannot learn on behalf of anyone else, any more than we can eat or drink for them. The practical details of any educational city will be worked out by itself. All we can do is rehearse the logical character of the city and think about the areas of life in which the question of life and death might know itself educationally.

J1: How should we begin, Socrates?

S: We should begin with what is already presupposed, namely, the question of the city.

J1: What question is the city?

S: The city breathes as the negation and preservation of collective life lived individually and individual life lived collectively.

J1: You mean the city lives the question of life and death.

S: Exactly.

J1: Which refers to the arrangements for the production, distribution and consumption of resources.

S: It does. And since the propertied city answers this question within the logic of mastery, so we might expect the educational city to do so within the logic of education.

J1: Perhaps it would help us if we explored the new city in relation to the old city, looking first at the way the collective life is lived individually, and then at how individual life is lived collectively.

S: Very well. Can we presume that both cities meet the same basic needs for survival?

J1: Yes.

S: Individual or social needs?

J1: They are the same. The needs are social because one life desiring to meet its needs meets another doing the same thing.

S: And from this the city takes shape?

J1: Our present city is shaped by those who exploit the needs of others. Ours is the propertied city, sustained through mastery and slavery where resources are made, sold and used to defend and extend this mastery and its property. A class of producers serves those who profit from this. This is the bedrock of injustice in our city.

S: Does the logic of mastery also define what people consider to be real needs in the city?

J1: I think so. Individual and social needs reflect propertied and masterful needs.

S: And do they appear to be natural?

J1: They do.

S: And things are created specifically to meet these propertied needs.

J1: Yes. But is this really sustainable? The propertied need for mastery to prove itself through accumulation can never be completely satisfied in-itself. Ever more human and material resources are exploited in pursuit of the illusion of total mastery. This is the very definition of unsustainability. It threatens the survival of the city. But I am unsure how the educational city could arrange this differently?

S: The need for preservation and the arrangements for production, distribution and consumption would not be for mastery.

J1: Such a city would understand life and death educationally.

S: Yes. As we said earlier, where one desire for preservation meets another, life and death experience themselves. Life is preserved in the experience of death, and therefore life needs death to survive – in both meanings of the phrase. In the logic of mastery life preserves itself by making death its slave and its property. In the logic of education life preserves itself in knowing death, or negation, as learning, and in learning that property is merely a surrogate for the work of learning.

J1: The I-life-and-death preserves the negation of death within it as education rather than as more property.

S: Yes. It does not master its vulnerability by enslaving it. It lives its truth of life and death as education, in the examined life.

J1: Does the examined life overcome the struggle with property?

S: The examined life *is* that struggle. It is the struggle between educational truth and propertied truth, exactly as the ancients knew in their own plan for the just city.

J1: If the propertied city creates resources that meet its never-ending need for mastery, will the educational city create resources which meet its equally never-ending need for education?

S: It will. But in ways that are sustainable.

J1: How?

S: What does life use to sustain itself?

J1: Objects, some of which exist naturally, and some of which are made by us.

S: And what is the truth of such an object, what is its quality?

J1: It is the quality of life being lived. And this suggests, then, that life, not value or use, is the truth of the object. But objects are inanimate. How can they be said to have the quality of life?

S: When they are seen as educational resources, or when we learn of objects not as property or as death owned, but as death learned.

J1: Then objects in this case are judged for quality not quantity, and as education not property.

S: Quite so.

J1: Then what is the educational truth of an object?

S: That its in-itself is for-itself by being for-another.

J1: How does that work here?

S: When an object is sold in the marketplace, it is sold as an object, an identity in-itself, as if its monetary value was naturally occurring. But really, the object is a commodity. Its value comes from mastery over those who make it. As such, anything bought or sold is only in-itself because it is already for-another.

J1: Then without such mastery over the other the value of the object would simply be found in its use.

S: But this in turn would value objects only as useful tools and use here would become another means of mastery over it.

J1: If the object is owned by someone, then I can see that others are enslaved in its production. But surely an object that is not owned can have its natural truth as something useful to humanity?

S: Would this use be the identity of the object in-itself?

J1: Yes.

S: But the philosophical revolution we spoke of has demonstrated that the very notion of an object in-itself, however defined, is a propertied identity.

J1: So even the value of use belongs to propertied logic.

S: It is propertied logic that prejudges something to be merely a thing. Even a city without private property that judged objects as merely useful things would still be a city of propertied logic. The educational city will have to learn to live both with and without the object in-itself.

J1: But since an object cannot think for itself it must be only a thing.

S: Yes, from the point of view of its master. That is exactly what was always said about slaves. Propertied logic has always said that an object which is for-us is not also for-itself.

J1: So, you are saying that if I don't hold the object hostage to being a propertied identity, I release it from the prejudice that it cannot be for-itself.

S: And then the object has its truth in what the master learns about the illusion of his mastery. It becomes not an object of use but a lesson in dependence.

J1: That doesn't mean it thinks for itself!

S: It means that it is real not as an object in-itself but as education. In educational logic the object for-us is also us for-the-object. It thinks us as much as we think it, and this is the for-itself of nature as an educational truth. Turning nature into property means destroying our educational relation to all natural objects. Such is the challenge of living the examined life with and without the object in-itself.

J1: Then educational truth resists ownership of nature and the masterful use of nature that follows from such ownership. But what is life without such ownership of natural objects?

S: It is life shared. Sharing is how an object participates in the quality of the examined life.

J1: So, I can only do justice to nature by living its education as sharing?

S: That is as much the freedom of nature as it is our own freedom.

J1: Then we must now explore how the processes of production, distribution and consumption can do justice to this educational truth of objects, or of the natural resources that serve the quality of life in the educational city.

S: You mean the city's educational resources.

J1: What are such educational resources?

S: They obviously include those needed for survival in the life-and-death struggle: food, shelter, clothes, etc.

J1: Then what makes them educational resources?

S: They unsettle the temptation to ownership.

J1: So, preserving the other as learning rather than as property is the key to educational resourcing?

S: It is. And production, distribution and consumption are just if they are true to this educational necessity.

J1: How?

S: By producing nothing that preserves the other only as its slave or its property.

J1: Then what kinds of things will be produced?

S: Who can tell? Circumstances will answer this question.

J1: Would there be a class of producers?

S: Everyone would live productive lives in living the examined life.

J1: Why? What is the educational truth of such work?

S: That work is for-itself when its in-itself is for-another.

J1: And what is justice here?

S: That this work negates and preserves itself as learning rather than as exploitation.

J1: So, there is no owner and no wage slave.

S: Nor is there a commodity or profit. The educational truth of work is that working as learning gains a mind of its own. What is produced is not an object, but the educational truth of the quality of life: individual life in the collective and collective life in the individual.

J1: Everyone works.

S: As they are able, yes.

J1: Are work by hand and by brain distinguished?

S: Not as they were in propertied logic as slave and master. Educational logic preserves the distinction not as work and leisure but as the for-itself of all human activity.

J1: So, work is not exploitative.

S: Nor is it masterful. That is why it is sustainable.

J1: And truth and justice are work?

S: Yes, they have to be worked for. They are difficult. But when difficulty is resolved in favour of mastery and property, then education is suppressed until such time as the injustice speaks of a different logic.

J1: Very well, Socrates. What about distribution, or the question of who gets what in the new old city.

S: In the present city the logic of mastery distributes life for some and death for others.

J1: So, in educational logic, how much should anyone have?

S: The educational principle would mean never having so much that the other is not preserved or is only preserved as slave or property.

J1: So, no poverty?

S: Material poverty for some is only a result of the educational poverty of others.

J1: But will some always have more than others?

S: In propertied relations some have more or less life and death than others. In educational logic that is inequality and injustice.

J1: This in turn would shape the consumption of resources in the city. We said that mastery consumes resources in fruitless pursuit of itself. Instead of this, could there be something called educational consumption?

S: Yes, in the sense that educational consumption preserves what it consumes because education is self-sustaining. Education is the logic and principle of sustainability.

J1: Do educational needs not increase?

S: They develop. The greater the need for education, the more sustainable education becomes.

J1: But how would one know how much to consume?

S: As we said, never so much or so little that what is consumed is not preserved, but never preserved as property or by exploiting slavery by mastery.

J1: So, in summary, Socrates, the educational city is able to produce, distribute and consume in ways where life and death sustain themselves by a logic of education and not a logic of mastery.

S: Yes.

J1: But distribution in the propertied city is mediated by money. Will there be money in the educational city?

S: What is money?

J1: The means of buying objects, or commodities.

S: What are commodities?

J1: They are objects made for profit. But they have a special quality.

S: What is that?

J1: They are valued according to a universal measure.

S: But a sausage and a rose have nothing in common.

J1: Money acts as their equivalence.

S: Then what is money?

J1: Money is the universal measure of paid work. Therefore everything has monetary value, and everything can be exchanged for money as if all were equivalent to each other. Money is the universal equivalence of all commodities which, perhaps somewhat ironically, is what the city tries to be for its citizens – their universal expression or common bond.

S: It seems like commodities have a stronger bond with each other through money than people have with each other in propertied social relations. Perhaps the present city will turn all social relations into money?

J1: It is on its way to doing just that. All communal activity in the city, the meeting of all social needs, gets turned into money, which everyone is then free to own more or less of. The social bond is lost to individual greed and exploitation and all this is shaped by the propertied logic of master and slavery. All social relations have a price. And everyone is invited to judge everyone else in such financial terms. It is as if money has become the real social life of the propertied city. Yet money has the appearance of neutrality.

S: It appears to treat everything equally and act only as a middleman, whereas, in fact, it is the social relation of injustice. Perhaps money has even managed to find its own mastery, its own propertied identity.

J1: As what?

S: As money in-itself, where money is no longer attached to objects or the labour within them.

J1: You mean capital?

S: Yes – money that is freed from death or dependency upon an object and is self-reproducing, and which can enter and exit the marketplace retaining an independence of its own. It is money become dependent only on itself.

J1: Money as an end in-itself, or money become invested in-itself.

S: And there is an inherent educational danger in such money markets.

J1: What is that?

S: Money making money for itself is an empty mastery. It is never for-another, never formative, and so it lacks an education for-itself. It makes nothing and has no self-educating social relation.

J1: So, what sustains it?

S: The confidence of the masters.

J1: Based on what?

S: Confidence in mastery.

J1: So, the truth of money has no substance?

S: Beneath the confidence, most people know this and especially those who try hardest to hide it. The collapse is ever-present.

J1: But the confidence, the capital, is the whole of the city's social relations.

S: Such is the frailty from which we retrieve the educational city.

J1: Surely a just city demands that this whole capitalized city needs to be completely overturned?

S: Is that not just more propertied logic and mastery?

J1: Then are *any* thoughts possible which are not already invested in this capital city?

S: Our vicious circles would suggest not.

J1: Not even critical self-education.

S: But we have also seen that this totality can be understood differently.

J1: You mean when the self-education of the capital city regarding its injustices creates new ways of being that do not belong to property.

S: Beware of being seduced by new masterful ideas of being. They would only reproduce the same injustice that is being opposed. The present city has already shown what happens when a political revolution exempts itself from the philosophical revolution, and what happens when the philosophical revolution is granted immunity from itself.

J1: Remind us, Socrates.

S: The philosophical revolution revealed that experience and objects presupposed and shared conditions of possibility, which moved truth from the object in-itself to the rules of such conditions.

J1: And its political revolutions?

S: One such revolution showed how the production of objects presupposed unjust conditions of possibility. This challenged naturalized and naive economics to recognize its propertied presuppositions.

J1: Did the philosophical revolution find a new truth?

S: No. It judged the revolutionary truth of education unknowable within propertied logic and substituted it with a notion of pure individual freedom.

J1: Did the political revolution find a new truth?

S: No. It judged the revolutionary truth of education unknowable within propertied logic and substituted it with a notion of pure collective freedom.

J1: Both replaced one mastery with another?

S: They did, by continuing to think according to propertied logic.

J1: So, neither could see an educational truth in the way that experience and production undermined mastery, and both turned to propertied logic for the truths of their revolutions?

S: It would seem so. They did not find the quality of life and death in self-examination. They did not find the meaning of the contradictions of their revolutions; they did not find the truth of life lived for-itself for-another.

J1: But, again, does all of this mean that the educational city will have property and money or not?

S: Remember, our just city is not a utopia. It is living education. As such, it will neither be mastered by property nor masterfully abolish it.

J1: Then its citizens will still have things, still buy things?

S: People will have things educationally rather than to own as masters and to profit from.

J1: But how can property be educational?

S: By being owned and not owned. Having things will not be an end in-itself. Its truth will be as property already for-another. As such, the logic of educational property is that the in-itself of anything we have to hand is for-itself for-another.

J1: And its principle?

S: The principle is that educational property is already other than mine, and its owner is not me. The educational necessity of such educational property is that it preserves itself when it negates itself, as it does me who is both owner and non-owner.

J1: And, as we said of the educational life of objects earlier, the negation and preservation of property and money is sharing?

S: In fact, sharing has always been the educational truth of property. To share something is both to have it and not to have it. This truth has always accompanied property. It has long been known that to share is educational and not masterful.

J1: I have seen so-called sharing where people are really only displaying their mastery.

S: There is masterful sharing in the propertied city. But there is also educational sharing, where my will over the external world is preserved not as mastery but as my learning of being for-another.

J1: That's hard to do.

S: It is.

J1: Perhaps people could also share money?

S: That would make money redundant.

J1: But even in the educational city there would always be some people who would exploit those who share what they have.

S: Perhaps. But educational sharing preserves such exploitation in a way that leaves the exploiter without purchase in the world. The examined life then addresses them in this dissolution of their power.

J1: What if the exploiter is an aggressive neighbouring city?

S: If their motive is for mastery of greater resources, then the educational city is unlikely to be an attractive target.

J1: Why not?

S: The educational city desires only sustainable and educational resources. It is not rich in the things that the logic of property craves. And it does not threaten the masterful resources of others.

J1: Not even by population growth?

S: Living with limited resources means that the city that seeks to know itself will learn the freedom and discipline required for a sustainable population, one that preserves its negations without slavery or property. This education about needs that are based in education and not in fear and greed can resist other more tyrannical solutions to population growth, especially those using concern for nature as a cover for the mastery of one kind of people over another.

J1: Even so, masters of other cities might still want to conquer and enslave the educational city.

S: Education might at some point have to defend itself against such enslavement. It might have to defend its own life and death in ways it would not choose.

J1: But war is just another shape of life and death.

S: War is the struggle to have mastery over life and death, to make life and death its own property. It is the attempt to own life and death. And victory brings ownership to the victors of the life and death of the other.

J1: Then wars are fought and resolved by propertied logic.

S: To the victors the spoils.

J1: Does war also have an educational logic?

S: All life and death is an education.

J1: Even if the immediacy of war is kill or be killed?

S: The immediacy still has to be planned for. But there is educational logic in war.

J1: How?

S: Every campaign, every battle, is for-itself because it is for-another. War is itself mastered by life and death. Combatants more than anyone else know this.

J1: Then how does one do justice to them?

S: By doing justice to this education about the illusory mastery of warfare. In the examined life, life and death have no immediate identity. To learn of one's vulnerability in relation to another human being, as combatants do all the time, is to learn the educational truth of the whole world and perhaps beyond this world as well. War brings its own education regarding the frailty of mastery.

J1: But as we said, there are times when one has to fight to survive. Can there be an educational war? Is it what we call the just war?

S: A war that does justice to life and death as education is one that educates itself.

J1: How? A just war is still a war.

S: It is. But a just war is prepared to preserve those it would destroy, not as the spoils of war, but instead as the educational truth that propertied victory erodes itself. Life always needs death to survive. The question, as always, is, will this truth be in the shape of property or education. The response to this question sows the seeds of justice or injustice for the future.

J1: Then why has the city always chosen property over sharing?

S: The logic of mastery shapes the choice. It ensures that sharing is made to appear nonsensical, unrealistic and easily dismissed as naive.

J1: Which leads me to a more general observation. People have always imagined what a better life for the city would be. But real life, or the logic of mastery, makes such visions impossible, and nonsensical. To choose the better way appears to be choosing self-destruction.

S: Then in this regard the new old city is not inventing anything new. It is releasing something ever-present. Educational truth has always been present in the city. But propertied education has always denied it a voice.

J1: Socrates, more questions occur to me. If we have educational property, will there still be crime?

S: Let us see. What is possession?

J1: Possession is my immediate having of something.

S: What is property?

J1: Property is possession across time and space. Even when the object is not in my immediate possession, it is still mine; it is still the will of the master over the object.

S: So, property is possession at a distance. And what is crime in relation to this?

J1: Crime restores the immediacy of possession. Either by force or by guile it negates the will of the master.

S: By the will of another?

J1: Yes.

S: But all property is already the will of one master over someone else.

J1: It is.

S: So, property by its own definition is a crime?

J1: Some have said so.

S: In which case, property is not only alienable by its own definition, it is also in-itself unstable and vulnerable to itself.

J1: Crime here exposes the instability of all mastery.

S: And the truth of this instability is found in educational logic.

J1: So, can there be crime in the educational city?

S: Of course. Some will seek security in property rather than in education.

J1: But if someone steals that which someone would have shared, is it a crime?

S: It is the violence and injustice of propertied logic in a city of the examined life.

J1: And is this perhaps a symptom of educational poverty?

S: If educational poverty is with us always, even in the new old city, then there will always be acts which defy educational truth.

J1: Then what kind of laws could the educational city have?

S: The existence of laws at all suggests mastery, while the absence of laws suggests the city is denied its own freedom to speak of its truth.

J1: Does such education therefore need different kinds of laws?

S: You mean something like educational laws?

J1: I suppose so. But what would they look like?

S: They would preserve education in the vulnerability of their own mastery.

J1: Laws that deliberately examined themselves?

S: Law as learning and learning as its own law.

J1: Lived how?

S: Law and learning lived as the examined life.

J1: Would these laws be written in stone?

S: Their truth would be as experiences.

J1: Of what?

S: Of individual and collective life and death.

J1: But laws are to be obeyed.

S: In propertied logic a law is merely in-itself.

J1: And in educational logic?

S: A law preserves itself in its vulnerability.

J1: But a vulnerable law will not be respected.

S: It will be respected because it will have a truth of experience which will also be the experience of its truth.

J1: A law that is not masterful—

S: . . . is a law that is trusted more than one demanding blind obedience.

J1: Why would it be trusted more?

S: Because trust in its authority is learnt, and the discipline it demands is experienced in learning.

J1: Then these are laws whose necessity is the logic of education.

S: These are the laws of the examined life.

J1: I am still not sure, Socrates. Would I have to obey these laws or not?

S: You would experience this question of their truth for yourself as your own education, your own freedom to learn.

J1: Do they regulate behaviour?

S: They command only that you understand their command to understand them as the necessity for self-examination. They are the necessity of the question become its own law from which the law itself is not immune.

J1: And what of the inevitability that someone won't want to understand. Are they a criminal?

S: They are like a teacher without a student. The law will always reveal the vulnerability of such a masterful stance in the world. But this is no criminal. This is evidence of poverty – material and educational. And to alleviate such poverty the law of learning commends doing justice to the experience of poverty.

J1: The justice of educational logic.

S: The justice that resides in living life and death as learning and not in its propertied resolution.

J1: Given everything we have said, Socrates, it does seem odd to think of the production and distribution of resources without exploiting others for profit, just as it does to think of property and poverty and law and war as having educational rather than masterful truth. But since we are exploring life and death as the collective life lived individually, would we say that the person living in the logic of education is a moral person?

S: What is a moral person?

J1: Perhaps someone whose principles involve care for others, and whose acts in the world are consistent with those principles.

S: What of his motives for action?

J1: His actions will have integrity. They will be true to his values and principles. A truly moral person will not compromise his beliefs at any price.

S: But actions seldom work out as planned. There are always unanticipated consequences.

J1: But if the intentions were sound, then the principles are still intact, and these are still the actions of a moral person. It is the world outside that lets him down.

S: And in some cases, the moral person, facing this difficult education, takes refuge in the beautiful soul.

J1: You mean the one who refuses to act at all in an unworthy world and withdraws into the safety of a poetic world of tragic and suffering integrity.

S: What the beautiful soul seeks to avoid is the corruption in the world of its pure principles and intentions.

J1: But his conscience will not let him compromise. What is wrong with that?

S: His conscience is closed to the educational logic of its own necessary presuppositions. As such, he is too much himself, and too little other to himself.

J1: Is this an education of the moral person?

S: It teaches of a new necessity, that of the contingency of morality in the world.

J1: And therein redefining the idea of the moral person?

S: Indeed. The moral person is not him who is master of his actions in the world, but him who learns that the truth of his actions belongs to the necessity of how their negation in the world is preserved.

J1: It sounds like education is asking the principled moral person to learn to compromise with the world.

S: On the contrary, it is asking the moral person not to avoid the necessity of educational logic in the world.

J1: And the educational logic of this learning is that morality is preserved in and as the loss of its mastery.

S: Yes. The morality of morality depends on its openness to the conditions of its own possibility. Morality as mastery of principles is closed to education. But morality open to the vulnerability of its mastery of principles is a new old morality, an educational morality.

J1: Would the same be true of the old idea of virtue?

S: It would.

J1: So, the virtuous man would be the man of educational necessity?

S: Yes.

J1: And can this virtue be taught?

S: It can be taught only by being learned. Education makes a
virtue of its own necessity.

J1: Then this might be how virtue can leave the path of hypocrisy
and bad faith that it has travelled in the city, carried by the
piety of those who believe themselves to be great-souled
men. But if we have redefined morality and virtue, is it now
inevitable that educational logic will redefine good and evil?

S: Let our daemon test us on this too.

J1: Could mastery be called evil?

S: Perhaps we should distinguish between mastery and evil. If
mastery is self-protection grounded in fear, then its truth
appears in learning of this self-deception. It is this education
that then provides the presupposition for evil.

J1: How so?

S: Evil is the practice of a mastery that knows and absorbs
its impurity as its own truth. The evil master knows
destruction as his own positivity, his own affirmation. He
makes the destruction of mastery truthful in a mastery of
destruction.

J1: Who or what does he destroy?

S: Everyone who has not admitted such destruction as their own
positivity and affirmation. He considers they deserve to be
taught this lesson in the truth of evil.

J1: What then is the distinction between wrongdoing and evil?

S: Wrongdoing is the untruthful mastery of one will over
another. It is uneducated. Evil is an educated mastery,
turning the illogic of mastery into an intrigue of pure
impurity. It is destruction practising itself in the world as an
aesthetic.

J1: How is it to be resisted?

S: An interesting question. Resistance is far from straightforward. In the logic of mastery one mastery resists another with a view to overcoming it.

J1: I have seen this. Those who resist are already within the paradoxical situation of having defined themselves within the reality they seek to overthrow and have to play by the rules that they oppose. In this logic of mastery, resistance seems able to resist everything except itself.

S: But when resistance is carried by a different logic, one in which this totality experiences its own extinction, then resistance also resists itself.

J1: So here the self-defeating paradox of resistance can learn of itself differently.

S: We might say that in educational logic resistance can preserve the negation of mastery differently than as interminable victory or defeat.

J1: And how would such educational resistance resist evil?

S: Evil knows its education, and this is its vulnerability. Its educational truth is always closer to itself than its property. Evil is resisted by exposing it to the education that sustains it.

J1: But how do I resist the evil of someone else?

S: Release the logic of education in them that is already resisting itself.

J1: How?

S: Show them that even in the evil they do, they are also already preserved differently than as evil.

J1: Redeem them?

S: Remind them that they are already other than the evil they adopt as their mastery.

J1: But education works slowly, perhaps too slowly. What if the evil person has immediate plans for genocide, or something utterly horrendous? What if he wants to teach the truth of evil to a whole race of people?

S: In such circumstances, education will want to practise an art of resistance to such pure impurity.

J1: Meaning what?

S: Finding ways to preserve the other as itself, so that evil is not met with evil.

J1: But will it always be successful?

S: The history of the city suggests that it will not.

J1: Then that is not good enough to prevent evil!

S: Not good enough for a mastery over evil, no. But in educational logic the good is in the necessity of education, not in victory.

J1: But surely education would want to be victorious over evil?

S: The educational principle of the good is not grounded in mastery. It requires to be learnt.

J1: Then the danger here is that anything goes? There is no moral law, no absolute principle of the good; for anything could be said to have been learnt at any time, justifying any action!

S: On the contrary, in the principle of education according to its own logic nothing is justified as good that is not also other to itself. Turning such scepticism into a dogma and then practising it as intrigue is evil. While evil refuses to lose the purity of its impurity and is another propertied logic, education can only justify actions that carry the necessity of more of itself.

J1: I do not see that such an educational principle guarantees the city will never commit another atrocity.

S: Neither do I. But education teaches us that evil does not defeat evil; it only reproduces it.

J1: So, can education always prevent the atrocity?

S: Again the history of the city suggests that it cannot.

J1: In which case, Socrates, sometimes the situation is so urgent that one logic of mastery must be met with another logic of mastery?

S: You want me to say that the logic of education must turn to mastery at such times.

J1: I see no other choice.

S: You forget that the logic of mastery is always part of the logic of education, and that the logic of education is always part of the logic of mastery. One learns of each in the other. Even at the moment of atrocity education will be present.

J1: As evil.

S: And therefore as able to resist its resistance to itself.

J1: Nevertheless, one atrocity may be needed to prevent another atrocity!

S: Then the city needs to prepare education to speak its truth precisely at such moments.

J1: It would seem so. But, still, in desperate times, education may have to wait. Sometimes someone just needs to be stopped by any means possible.

S: In which case it seems opportune now for us to explore how the new old city might better prepare itself in advance of such horrors. Let us encourage our daemon to speak of ways in which the just city might embody the negation and preservation of life in death, and death in life, in the collective educational shapes that individual lives take.

J1: Is it obvious what we mean when we speak of the collective life?

S: What do you think?

J1: Yes and no. The collective is life lived in common with others. It is our external life, not our internal life. But I would say that even this external life is also lived internally by each of us.

S: Is collective life like being part of a crowd?

J1: It can be.

S: And is a crowd external or internal?

J1: Both. It is a very powerful external force but is able to create the most intense internal feelings.

S: What are these feelings?

J1: They are feelings of being overwhelmed by something greater than the individual, a heightened sense of belonging to a collective energy, to something powerful, something for which one would sacrifice oneself.

S: Is this a loss of rationality?

J1: It can be. A crowd acts on emotions and can make one much more spontaneous and much less reflective than when one is on one's own.

S: And would you say this is a good or a bad thing?

J1: Both. The collective needs a sense of belonging, something which will enable the submergence of selfish desires in favour of self-sacrifice for the good of all. No city could defend itself against its enemies without this sense of collective will and strength. But in the absence of reflection and thinking, these same collective forces can give way to mob mentality resulting in acts of extreme barbarism. Such energy can also be manipulated by individuals or groups for their own ends.

S: Is education the key to mediating the immediacy of collective life, just as it is the key to mediating the immediacies of individual life and selfish desire?

J1: If it is, the individual and the collective share this educational truth.

S: Just as the individual without the collective is blind, so the collective without the individual is empty. Each without the other is the absence of education.

J1: So, together they do justice to the whole?

S: Together and apart. The negation of each is preserved in the other. Both are for themselves when they are for-another. The shapes this takes are the shapes we call the city.

J1: And the city supports justice or injustice depending on the logic of these shapes.

S: Are we agreed that collective life presupposes that no one of us is self-sufficient?

J1: Yes.

S: And that the common settlement or the city is an arrangement for the production, distribution and consumption of necessary resources?

J1: Yes.

S: And, finally, are we agreed that the institutions of the just city will represent the educational truth of the just city?

J1: Yes, they will carry the truth of the city's examined life.

S: Then in our thinking about collective life, let us consider how the institutions of the educational city might do this by referring again to the cities of both logics.

J1: Before that I want to ask, is the common settlement answering a natural need? If the city intervenes in natural events and processes, is the city master of nature?

S: Here we will need to distinguish between nature understood within the logic of mastery and nature understood within the logic of education. What is nature within the former?

J1: It is where nature is an end in-itself, following its own laws, or where nature is its own identity and mastery unadulterated by human intervention.

S: So, it is like the object in the cave rather than the shadows. It is the original and not the copy.

J1: Yes. This is the beauty of nature.

S: But this version of nature is one-sided. It suggests a divide between itself and what we call thinking. It means that its mastery is never reflective, never for-itself or self-conscious, having no culture, no art, no religion, no philosophy and no freedom. Hence, animal life is judged inferior to human life.

J1: But it also means that nature doesn't traduce life and death into private property.

S: Yet it suggests that nature leaves life and death unmediated. And this is why nature is judged barbarian. Natural justice is the law of survival according to strength and brute force. Reason thinks it can improve upon this by overcoming nature, including by introducing property. That for which nature is so valued, its purity, is also that for which it is condemned, its lack of reason.

J1: So, nature in-itself is both beautiful and barbarian. It is somewhat ambivalent.

S: As is every object in-itself that our daemon has brought our way. But the educational city lives without the certain identity of the object in-itself. So, should our city also live without nature in-itself?

J1: Live without nature?

S: Not without nature, but without nature in-itself. Let us explore this in two of the most fundamental identities of nature: man and woman.

J1: The city long held the view that man was by nature superior to woman, equating woman with the simple immediacy of nature in-itself, and man with the rational power of the human mind in-and-for-itself. Woman embodied natural functions like childbirth and childcare, family, domesticity and the irrational life of emotion and its frailties.

S: And man, armed with rationality, embodied social functions like work and law. As reason was deemed superior to nature, so man was deemed superior to woman.

J1: Some women enjoyed the natural life, believing that those who wanted to be equal to men renounced their femininity. Others saw this naturalized conception of women as a domination by men, enabling women to be exploited physically, economically and legally.

S: Is the ambivalence of nature in-itself also reproduced in the family?

J1: Yes. What to one woman is her joyous natural role as wife and mother, living her true purpose, is for-another woman a slavery to her master's will. This provokes a crisis for family life.

S: Does the crisis of the relation to nature in-itself spread beyond the family?

J1: Indeed it does. There is uncertainty about male and female identity, about the nature of the body and its being accessorized by technology, about procedures for creating babies which might make men and women largely redundant, about the appropriate length of life and whether it is natural to sustain life by drugs and other interventions, about the rights of animals, about the state of the city's natural environment, and the extent to which the human should intervene in nature, by design or just through carelessness.

S: Nature in-itself enters its own life-and-death struggle when the struggle becomes conscious of itself.

J1: That is an interesting way of putting it, Socrates. You mean that reason might be nature's self-consciousness?

S: Perhaps reason is the necessity or the nature of nature known to itself.

J1: But if we follow the logic of mastery here, reason takes itself to be all life, defines nature as barbarian and justifies making nature its property.

S: Then nature and reason, and woman and man, are cultures of the life-and-death struggle enacting the logic of mastery and slavery.

J1: If this is the conflict the city endures within the logic of mastery, how different might it look within the logic of education?

S: As always, the logic of education lies within our description of the logic of mastery.

J1: How so?

S: Is nature to be known as the necessity of its being already presupposed?

J1: Yes. It already presupposes the living and dying of life and death.

S: Then nature is the presupposition and it is the presupposition being known as nature.

J1: To know nature is naturally, or necessarily, also to be in relation to nature.

S: A vicious circle for mastery, but a truth for education. Since necessity is often what is meant when someone speaks of the nature of something, then, as we did just now, might we call this the nature of nature?

J1: Yes if we mean the nature of nature is the necessity of its presupposition.

S: There are two elements in this necessity of presupposition: that nature in-itself is always already for-another; and that in being so the nature of nature is also for-itself.

J1: But people would question how nature can ever be for-itself? It is not self-aware.

S: We had this same discussion regarding the object. In the logic of mastery nature is not allowed to think itself because that would corrupt its immediate beauty.

J1: And in the logic of education?

S: Necessity knowing itself is the truth of educational logic. So, the nature of nature, in-itself, for-another, for-itself, is the educational truth of nature.

J1: So, we are nature knowing itself?

S: We are life and death presupposed as its own truth, yes. Nature is negated and preserved as education.

J1: I have long felt that we have got our relationship to nature wrong. An educational relationship to nature seems much better. It suggests a sustainable relationship for nature and the city. So, what does this educational truth of nature mean for the nature of man and woman?

S: What is the status of the male master within the logic of mastery?

J1: I suppose that man is the in-and-for-itself, and woman is the for-another or is nature mastered by him. The for-itself here is man's male-centred self-awareness projected as all reality, as common sense, so that the world is a mirror of the master. It is how man makes the world the same as himself, and how he condemns as broken anything that is not the same as himself.

S: And what is the contradiction in this logic of mastery?

J1: That man's mastery in-itself is already vulnerable in its dependence upon that which it masters – nature or woman. So, his self-consciousness, his for-itself, his freedom, is not of mastery at all but of vulnerability or being for-another.

S: And whose truth is vulnerability?

J1: Nature or woman.

S: Why so?

J1: Because nature or woman is defined as for-another.

S: So, nature or woman is also now the truth of the vulnerable master who is also for-another.

J1: I presume that the educational principle at work here in this logic of male mastery is that man – the master – is already other, and the other is not man.

S: What kind of truth is left if each is neither themselves nor the other?

J1: An educational truth – that each has its truth in the learning that negates them and preserves them differently.

S: And what is the educational logic of this truth?

J1: That neither man nor woman is independent of each other. That their identities in-themselves are illusory propertied identities of mastery and enslavement. And that, perhaps, educationally, this relation can be learned and lived differently.

S: If so, what would you say is the educational necessity that reconceptualizes the illusions of the identities of man and woman?

J1: That their relations are presuppositions of shapes of life and death.

S: And what does educational justice demand here?

J1: That propertied nature be negated and preserved as an educational relation, or that nature be lived as the examined life. Man and woman learning that what they are is also what they are not; and learning too that while this is nonsense in the logic of mastery, it is truth within the logic of education.

S: But our discussion has also shown something else in this relation.

J1: What?

S: When we told the story of life and death, it was the mother who was both the immediacy of life and death – in giving birth – and the universal mediation of life and death by itself – its whole negation and preservation of itself. While the hunter acts only on immediate needs, the mother carries love as the circle or, better, as the eternal experience of life and death.

J1: But this sounds like the old stereotype of woman as an unreflective circle of nature, while man can rationalize survival and turn it into the rational city.

S: In the logic of mastery the circle is either unreflective or is dismissed as a meaningless repetition. But in educational logic this circle is reason knowing itself. It is its universal educational self-experience.

J1: Then educational truth is woman?

S: Not as the mastery called nature and not as the mastery called essence. But perhaps as the redefinition of truth within the whole circle of life and death. However, educational truth is an experience for anyone and everyone who learns to live life and death as the struggle of negation and preservation. To want to assign the universal here exclusively to mother or hunter, to want to fix it one way or the other, is to seek to master the educational truth that only exists within them because it already exists between them.

J1: Do you mean that life and death, sustained both immediately and universally, is somehow between man and woman? If so, then the truth of education speaks not so much of their masterful identities but of movement within and between them?

S: It speaks of the educational truth of such movement as learning.

J1: Should we then get rid of the verb 'to be' as you once suggested? Should we no longer say that someone is a man or is a woman?

S: Yes and no. Negate and preserve them together and apart and learn this truth. Let their characteristics be those of educational nature not masterful nature.

J1: You mean that man and woman can be true as change?

S: What else can educational truth be but the unchanging truth that education means change? And if education is not true to itself, and does not do justice to itself, then it is unjust.

J1: Then is this truth of education changing or unchanging?

S: In the logic of mastery one demands a masterful answer to such a question. In the logic of education, the answer to such a question learns that it can only be of one of them by also being for the other one.

J1: Very well, Socrates. Perhaps we should now return to the institutions of the educational city and reflect on the nature of the nature of the family, and the nature of the nature of the marketplace.

S: Well put. What is a family?

J1: It is the institution by which the city arranges the birth and death of succeeding generations.

S: So, the family preserves the city.

J1: The propertied city preserves itself through the propertied family. The logic of mastery allows for propertied relationships between its members, both between its adults and between its adults and their children.

S: Perhaps educational logic can redefine the idea of the family, finding within it an educational truth.

J1: How?

S: Perhaps in educational love, in educational emotion, in educational child development and then in educational relations that redefine the inner world of the family in its relation to the wider city.

J1: What is an educational logic of love?

S: We have seen this already. It is the experience of life and death in the circle of birth and dying. It is the love that preserves itself in the negation of its propertied forms.

J1: We called it mothering, for it is life loving itself, and we have also called it learning, which is also life loving itself. But what of erotic love, Socrates, does that have an educational logic?

S: Desire, learning to give to and receive from that which has moved it, has its own educational logic. The erotic is mere mastery and slavery until it lives this relation, this love, as educational truth that preserves its struggles as learning.

J1: And what of an educational logic of emotion?

S: It is, as always, the necessity of negation and preservation.

J1: Can you explain?

S: Why do we cry?

J1: Because we feel sad.

S: And why do we feel sad?

J1: Sadness is loss or negation.

S: If sadness is loss, what are tears?

J1: Tears express the sadness at the loss.

S: So, tears carry sadness from inside to outside?

J1: Yes. They give loss a reality in the world. They make the nothing into something, the absence into presence.

S: Then we should not be sad about tears or fear them.

J1: Why not?

S: If you cry, you must know the sadness and the loss.

J1: You mean I must have learnt of it on some level in order to be able to cry.

S: Tears express this learning. They preserve what is lost and give the loss real existence.

J1: Is the same true for laughter?

S: Have tears and laughter not always been close together?

J1: They have.

S: As with tears, do we laugh when we learn something, or see something differently, or when we understand something differently?

J1: We do.

S: Then laughter, like tears, preserves what is lost. This is perhaps why we often laugh and cry at the same time. There is joy in our sadness, and sadness in our joy, because each knows the education that is carried in the other. Laughter preserves the negation of sadness, and sadness preserves the negation of laughter. These are truths that mourners and comedians know all too well.

J1: What of love and emotion in the institution of the family?

S: In the logic of mastery the love of life, the cycle of birth and dying, is propertied. The one who carries life for its own sake is mastered by the one who takes himself to be all life and has the risk of death in birth kept safely at arm's length.

J1: You mean the love of life becomes his property as mother and wife?

S: This has been its reality in the city.

J1: Then what is its educational logic?

S: Life preserves itself by learning of its truth not in the owner but in the bearer.

J1: Can the circle of life and death be restored here?

S: Not as a merely rotating circle. But as an eternally falling circling, or as an experience, yes. Love of life by its own gravity falls into itself and parents are negated and preserved in the falling. This is their learning about their being life and death.

J1: What of an educational logic of childhood? In the logic of mastery, the child is property. How is this different in the logic of education?

S: Parents lose their identity in-itself and the child expresses this negation educationally. It preserves the negation of its parents as their love given reality in the world. Here the child is not their property; it is the educational logic of their love. It is their laughter and tears.

J1: Does this mean a family can be defined educationally only if it has children?

S: Not at all. A family can define any outward expression of learning between people, whether bound by erotic love or the love of the examined life, or love of shared life and death. A family could be people who laugh and cry together or who preserve their negation together emotionally. A family can be those who live and die together.

J1: So, at times a city could be a family?

S: Yes. They are cultures of life and death lived individually collectively and collectively individually.

J1: What of the defenders of the city, are they a family?

S: Defenders are asked to forge bonds between each other where they trust their lives – their negation and preservation – to their comrades. Theirs too is a culture of shared laughter and tears, of loyalty and sacrifice. When this family's blood is spilled, it is as an educational culture of life and death.

J1: And without such educational truth this family of guardians is merely violence.

S: Self-examination negates and preserves the defenders educationally.

J1: Very well. Now the ancient plan for the city also redefined the family in an educational way for its leaders.

S: Our new old city might do this for everyone.

J1: What then of a child's education?

S: Within the logic of mastery a child's education involves learning its own mastery by means of the mastery that others have over it. The child conforms until such times as it becomes the adult who then imposes conformity on others. This education does not encourage the examined life. Negation is seen as weakness, thoughtfulness is seen as slavish and preservation is achieved at the expense of such weakness.

J1: And within the educational city, how different will this be?

S: The child will be able to live the logic of education as the ages and stages of its own development.

J1: How so?

S: The child begins as the prisoner of shadows. But a knowledge beyond the immediate senses is soon required because the objects are not always present at hand.

J1: They are preserved in their absence by recollection in the memory.

S: The child learns to recall objects by using their names. This becomes the idea of an object.

J1: And so, the child learns of ideas.

S: And sees that the names and ideas of objects are shared in common. In conversations the city becomes an ordered place where one can speak to others and be understood by them.

J1: And grammar and number are the rule-based ordering of this communication and understanding.

S: And art and creativity are a vital part of this communication, as is learning of the body and the freedom and discipline that it teaches.

J1: Let us hope that such education will not be suppressed in the city of educational logic as it has been in the city of propertied logic and that it is made available to all ages.

S: Childhood is the time of the immediacy of these rules, but it will not be long before children negate these immediacies, testing them and questioning them. It is not long before 'why' is established in the vocabulary of the child's development.

J1: Are the rules necessary?

S: Your question presupposes them. Education is always the struggle of discipline and freedom. It cannot avoid this and remain educational at the same time. The new old city will know the necessity of this mastery, and its vulnerability, for the education of its children. The alternative is simply to avoid mastery in childhood and give children no experience of it or of its vulnerabilities, in which case mastery could become the attraction of the forbidden fruit. The educational city will not shy away from letting its children have an experience of mastery.

J1: But how is this different from a masterful education?

S: The logic of this education is not to create propertied masters and will not be cruel or despotic or tyrannical. It will always be mediated by the self-examination of the parent or teacher or public servant. This is a knowingly vulnerable mastery. The goal of such education is the exposure of the illusion of direct mastery in-itself. Educational logic determines that the more the teacher's mastery refuses to be a surrogate for the student's learning, the more the student trusts this as an educative authority. But the city must be brave enough to expose itself as a mastery to its children, so that they can learn for themselves that the exposure is not for mastery but for education. This is the risk of the examined life that the new old city will take as part of its educational truth. Only in the risk of freedom is freedom learnt.

J1: So, children are exposed to the mastery of things in-themselves, and thus to the vulnerability and frailty of such masterful identity. What next?

S: The immediacies of early education become increasingly subject to the child's questions. Now they begin to learn the power of the mind's mediation of the shadows.

J1: With the doubts that accompany it.

S: And the crisis this brings.

J1: Does this crisis have a name?

S: It is called youth. The youth is neither child nor adult. It is negation preserved neither as mastery nor as education.

J1: How does youth respond?

S: At times sceptical, rebellious, lethargic, indifferent to a world it sees as hypocritical, a world pretending to have an authority that it neither has nor deserves. And youth despairs as much for itself as for the world and seeks an identity in this despair.

At times here it will cling to anything that seems to offer authenticity in the face of this crisis of inauthenticity.

J1: This is mediation still clinging to immediacy?

S: Yes. A kind of idealism of mastery in a world of compromises, an idealism of solutions to problems. An idealism born of impatience.

J1: What happens?

S: Mediation rebounds on such idealism and rediscovers itself.

J1: By the emergence of the adult?

S: In the sense we are talking about – of the educational logic of personal growth and development – yes. Here is where serious life begins, as they say. Mediation has negated the world of sense and shadows but become a kind of youthful mastery. Now it will re-educate this youthful mastery. In the educational city the name of this work is reason. Here is where education steps into its own universality, for if everything is mediated, and mediation is education, then everything is education.

J1: How does this reason not become another mastery?

S: We will need to look to other aspects of the city to understand this. But as we have acknowledged, mastery is a temptation even in the educational city.

J1: And I would suggest that one of the ways mastery tempts this adult would be in the marketplace, or the sphere of needs where resources are produced, distributed and consumed. In the logic of mastery the market is a brutal place, incapable of social justice. Everywhere masters enslave others as surrogates for vulnerability: legal slavery as well as economic slavery.

S: As we have said before, production is by the enslaved who are not masters of land or resources. Distribution is controlled by those who own this production. Consumption is decided according to wealth. And the market is the organism that pretends such arrangements are natural and inevitable.

J1: So, as a culture of mastery and property, the sphere of needs is really the sphere of exploitation and profiteering, of inequality and injustice.

S: Quite so.

J1: Yet what we call civil society is also the sphere of rights and protections.

S: Only of rights and protections that are property-based. Equality is defined by the masters in their own image, including the equal right for some to have more life and less death than others.

J1: So, the educational city will need a market which is not property-based.

S: Be careful. As we have said before, to abolish property would be an act of mastery by a logic of mastery. It would hand the life-and-death struggle over to a culture of unmediated power, unless somehow resources were unlimited. It would put an act of mastery at the very heart of the educational city. Instead, the educational city needs to learn its way out of property. Remember the dilemma our daemon keeps repeating for us. No justice with property, and no justice without property; both are the logic of mastery.

J1: But within property the sphere of needs produces, distributes and consumes by means of the mastery of the free market. When resources are depleted, it preserves itself by creating new desires and new appetites. This in turn reproduces the enslaved, ensuring the free market again preserves itself at their expense.

S: Property ensures it always appears to be the solution to its own problems.

J1: Then how different does the market look in an educational city, Socrates? How different is it when working with the logic of education?

S: The market learns different truths about itself.

J1: How?

S: In perhaps four ways. First, the needs that preserve the market and property are re-learnt as shadows of mastery.

J1: You mean they are false needs.

S: Yes.

J1: But we all need food and shelter and clothes.

S: We do. But these have become propertied needs within the propertied culture of life and death. They can exist differently in educational culture.

J1: Go on.

S: Second, there comes the learning that objects which are desired and possessed are really conveyors of self-harm.

J1: In what way?

S: Objects are produced by people who make what they do not own, for others who own what they do not make. The makers see their making sold for profit. The most basic and important aspect of life and death, the activity by which we shape our material existence, is reduced to the value of market commodities.

J1: The very activity of life and death becomes propertied.

S: It does. As does the relation between the makers to each other and the relation of each maker to itself.

J1: So, needs are shadows, and life activity or making is self-harming. What else?

S: Third, the act of self-harming reproduces itself in the marketplace when these same objects are bought and sold.

J1: But market freedom – or shopping – is an expression of personal freedom! So how is shopping self-harming?

S: In buying back the objects of self-harm, the makers purchase their own torment.

J1: As if life, lost to pain, is only able to return to itself as more pain. But, Socrates, shopping is choice, and choice is not pain!

S: Really? In the propertied city choice for one person is often the absence of choice for someone else. As one person gets what he wants, so someone else loses out. And the more choice there is, the greater is the illusion that everyone is benefiting.

J1: This is choice defined in the logic of mastery?

S: It is choice as mastery.

J1: So, what is choice in educational logic?

S: It is choosing to preserve choice differently – not as mastery but as an education about mastery. Not always getting what you might think you want is an educational truth.

J1: And so masterful choosing is unsustainable?

S: Yes, in two ways, these being the fourth re-education of the market. It is unsustainable because mastery in-itself and its freedoms and slaveries and injustices are unsustainable. And it is unsustainable because the recreation of needs, or shadows, that it relies on is never satisfied and cannot ever sustain itself. It can only ever outrun itself. The city's limited resources cannot sustain this ever-expanding creation of shadow needs.

J1: So, the market learns of the injustice of its ever more desperate measures to preserve itself in the face of its unsustainable logic of mastery. And these, then, are the four elements of the market's re-education regarding its own injustice.

S: They are.

J1: So, in this fourfold education life and death are preserved differently in the marketplace than as mastery and property. This obviously changes the market and the city.

S: It is changed by its education. And to do justice to this education is now its most fundamental challenge. It can do so by serving its own educational necessity and its own educational needs, rather than its masterful needs.

J1: So, what are educational needs, and how does the market meet them?

S: Education needs its own truth. In the educational market, production, distribution and consumption will serve this need.

J1: Even the basic needs of food and shelter?

S: Especially those. If the market serves life and death as educational needs and not as propertied needs, then the market will be just at the most elemental level of individual and collective life and death.

J1: An educational market doesn't sound quite right.

S: Then let's call it the sphere of educational needs, no longer determined by false needs.

J1: And none need to starve or suffer because of such false needs.

S: False needs are created by profiteering. Real needs learn of their own truths.

J1: So, the sphere of educational needs will strive to be just. And the market will be just if it does justice to its own educational truth.

S: Perhaps we can put it like this. The logic of educational needs is that such needs are true when they are already for-another. The educational truth of such needs is that the selfish need is already an untruth.

J1: Then what of the relationship between the family and the sphere of needs?

S: In the logic of property they were often at odds with each other. The family competed for time that the markets, or the world of work, required for the enslaved. And the market had attractions that encouraged new young masters to leave the family. Each destabilized the other.

J1: And in the history of the city there are examples of families who, in the teeth of such instability, pursued their own particular mastery. Families have ruled the city as gods, emperors, tyrants, cartels, all seeking some kind of immortal dynasty, using fear and brutality. Some learnt to hide their terror behind the legality of market trading.

S: Such terror perhaps feared education above all else.

J1: In the past, family was seen as the natural sphere, civil society as the social sphere and the city as the rational state that subsumes them both. Is that the case in the educational city?

S: Perhaps not. Nature and the social were defined like that within the logic of identity. In the logic of education, nature, as we saw, is the nature of nature or already other in its own education. The family need no longer be defined within the logic of mastery as opposed to the social. But equally, the sphere of needs defined within the logic of mastery presupposed human nature as being mastery and slavery. The nature of this nature is also educational. The sphere of needs and of the family has nature and the social already within and between it. Their opposition, now within the logic of education, is educational.

J1: And how is this educational truth lived?

S: Their difference is the learning we call the city.

J1: How so?

S: As we saw, the family preserves life and death across generations, and the market preserves life and death within generations. The city preserves the family and the sphere of needs as its own comprehensive self-examination. The whole relation, for-itself, is the educational city.

J1: So, we could not describe the city as geographical?

S: It is not a territory. It is not a formal boundary. Its boundaries will be defined by its learning.

J1: Will the city have walls?

S: It will not be afraid to symbolize its own limits, but not as walls that close the city off to its truth for-another.

J1: And this will be called the educational city or the rational state perhaps?

S: The new old city is the city of comprehensive education. It is the rational state lost and found in that which it contained but suppressed – that its truth is learnt not imposed.

J1: What is the difference?

S: The educational city is the comprehensive experience of the vulnerability of the rational state in-itself. It has this individual and collective experience of freedom and discipline as its own continuing education and its own truth.

J1: And how do people in the educational city live such educational freedom and discipline?

S: As teachers and students.

J1: The old city of mastery and slavery is to be the new old city of teaching and learning?

S: Teachers and students are the citizens of the examined life. As the old city preserved the life-and-death struggle as mastery and slavery in property, so the new old city preserves the life-and-death struggle as teaching and learning in education.

J1: A city of teachers and students.

S: Yes.

J1: But even these terms have been defined within propertied logic. The teacher is the master who owns the knowledge that the student, or the enslaved, must pay for it in one way or another.

S: Then the new old city will redefine teacher and student within educational logic.

J1: How.

S: We saw how the master's life avoids its educational truth by owning property. And we saw that this is unsustainable, both according to its own logic and in alienating the master from the meaning and quality of life. We saw, too, that the enslaved live this truth for the master.

J1: So, is it the enslaved who are the truth of the educational city?

S: Again, we must be careful here. In the logic of mastery this idea would mean the overcoming of one masterful identity by another. One unsustainable mastery would replace another.

J1: And this is different in educational logic.

S: The enslaved, and the city, achieve a mind of their own educatively not masterfully.

J1: So, the truth of the enslaved, the mind of the for-another, is as student *and* teacher of the examined life?

S: The enslaved are the educational truth of the master, and this truth is teacher and student to and of itself for-another. This does justice to its own educational logic, preserving its negation as the experience of learning, not as mastery.

J1: Is . . . are. . . the teacher and student one person?

S: It, they, is, are, individual and collective, soul and city. The freedom of the soul and the city is for-itself for-another.

J1: Lived as education?

S: Lived individually and collectively in and as the examined life.

J1: Finally, then, we can speak of the logic of the educational city.

S: Let us try. It is free when it is other to itself, and it is other to itself when it lives the discipline of its own self-examination.

J1: And this is a just city because life and death are preserved
   not as property and mastery and slavery but as education and
   teaching and learning.

S: Only when the city risks its own education is it doing justice to
   its own freedom.

J1: But many might say that a city of logic, even an educational
   logic, is still mastery.

S: The new logic is the eternal self-destruction of the old logic of
   mastery. Its openness to this is its greatest defence against such
   tyranny.

J1: Very well, Socrates. Our educational city is a city of teachers
   and students. But where is the centre of government? Or, if the
   city is government by its own education, is there a centre of
   education?

S: Perhaps educational government needs something like a
   House of the City, a place one leaves and returns to on one's
   educational odyssey through life and death.

J1: A place of learning?

S: Yes, but of learning defined according to educational logic.

J1: Why would it exist?

S: It is its own necessity.

J1: So, it would be the House of educational logic, principles and
   truth?

S: Yes. It is the candle casting the city's own educational light and
   shadow. It is where the city learns itself.

J1: Is it also the House of justice?

S: Yes.

J1: Is it an upper world?

S: Yes and no. The upper world is only the city's experience of
   itself.

J1: Is it transcendent?

S: No, because it is for-another, not in-itself.

J1: Is it metaphysical?

S: If you like, but it lives in our experience.

J1: And is this House of the City a physical entity?

S: It is a building, but in entering and leaving the building, people are also coming and going from themselves.

J1: In a mystical sense?

S: In a logical sense.

J1: What goes on in the House of the City?

S: It is a House of educational government.

J1: Then how does it govern educationally?

S: It teaches educational logic and truth through a curriculum that is the city's own life and death.

J1: Does it teach immediacies, I mean, does it teach of the in-itself?

S: It does.

J1: To children?

S: To anyone beginning to learn something for the first time. Any new beginning requires the immediacy of new names and objects and requires us to become as a child again.

J1: Does the House also teach for the experience of the mediation of such immediacies?

S: It does.

J1: In the old city this meant seeing that the shadows were only copies of objects, not truths in-themselves.

S: This is true in the House too. Immediacies and truth in-itself are similarly vulnerable.

J1: Does the light that creates the shadows then blind those who turn round to look at it?

S: It does. In the logic of mastery, education would remaster such doubts and anxieties with new immediacies. But in the House no mastery survives the relation to its own light unchanged.

J1: And when mastery learns that nothing sustains an identity in-itself free from this mediation, so it is tempted by the dogmas of stoicism, scepticism, cynicism and perhaps seeks entry to the playground of intrigue in the pursuit of power.

S: But in the House, this is an educational experience where the light of the in-itself is for-itself by being for-another. This is what makes for a comprehensive education.

J1: How does the House practise such comprehensive education?

S: In its openness to the illusions and injustices of mastery.

J1: Does this include what we might call cultural education?

S: It does. Its curriculum includes the ways that the city has tried to mediate its mastery. We know this education for-itself as the arts, sciences, humanities, religions, etc. But in the House, these are now taught comprehensively, within the educational logic of these experiences.

J1: And does this include an education about the logic of mastery?

S: That is one of its most important elements. As we said before, in teaching itself about mastery, the city is learning about itself. To suppress this would be another unchallenged mastery.

J1: Does this include learning about the injustice of the propertied logic of mastery?

S: Yes, and the masteries that attend gender, and race, and environment, and nature, and animals, and technology, and even personal relationships. In all of these ways the curriculum is the city's work of self-examination. Here the House is the candle – the light and the shadow of the city. This is its self-government.

J1: Many might still say that the educational city has not eradicated mastery.

S: Perhaps. But it has preserved its negation differently from being just more mastery.

J1: What does this mean for government?

S: Government as self-examination is government in which freedom is to learn. This requires government to risk itself as teaching and learning. Its authority is the vulnerability of its mastery.

J1: Are the teachers also rulers?

S: Rulers as defined in the logic of mastery are now students and teachers of the logic of educational government.

J1: Who are the teachers in the House?

S: Anyone can be teacher or student in the House at any time.

J1: And what do they teach?

S: Whatever content they teach, they do so within the experience of its educational truth.

J1: But the danger must be that teaching which risks mastery becomes mastery.

S: It is. The risk is not that the curriculum and its teachers will not be mediated. They will. The risk is that, tempted by a logic of mastery, this mediation is suppressed, avoided and turned into the property of masters.

J1: And what will oppose this?

S: What else but its own continuing education?

J1: But, Socrates, even here there is mastery. This education is not as open to its own negation as it might seem. The structure of the curriculum and the pattern of learning look like they are already planned in advance. Surely this is a mastery even of the mediation of mastery?

S: A good point, one that has been made several times in our discussions. But remember, this curriculum is a track laid down by experience about experience, as something presupposed. It is its own necessity, the nature of the nature of teaching and learning. To avoid this necessity in advance is to resolve life and death as property relations.

J1: So this is different from a curriculum within the logic of mastery.

S: In the logic of mastery, planned educational outcomes perpetuate mastery. In the logic of education, the curriculum and its teachers practise an openness to and not a mastery of educational freedom. Mediation of educational authority happens anyway. It can either be suppressed or embraced.

J1: So, what is a threat to masters is a truth to teachers and students, or to citizens of the educational city. And the House, as the curriculum of the city, is the openness of the city to education not its refusal.

S: It is. Educational logic has to be experienced – that is its life. This city lives it by the truth of self-examination. It knows itself. It is the light and shadow, the life-and-death of itself as its own free self-governing.

J1: And this freedom, this education, is the fire at the heart of the city?

S: The House is the candle of the city whose citizens learn in the light of its shadows.

J1: No philosopher kings this time?

S: No. In place of privilege there is comprehensive education.

J1: What counts as authority?

S: The authority of the comprehensive citizen is in being the teacher and student who lives and who live the examined life.

J1: And such authority is not in property but in education?

S: It is in having life and death as one's vocation lived as the examined life.

J1: How would such authority not form itself into a hierarchy or an elite?

S: Perhaps the danger is never entirely absent. But the safeguard is education itself. If teachers are tempted to turn self-examination into propertied mastery, then the defence against this, as always, is only continuing education and learning.

J1: Presumably any such mastery would be unacceptable to the educational city.

S: Indeed. Propertied masters would be seen to be practising an unjust authority, not only unjust to its citizens but unjust to education and to the truth of the city.

J1: I see this. But it's still likely there will be leaders and followers, thinkers and those who let others think for them. The city will still be divided into those who know and understand and those who do not.

S: Within propertied education this is an apology for privilege and a prejudice that divides human beings into the educable and ineducable. But in a city where wealth is learning, such prejudice impoverishes the city. And which human being would knowingly choose the impoverishment of allowing someone else to live and die on her behalf?

J1: But people might say that the teacher and student relationship is always hierarchical!

S: You are forgetting that educational truth orbits according to its own gravity. Every teacher remains student to herself in her relation to others. Such an education could never be completed or finally mastered.

J1: So, everyone will be a teacher and student in a city of comprehensive education.

S: Yes. This is the way that the educational city holds together the individual and the collective, as the old Republic did by the soul and the city.

J1: The old and new cities are not so different from each other then?

S: In this respect, perhaps they are not so different. The inner life and the outer life were always a struggle with each other. Education, then as now, is the soul and the city lived as the examined life.

J1: But without an elite class of rulers, the new old city is in fact very different from the old city.

S: It appears that the city has only ever known various shapes of government by a privileged class, and that for almost all of the time, this privilege has been justified and preserved by an elite education. Because the city works with the logic of mastery, it has not yet experienced its own democratic education.

J1: It does have equality.

S: Its equality within the logic of mastery merely means that everyone is entitled to be more or less equal than others.

J1: But in terms of government, more people are represented now in the city than ever in its history.

S: And yet still education serves the masters. And when the masters are corrupt, they take the integrity of democracy and of the education it requires down with them. Democracy degenerates into a system where power is gained and held by promising people what they think they want, or what they are told they want, a system where votes can be bought at almost any cost by those with wealth and power. Democracy of the many is so easily manipulated by the few.

J1: Yet still most people respect the idea of democracy as the best form of government. It is hard to think of a better system than one where leaders know that they can be removed from office by the votes of the citizens and accept this removal as the safeguard against demagoguery, others and their own.

S: Educational justice commends that we negate the mastery of the few who control democracy and preserve this negation differently than with more of the same. We need to think of democracy differently within the two logics. Within the logic of mastery democracy is propertied and masterful. But within the logic of education, democracy – now requiring the examined life – cannot have itself shaped by the privileges of those who wish to preserve their mastery of it.

J1: This is something our own city may urgently have to attend to, Socrates.

GUARD: I am sorry to interrupt you all, but the hour is late and I have duties to attend to away from this cell. I must ask you all to return to your rooms now.

J2: One last thing, Socrates. Something has been haunting me right through our discussion.

S: What is that?

J2: This new old city we have imagined will never happen.

S: Must we think less of our words just because we cannot prove such a city will be possible?

J2: No. But it's still just a vision!

S: Where there is no vision, the people perish.

Part 3

The Apology

Book 18

JUDGE: The Court will come to order. Thank you to the jury for spending the day of the festival in sequestration. I hope you all managed to make good use of your time. Today the accused will be offered one last opportunity to mount a defence against the charges that have been brought, before the jury retires to consider its verdict. Socrates, are there any last words you would like to offer the court?

S: Such an ominous tone to your invitation. But I am no stranger to such dark forebodings. I have previously been charged by the city and placed before a jury to await judgement on my life. I think you will all know by now that at my first trial I explained how my life of education and self-examination came about – how the oracle at Delphi told a companion of mine that I was the wisest person in the city and that, not seeing how this could be true but knowing also that the god could not lie, I set out to try to understand this conundrum.

I questioned the wise in the city and discovered, to my surprise, that despite appearances, I might have a wisdom they lacked. On questioning these people – they were of course the most powerful, the most influential and the most prominent in the city – I found that they invariably pretended to know things which, after being questioned about them, they were clearly ignorant. What was even more significant was that they did not seem to know this ignorance. I was different from them in this respect. Like them, I knew nothing much, but unlike them I was fully aware of my own ignorance. Indeed, I knew this better than I knew anything else. On this alone, then, I thought myself wiser than them; that where they thought they knew things and did not, I knew that I did not know such things.

Which of us, do you think, is the wiser? The one who is blind to ignorance or the one who sees it? For these kinds of questions, and for this strange sounding wisdom, I was tried in the old city and had the death sentence passed upon me. It became clear that the city's statesmen did not want to be reminded of the fraudulence of the knowledge which authorized their rule. The powerful did not want their ignorance exposed under the scrutiny of philosophical examination. They did not want to be challenged by a thinking, questioning city.

Of course, I understand that most people are not what they seem to be. I understand that most people practice some kind of fraud in their lives and that no one wants to be embarrassed by having such things exposed. I understand that most people care too much about what people think of them, and too little about what they really are. And if your fraud happens to be in regard to a pretence of knowledge and understanding, then of course you will fear examination by others and will avoid self-examination.

But underneath this fear of exposure lies a different way of life, one that, instead of pretending to be something that someone is not, is lived instead in the search for what someone is. It is a life lived open to learning about one's own ignorance. And in such a life, truth can be found in the questions that it asks. For there are two responses to questions: cover up one's inadequacies or live in the truth of one's incompleteness. Live the life of intrigue and duplicity required to mask one's ignorance or live the examined life that embraces it.

As I have said, my first jury found me guilty of the charges, sentenced me to death and tried to save the city from further examination. But despite this, the fact that today I am again on trial shows that the examination of the city has not died. It continues to live. And it shows that I have not died. It shows that I too continue to live. The death sentence did not put an end to questions, and thus I live on. But I am retried every time there is an attempt to stifle education and examination and questioning in the city. And since the attempts at such suppression are all pervasive, so too, my trial never ends. This unceasing trial is where I live my death over and over again, and as such it is where my death keeps coming to life. Wherever education is denied, it is there you will find me. And since education is continuously denied, I am ever present in the city, even if unrecognized.

Perhaps the reason my trial is perpetual also goes beyond each attempt to rescue a reputation or to protect a privilege. My first trial and its outcome summoned a response in the city that has endured through the ages. The city experienced my educational life and death as dividing itself into two halves which, when put together, did not add up to a whole. Thereafter, any wisdom attached to the examined life was rent asunder and only ever understood from one half of this divide or the other. On the one side, knowing was separated from not knowing and became the mastery known as dogmatism. On the other side, not knowing was separated from being known and became the mastery known as scepticism.

Ever since, the city has lived this experience of the examined life as a civil war between these two irreconcilable opponents. My life and death is the life and death of education fought out as this civil war. And I am present but unseen – unseen like those who are deemed ineligible to participate in the civil war – every time this one-sidedness creates for itself contradictions that it cannot solve.

But today my trial is different. It has been the condition of the possibility of my visibility. Whether it will also prove to be the condition of the possibility for the visibility of those forced to endure the city's injustices, remains to be seen. Who knows how deep the self-examination of the city must be for that to happen? But today my return is at least a small step towards what is required.

And why am I visible now? It is because the city has done something here it has not done before. Since the conclusion of my first trial, I have been retried each time the forces of dogma prosecute scepticism as the destroyer of worlds and as a sickness in the city that dissolves truth and leaves nothing in its place. I have also been retried each time the forces of scepticism prosecute dogma for its arrogance as the builder of worlds, armed with an absolute certainty regarding the truth of how things must be. Each one-sided trial reproduces the broken middle of the city. Such a city learns of itself only through the lens of this civil war. Such a city does not examine the presuppositions of life and death and property that drive the war or that form the image the city has of itself. In the absence of such examination, my life and death has become the battlefield upon which the two sides practice their warcraft.

But in this latest trial, a despairing city has made a despairing move. This trial is still a one-sided trial but in a different way. In this trial both sides of the civil war became allies and joined forces against me. Their common enemy is education, and especially the philosophical self-examination that would expose the presuppositions that their opposition to each other relies upon. And they have come to see that their endless trials risk promoting exactly such exposure. They have come to see that the danger of these trials is that on each and every occasion, regardless of the outcome, education commends itself against the logic of their civil war. It commends itself because the civil war, and the eternal trial, is forever unwinnable.

So, the two sides find that their self-interests are served by working together. The allies begin to see that the true victory of the civil war will not be a one-sided victory for one side or the other, but the victory of one-sidedness itself against the examined life. Such a victory would finally put an end to the trials that open up the city to the risk of learning about itself. Such a victory would finally close the door on all such trials and tribunals. And so, in this current trial, the civil war pursues its own victory by putting education on trial once and for all.

Now, perhaps for the first time, I can be found guilty by both sides at the same time, for they have conspired in bringing their charges against me. If I am found guilty of the dogma of elite truths, then I am guilty of the injustice that flows from them. And if I am found guilty of scepticisms that are contrary to privilege, I am guilty of the injustices that are required to compensate for them. At one and the same time, education is convicted of being the source of injustices that flow from education and of the injustices that flow from opposing such education.

What, then, is the nature of such a victory for the allies? They believe that in victory, in defeating the education that exposes their common presuppositions – in finally laying Socrates to rest – no new trials would ever be required in the city. If one-sidedness defeats examination, it can finally prevail in the city without risk to itself.

And I hope you can see that the result of such a victory is a city of endemic injustice. Injustice becomes a casual way of life, responded to only by anger, or ignorance, or intrigue. The only learning that survives is that in which the city learns to live with injustice, learns to be an unjust city, a city in which injustice becomes a way of life. The examined life will have finally been defeated.

This was promised to me, or perhaps threatened to me, very recently as the sentence of a life lived in just such a playground, where examination is meaningless, critical thinking is shameful and ruse is the new expression of the good life. It was stated very clearly that sentenced to such a life in the playground, I would not return again, for in a city where all questions are indifferent to themselves, there will be no questions worth asking, and I will be redundant.

But for those who would welcome such an outcome, I say beware of what you wish for. The nature of education has its own laws. When indifference exerts a great force on the mind, the mind exerts an equal and opposite force in return. That is what prevents indifference being indifferent to itself. Some have said that indifference will be the end of the history of the city. But it will not be. There will be no last question, because the question of indifference is, like all questions, a shape of life and death; and like life and death, the question returns. Indifference cannot be the end because indifference will disturb itself. Thoughtlessness troubles its own unrest. And, too late, it is already another question. Experience resists its own inertia because it is always pulled away from itself by the gravity of education, and it is always changed in doing so. This is the force of gravity that attracts experience to education. If there is hope for the city it lies here, in the orbit of educational experience that resists the straight line of indifference.

And so, you have made a mistake in putting me on trial together. For you expose the shared misunderstanding that sustains the civil war. Here, for the first time in a long time, the civil war of one-sided thinking faces itself in its allied prosecution of the examined life. It risks the trial of all trials. And this time, because of that, it faces an examined life that is learning again about itself. You have risked the city learning that what it thinks it knows about itself, in fact, it does not know. You have exposed one-sidedness to itself. You have risked exposing to self-examination the misunderstanding of its civil war. And you have allowed the city, on one of its festival days, to do the work once again required for the city to know itself. Obviously, I do not know what verdict the jury will reach. But I have confidence that this is a jury that will show fidelity to the examined life. I believe it will be open to thinking. That such a jury exists is a blessing for me. It shows that even within the afflictions of the city, life and death is still open to itself in ways that inspire sadness and joy, tears and laughter, in the love of learning. All is most certainly not lost. The city should credit itself that, even in such a perilous condition, it can find jurors that understand city matters.

Perhaps some will say that I am still being ironic. The city might want you to think that I am mocking this trial of trials. Let me tell you, I have always meant what I said. But what has changed, now, is that whereas before I knew only that I did not know, now I know what it is that I know I do not know. It is the truth of the examined life, the truth of education.

The accusation of irony came from a city that could not understand its experience of me. What I was saying had to be accepted or rejected. Any other response could not be taken seriously. And so, the city's difficult experience of me and my life, and the discomforting contradictions that issued from this kind of self-examination, was explained away as ironic. But what the city dissolved into irony, I have come to experience as having a truth of its own, a truth called learning. I have found that learning has its own necessity. I have seen it appear in my conversations with people, and it is ever present in the city in each of my retrials. It is a necessity of the city itself, and it is a necessity that the city knows, but fears – the necessity of self-examination.

What is this educational necessity? When questions are treated one-sidedly in the civil war, answers are accepted or rejected. But as education has its own laws, so questions have their own truth. Questions are the life and death of education, its force of gravity. Think of questions not according to the logic that defines the bud, the blossom and the fruit independently of each other but according to the logic that defines them as the process of growth, decline and return that is life and death. The bud becomes the blossom, and blossom becomes the fruit, and the fruit dies. But in death the seed falls to the ground, takes root, grows and buds again. The process is presupposed as that in which life negates and preserves itself. Our experience of this life and death is our experience of education. To live its truth is to live the examined life. My old life now has its own old and new educational logic.

If the city is to do justice to itself, then it needs to do justice to its own educational necessity. If the jury ignores this educational necessity, then it can deliver another one-sided verdict. If it turns the necessity into dogma, or into scepticism, either way, it will find me guilty as the the source of injustice. And no doubt in their deliberations the jury will feel the comfort that comes from the one-sidedness of simple acceptance and rejection. The trial invites the jury, once again, to the superficiality of what appears to be serious and profound within the logic of the civil war. This superficiality defines what thinking in the city is supposed to look like and what it is supposed to do. But if the jury does justice to education, it will find a different necessity in its own thinking and its own experiences than the one which drives the civil war.

Of course, the death penalty still remains an option for the city. I will remain the surrogate experience of life and death until such time as it is able to speak this experience with its own voice. For the longest time I have been patiently waiting to be tried not as a surrogate for the life and death of the propertied city but for the life and death of the examined life, for my own life and that of the city.

But is now the time for education to find its voice? The civil war leaves the city extremely vulnerable to being manipulated and overcome by the mastery of authoritarian leaders and the proprietors who sponsor them. Aided by their sophisticated propaganda, the ambivalence of democracy – its reproduction of power and privilege, and its desire for peace and justice – is slowly turning into visceral anger, on the one hand, and disillusioned scepticism and cynicism, on the other. Belief in anything called truth in the city is crumbling. And education, the formative activity that enables the city to learn about itself, seems to be collapsing in exhaustion and fatigue, without a vision of itself, or for itself. Life in the city, and perhaps beyond the city, is in a state of paralysis, held fixed by the blinding light of petrifying rational paradoxes that it experiences in all forms of social relations. If the city cannot learn something new from these paradoxes, then myriad possibilities of barbarism will feed on this. Is now the time for education to find its voice? If not now, when?

The verdict

JUDGE: Have you reached a verdict upon which you are all agreed?

JUROR: No, your Honour.

JUDGE: Have you reached a majority verdict?

JUROR: Yes, your Honour, we have.

JUDGE: Then do you find the accused guilty or not guilty of the charges?

JUROR: We find the accused guilty of continuing to seek truth and justice in the city.

JUDGE: Let the court record a verdict of guilty. Do you have any recommendation for sentence?

JUROR: We would ask that you sentence the accused to death; and we would ask that you sentence the accused to life; and that the sentences be served in the city concurrently and freely by the accused continuing to live the examined life.

SOCRATES: . . .